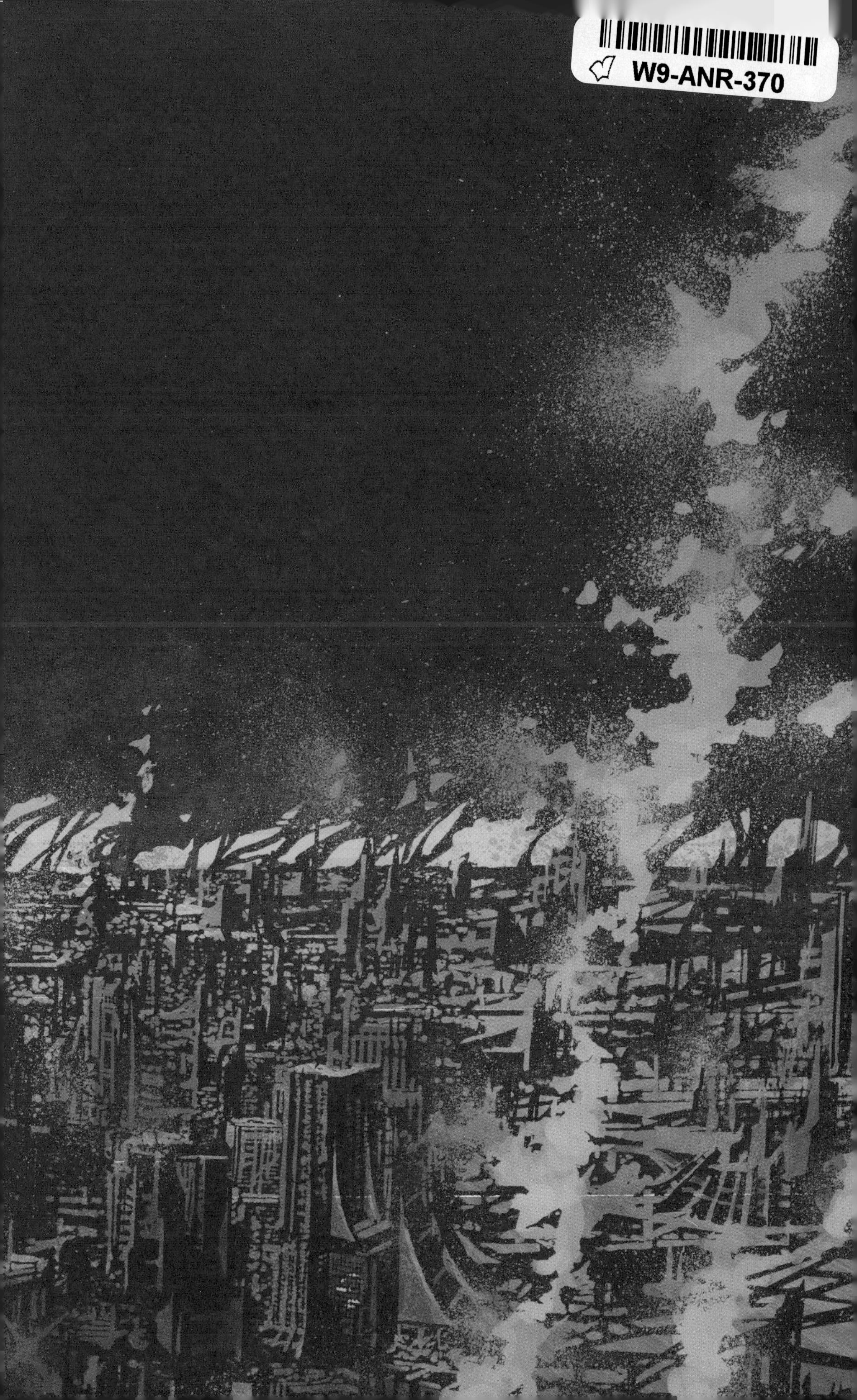

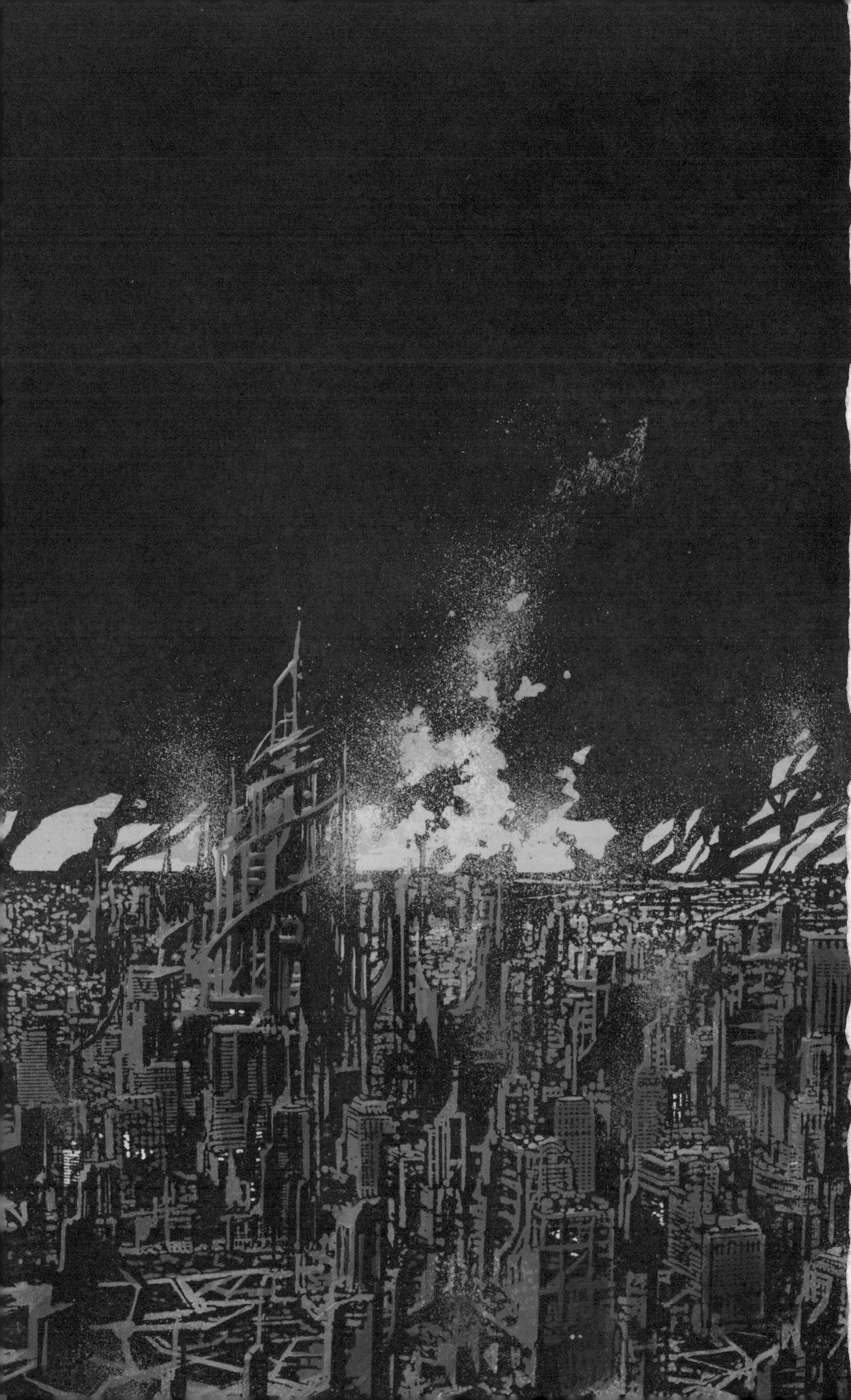

EVERLAST

A GRAPHIC NOVEL

Written and Created by
CHAD MICHAEL MURRAY

ARCHAIA ENTERTAINMENT LLC
WWW.ARCHAIA.COM

BUFFALO BOY PRODUCTIONS ™
WWW.BUFFALOBOYPRODUCTIONS.COM

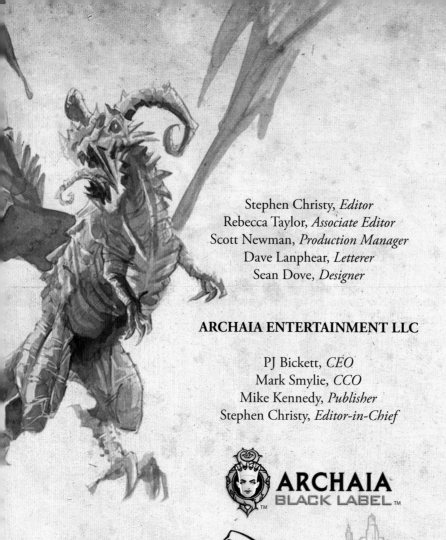

Stephen Christy, *Editor*
Rebecca Taylor, *Associate Editor*
Scott Newman, *Production Manager*
Dave Lanphear, *Letterer*
Sean Dove, *Designer*

ARCHAIA ENTERTAINMENT LLC

PJ Bickett, *CEO*
Mark Smylie, *CCO*
Mike Kennedy, *Publisher*
Stephen Christy, *Editor-in-Chief*

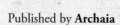

BUFFALO BOY PRODUCTIONS™

Published by **Archaia**

Archaia Entertainment LLC
1680 Vine Street, Suite 1010
Los Angeles, California, 90028, USA
www.archaia.com

EVERLAST Original Graphic Novel.
September 2011. FIRST PRINTING.

10 9 8 7 6 5 4 3 2 1

ISBN 13: 978-1-932386-97-4
ISBN: 1-932386-97-1

Printed in China.

A Message from THE AUTHOR

To all that have opened this book, awaiting its journey,

First, I'd like to thank all of you. You've inspired me to inspire. This book has been its own adventure for me. The story originated from a man who rang my doorbell, preaching about the End of Days and how one hundred and forty-four thousand people would be saved. Now, what he was selling may not have been for me, but after he had left, I couldn't put down the thought of this small percentage of people being left to reign. Thus, my first character was born: Derek Everlast. His mission in life, to find those chosen people and protect them from the End of Days.

Derek is so very dear to my heart because he lives a tortured life. Based on his knowledge of future events and his inner gift the Nudge, which guides him to select individuals, he ultimately has to venture forward a lonely man. Love and friendship aren't an option, because he knows that most people won't make it when the world ends. He spends his days watching and thinking about the day when humanity will gather up all its positive light and finally feel whole.

We were very fortunate to get the talented artists we did for this book! Our object in having four main artists was to convey this story through each character's eyes. You'll notice we start with a dark, realistic style that projects Everlast's version of the world. When Everlast meets Melissa, we transition to a cartoon style—dark, yet animated. Our third style shows our story through the eyes of our villain, Stavros, exaggerated and distorted like all supervillains. The last section shows the world through the eyes of Naomi, our strong-natured and beautiful female lead. The delicate watercolor shows how she can take all the negativity surrounding her and turn it into something beautiful.

As an actor, we all dream of finding characters we relate to and find intriguing. I believe each character created in Everlast has those qualities. From the cool wisdom of Hutch to the tough street girl in Melissa, from a villain whose intentions are true and right in his own mind to our lonely hero who seeks no validation in his victories but is so very human and flawed.

From my heart to yours, I truly hope you enjoy this story. I hope it transports you to a place of excitement, longing and satisfaction. Enjoy the ride!

Cheers,

Chad Michael Murray
Los Angeles
July 2011

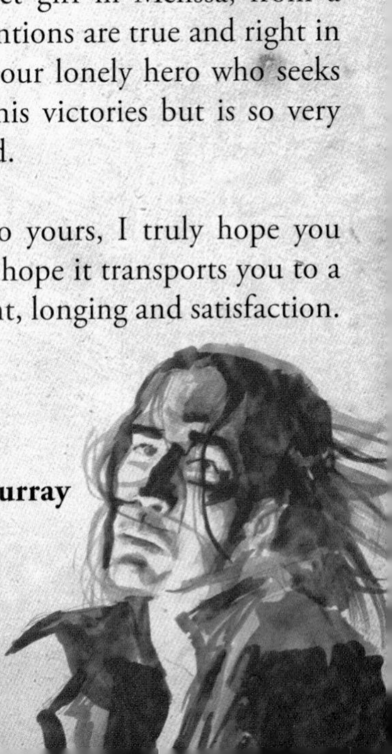

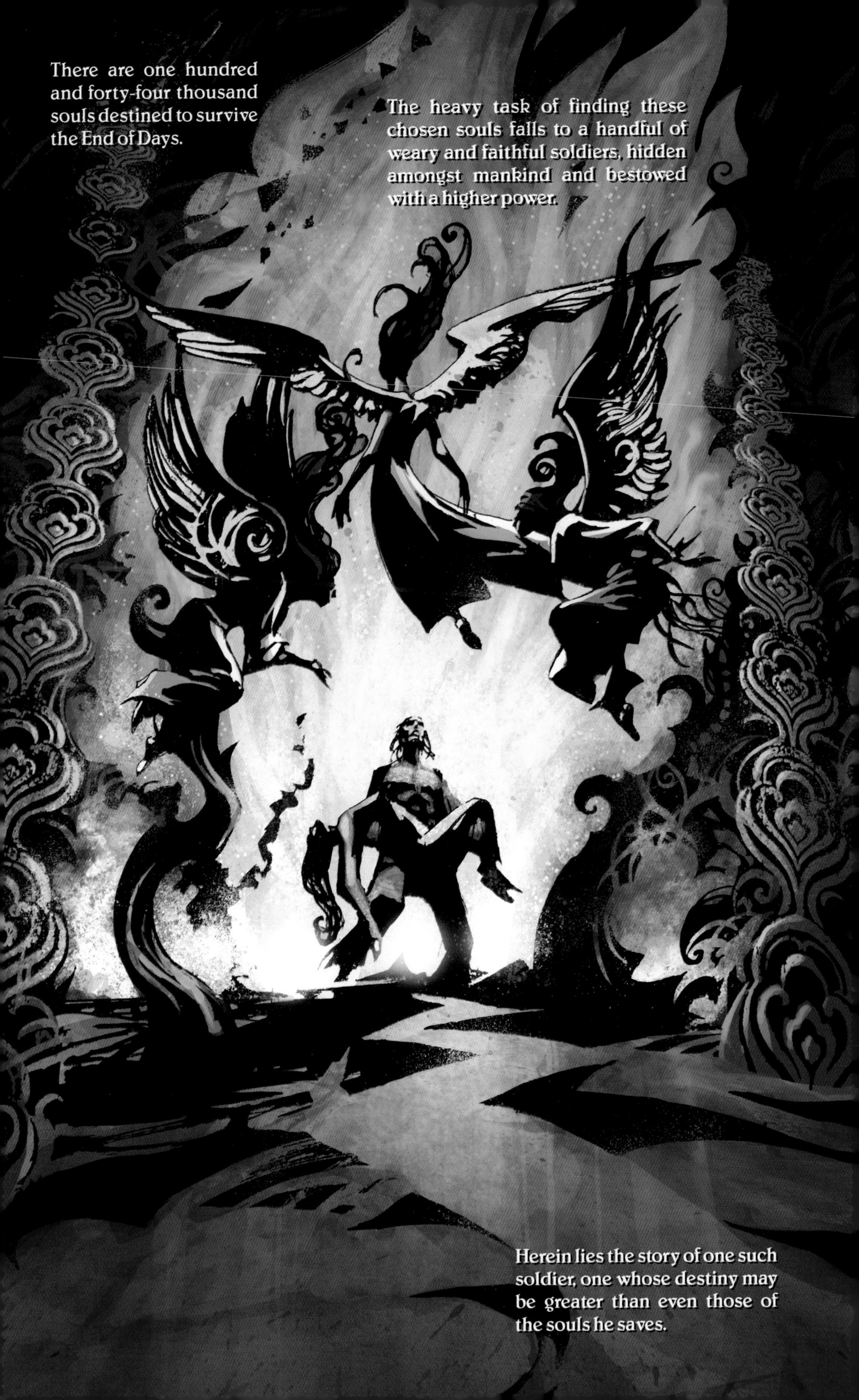
There are one hundred and forty-four thousand souls destined to survive the End of Days.
The heavy task of finding these chosen souls falls to a handful of weary and faithful soldiers, hidden amongst mankind and bestowed with a higher power.
Herein lies the story of one such soldier, one whose destiny may be greater than even those of the souls he saves.

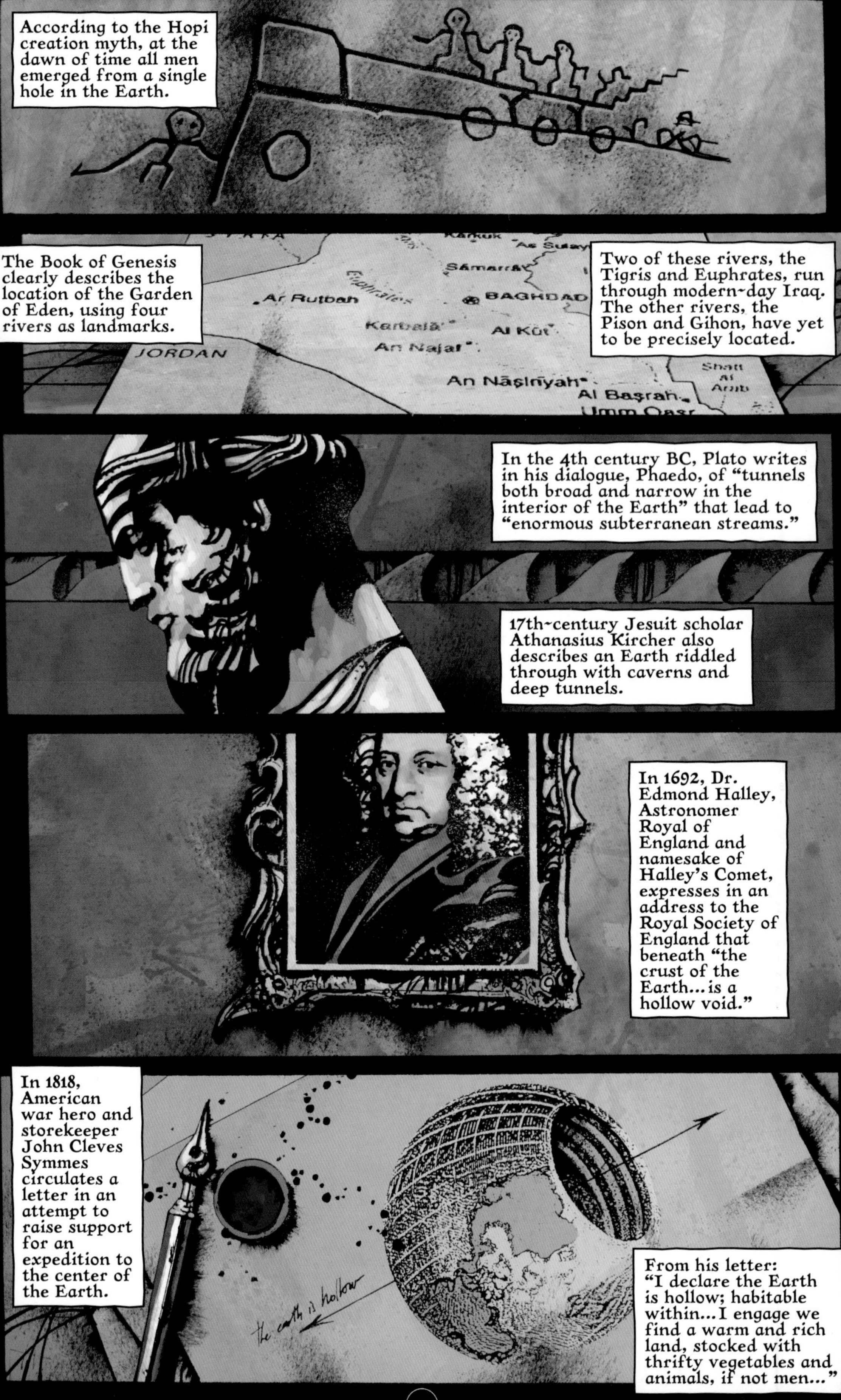

According to the Hopi creation myth, at the dawn of time all men emerged from a single hole in the Earth.
The Book of Genesis clearly describes the location of the Garden of Eden, using four rivers as landmarks.
Two of these rivers, the Tigris and Euphrates, run through modern-day Iraq. The other rivers, the Pison and Gihon, have yet to be precisely located.
Euphrates
Sāmarrā'
Ar Rutbah
BAGHDAD
Karbalā'
Al Kūt
An Najaf
JORDAN
An Nāşirīyah
Al Başrah
Shatt al Arab
In the 4th century BC, Plato writes in his dialogue, Phaedo, of "tunnels both broad and narrow in the interior of the Earth" that lead to "enormous subterranean streams."
17th-century Jesuit scholar Athanasius Kircher also describes an Earth riddled through with caverns and deep tunnels.
In 1692, Dr. Edmond Halley, Astronomer Royal of England and namesake of Halley's Comet, expresses in an address to the Royal Society of England that beneath "the crust of the Earth... is a hollow void."
In 1818, American war hero and storekeeper John Cleves Symmes circulates a letter in an attempt to raise support for an expedition to the center of the Earth.
the earth is hollow
From his letter: "I declare the Earth is hollow; habitable within... I engage we find a warm and rich land, stocked with thrifty vegetables and animals, if not men..."

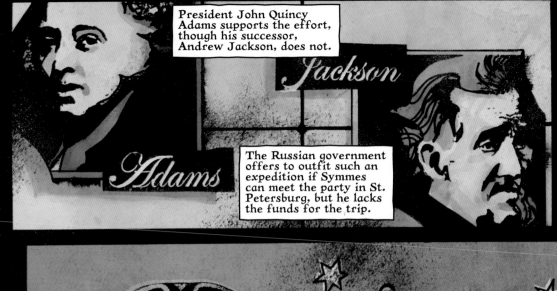

President John Quincy Adams supports the effort, though his successor, Andrew Jackson, does not.

The Russian government offers to outfit such an expedition if Symmes can meet the party in St. Petersburg, but he lacks the funds for the trip.

In 1906, William Reed states in his book, *Phantom of the Poles*, "The Earth is hollow... In the interior are vast continents, oceans, mountains and rivers."

In 1908, Willis George Emerson writes *The Smoky God*, the biography of Norwegian sailor Olaf Jansen, who claimed to have lived for two years after a shipwreck in the Earth's interior amidst a civilization whose capital city was Eden.

In 1920, Ferdynand Antoni Ossendowski publishes *Beasts, Men, and Gods*, discussing the legendary underground city of Agartha (known as Shambhalla in India), where the Masters, or spiritual leaders of humanity, dwell.

In a 1947 interview, Rear Admiral Richard E. Byrd of the United States Navy proclaims, "that area beyond the Pole is the centre of the Great Unknown."

In a 1956 aerial expedition, while still in radio contact, his party penetrates to an unknown iceless land 2,300 miles beyond the South Pole.

And returns.

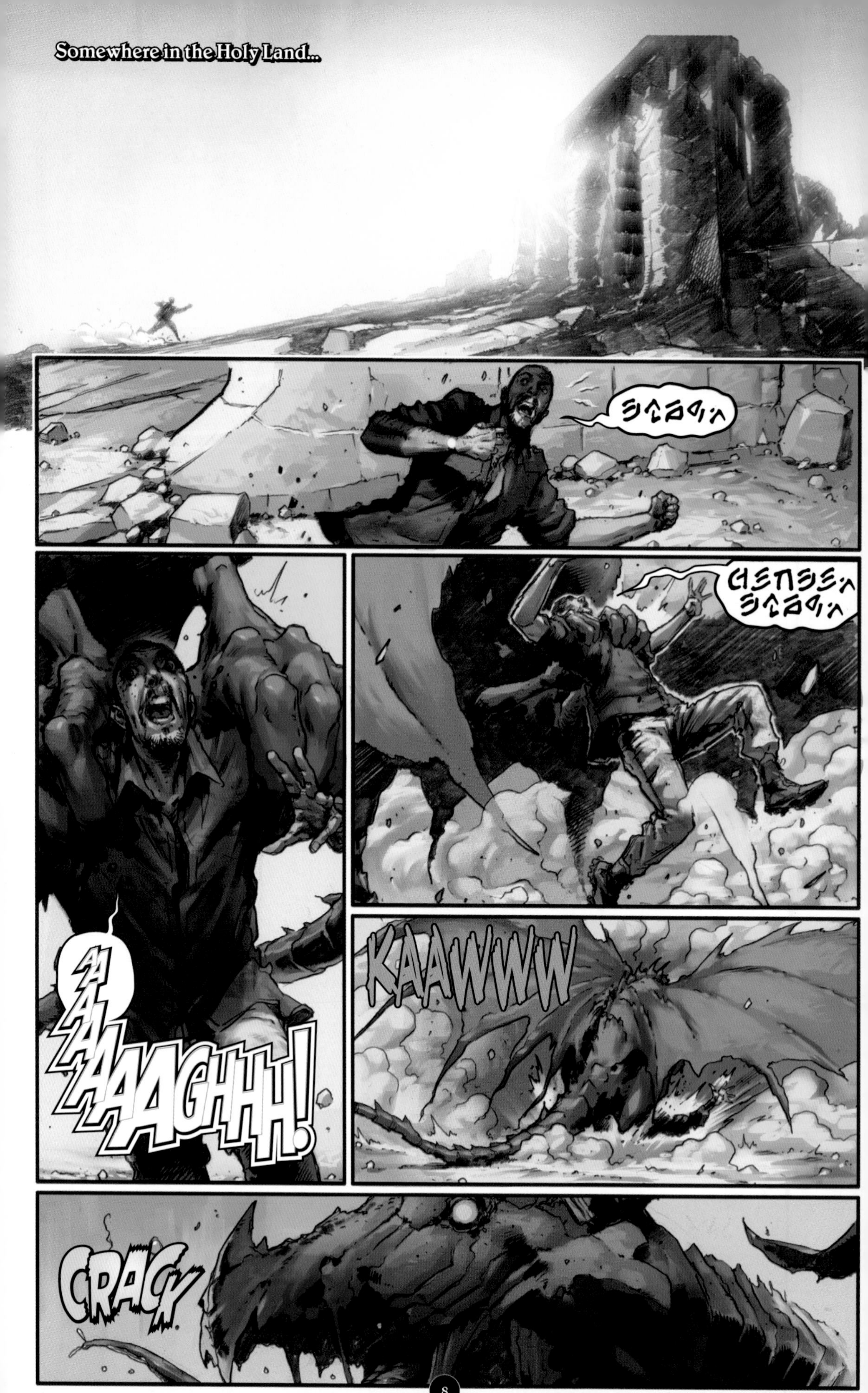
Somewhere in the Holy Land...
AAAAAAAGHHH!
KAAWWW
CRACK

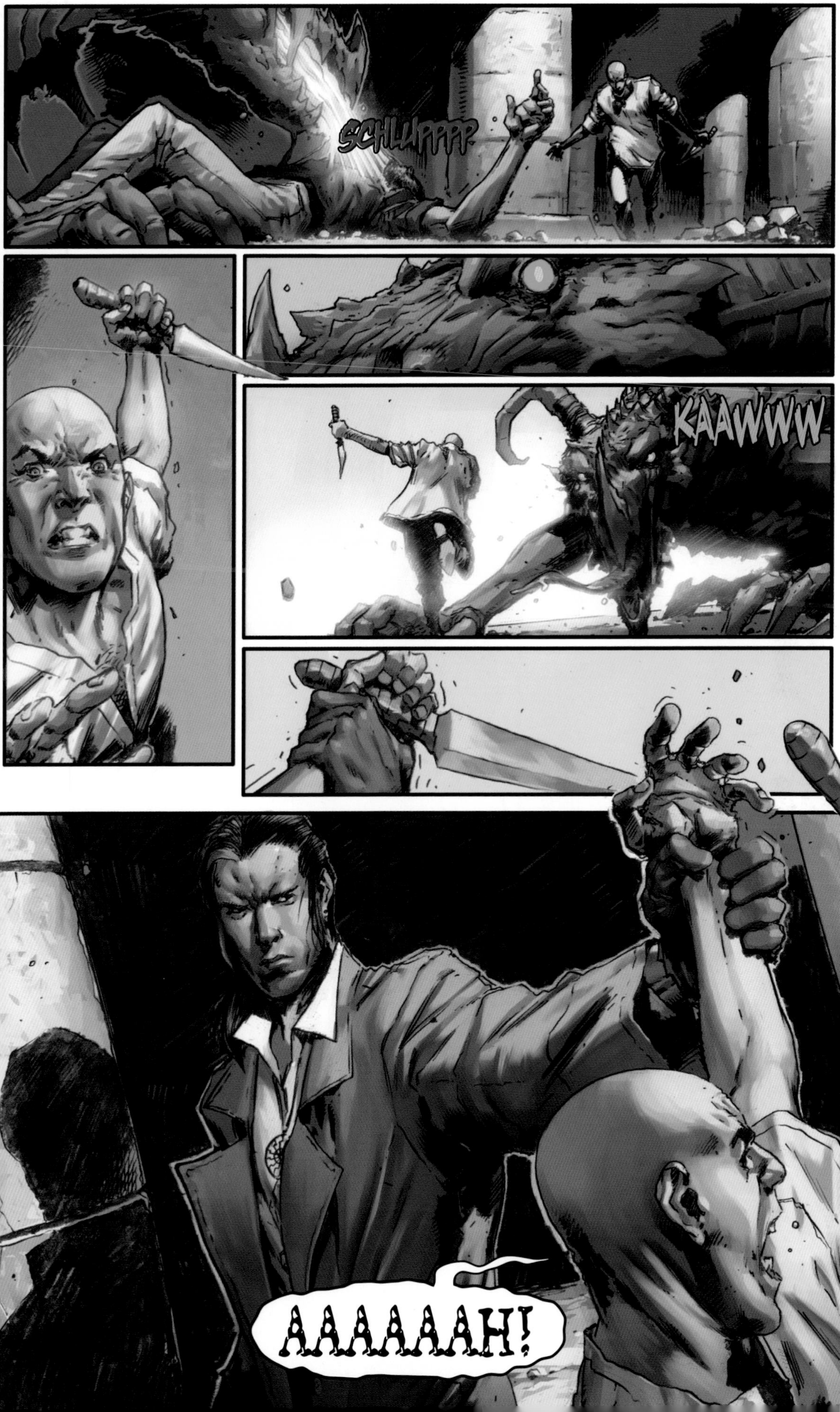
SCHLUPPPP
KAAWWW
AAAAAAH!

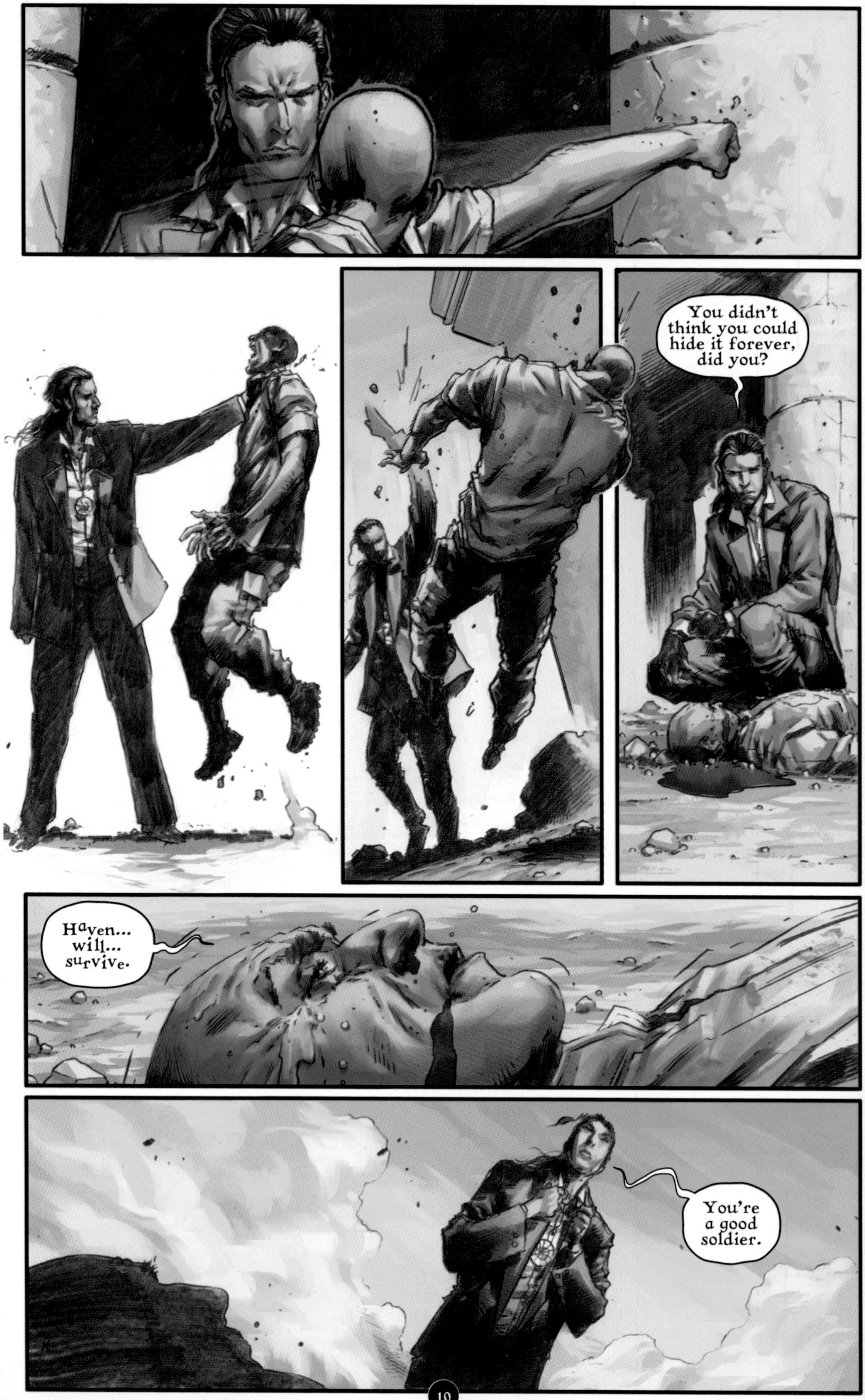
You didn't think you could hide it forever, did you?
Haven... will... survive.
You're a good soldier.

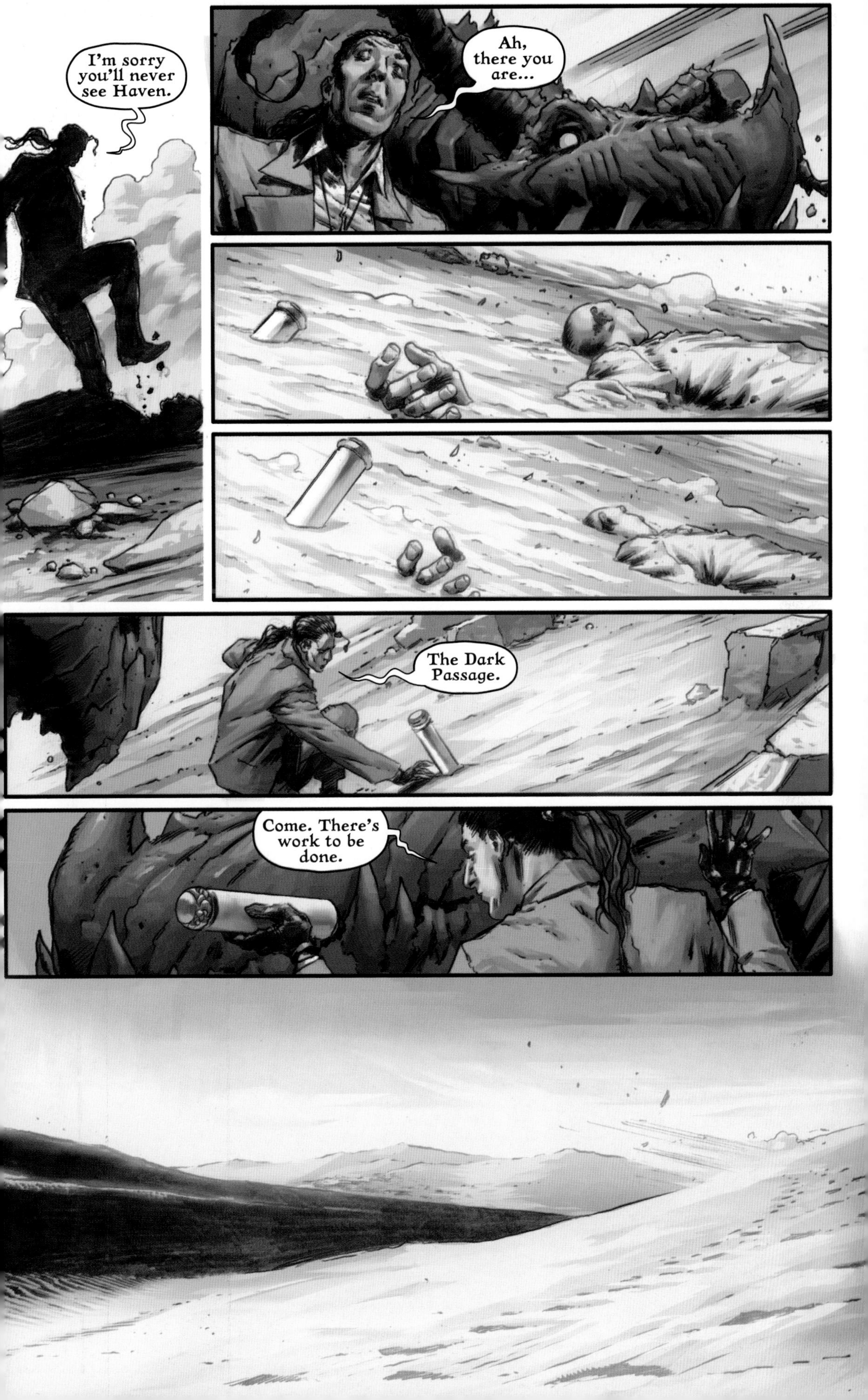
I'm sorry you'll never see Haven.
Ah, there you are...
The Dark Passage.
Come. There's work to be done.

Written and Created by CHAD MICHAEL MURRAY

Art by DANIJEL ZEZELJ,
ROBBI RODRIGUEZ, ANDREW HUERTA,
JK WOODWARD, and TREVOR HAIRSINE

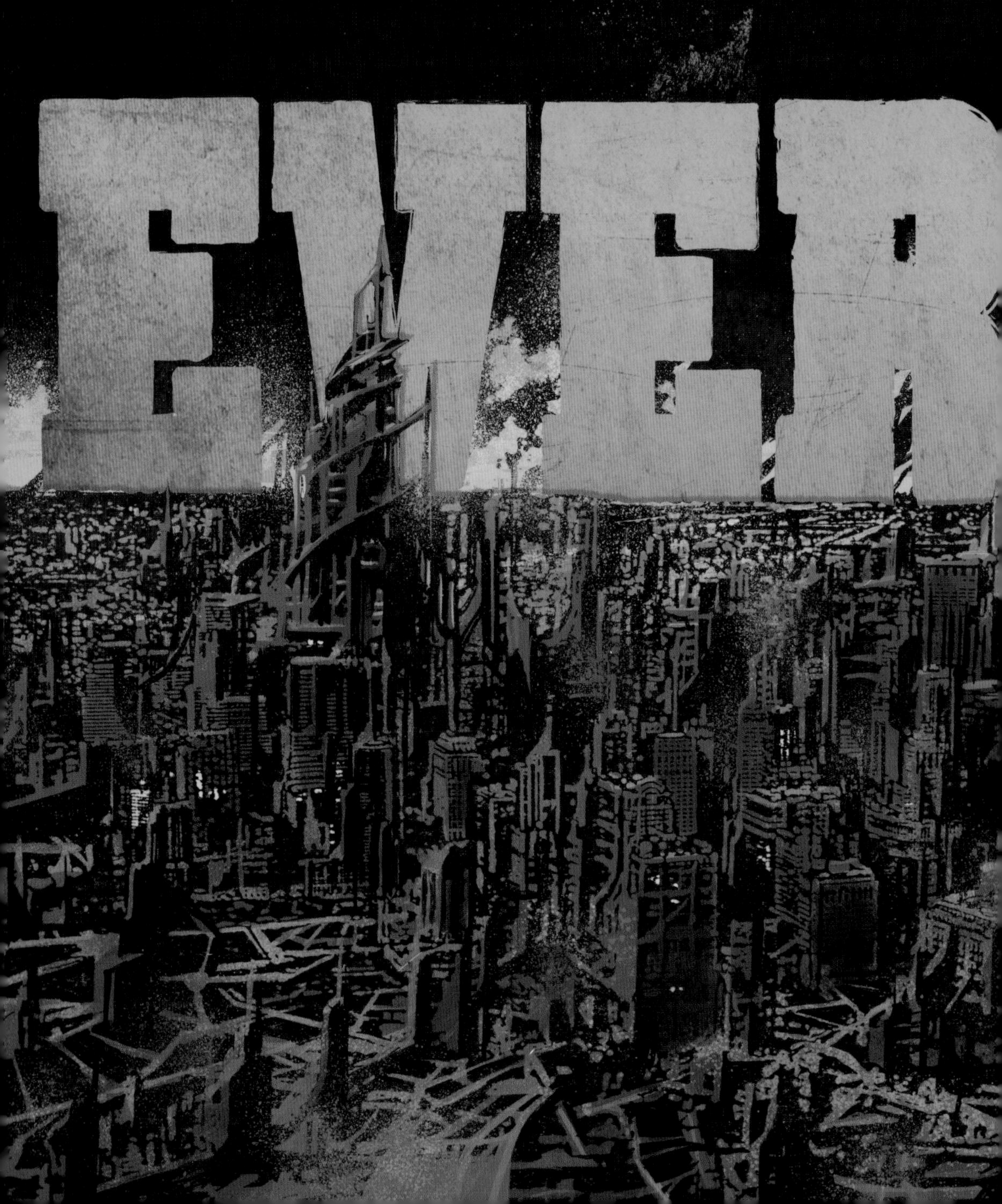
EVER

Colors by SCOTT KEATING, MARK ENGLERT,
RACHELLE ROSENBERG, and LIZZY JOHN

Executive Editors CHAD MICHAEL MURRAY
and DAN BARENTINE

Special Thanks to CALEB MONROE

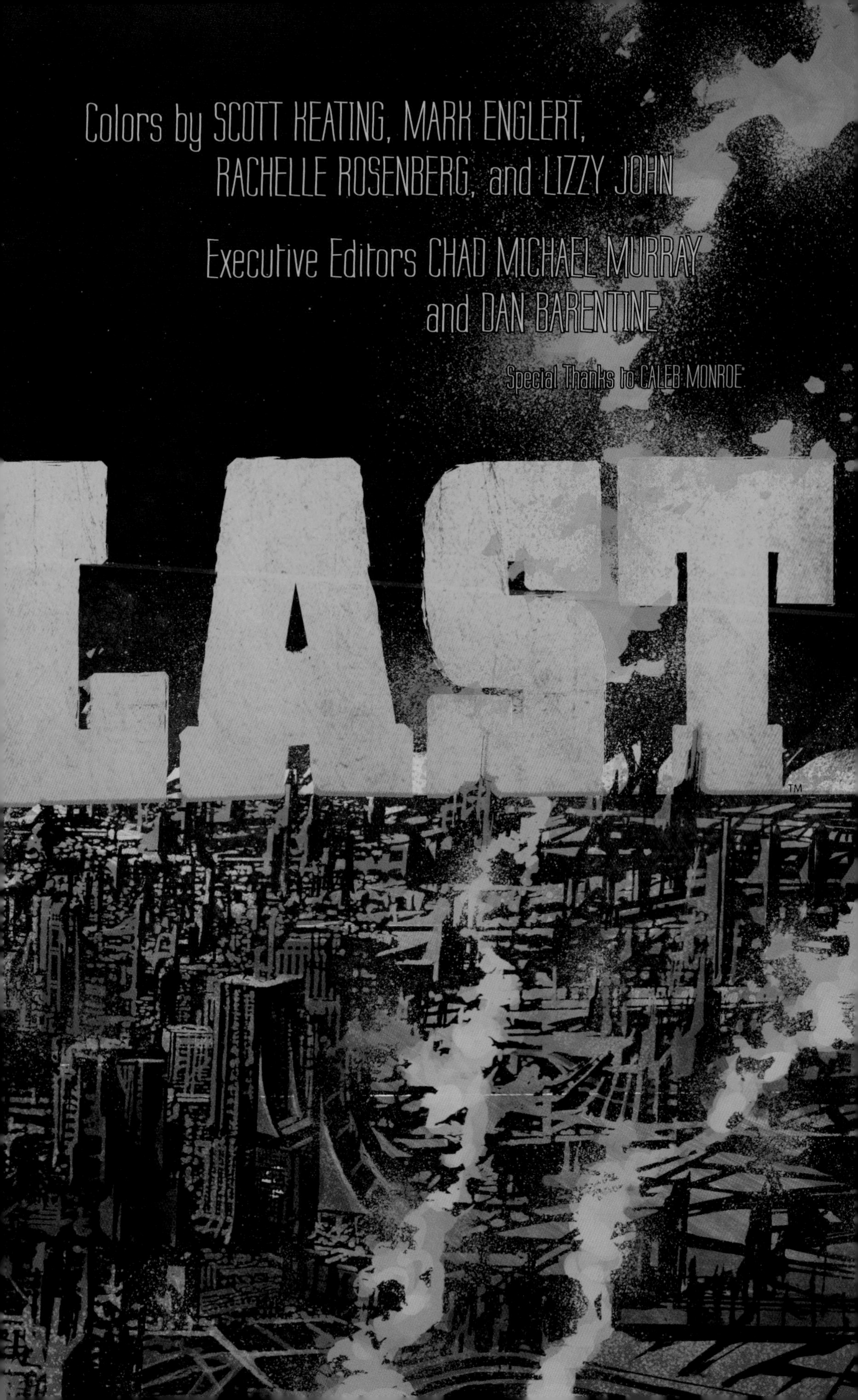
LAST™

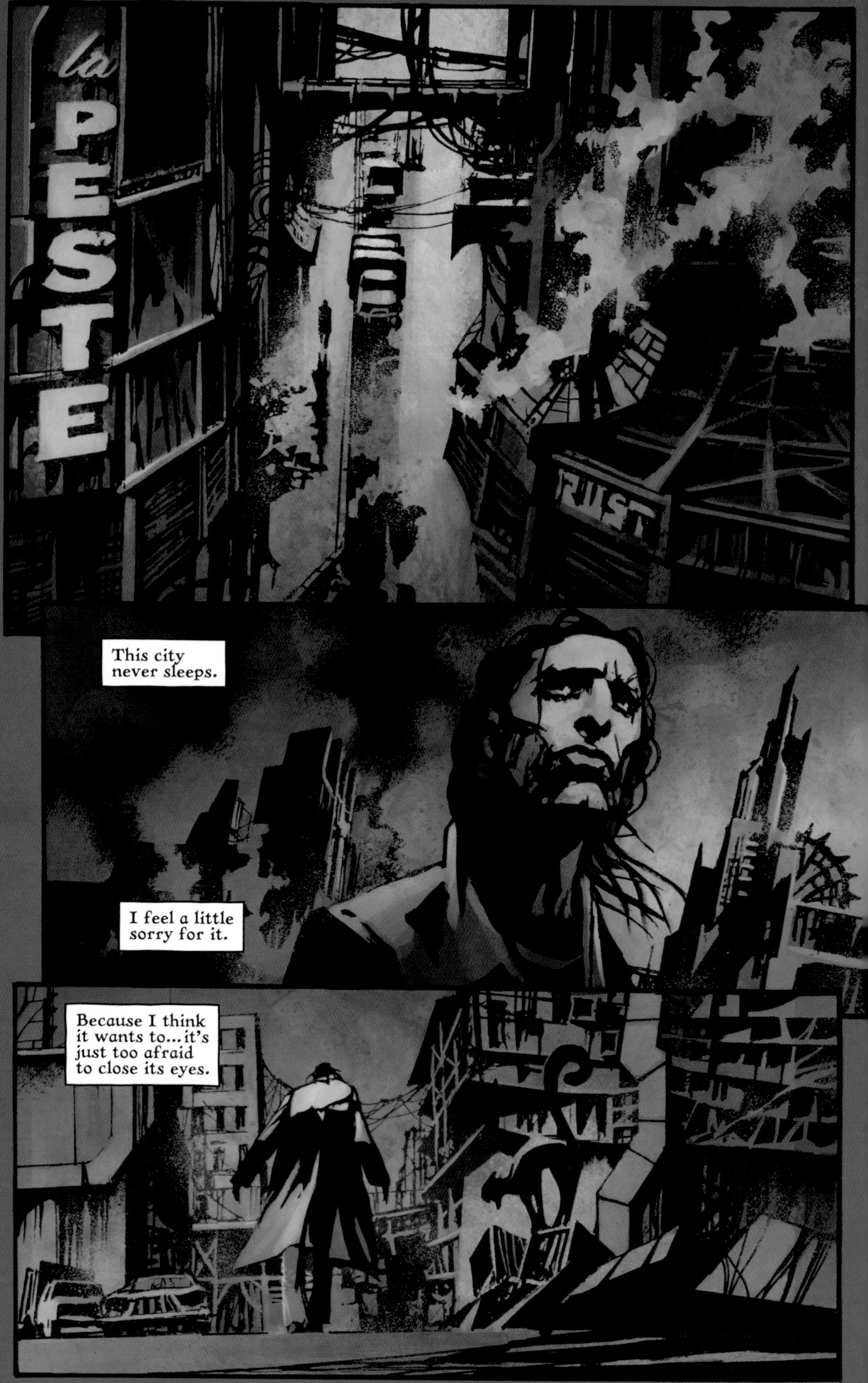
la PESTE
This city never sleeps.
I feel a little sorry for it.
Because I think it wants to...it's just too afraid to close its eyes.

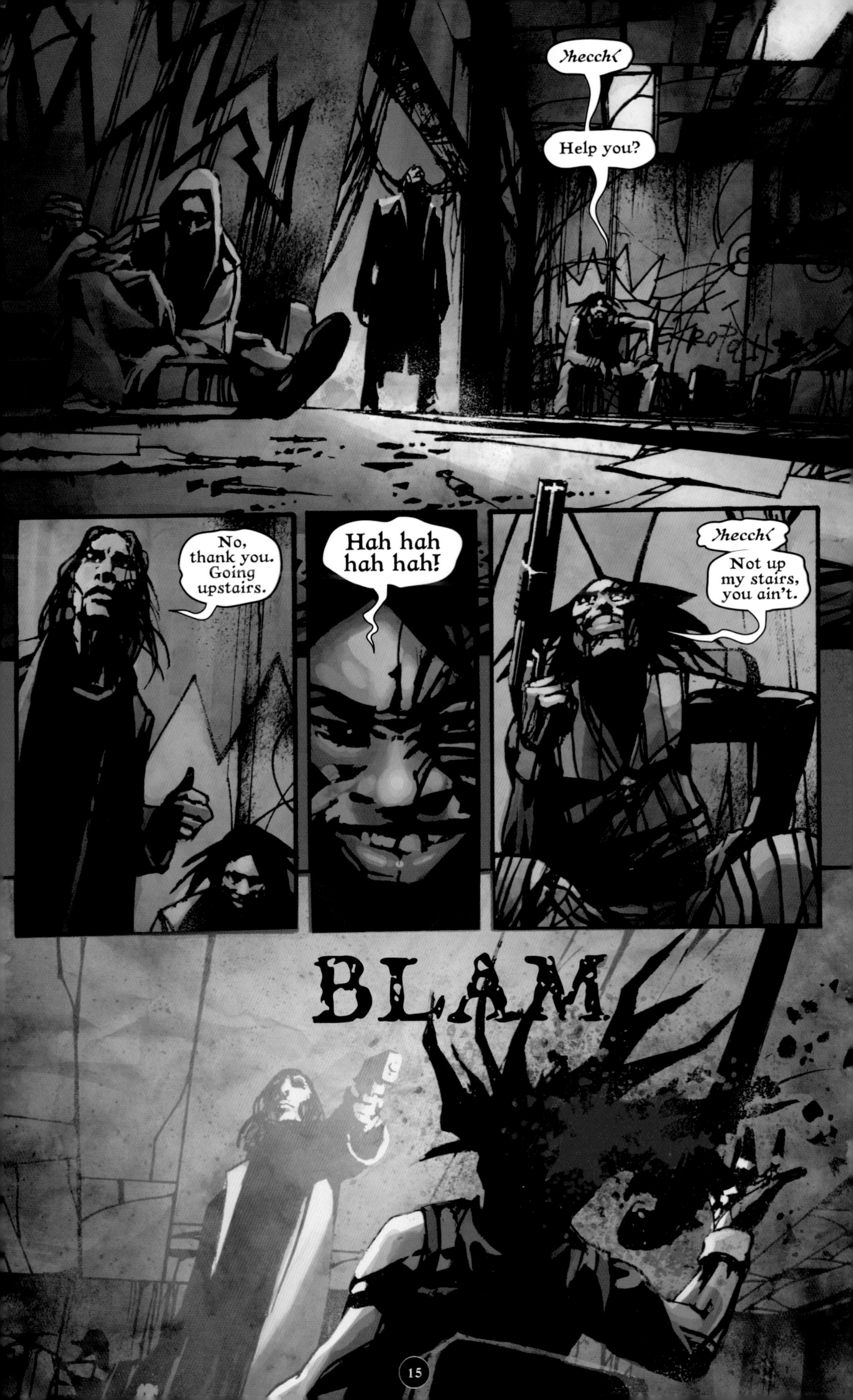

>hecch<
Help you?
No, thank you. Going upstairs.
Hah hah hah hah!
>hecch<
Not up my stairs, you ain't.
BLAM

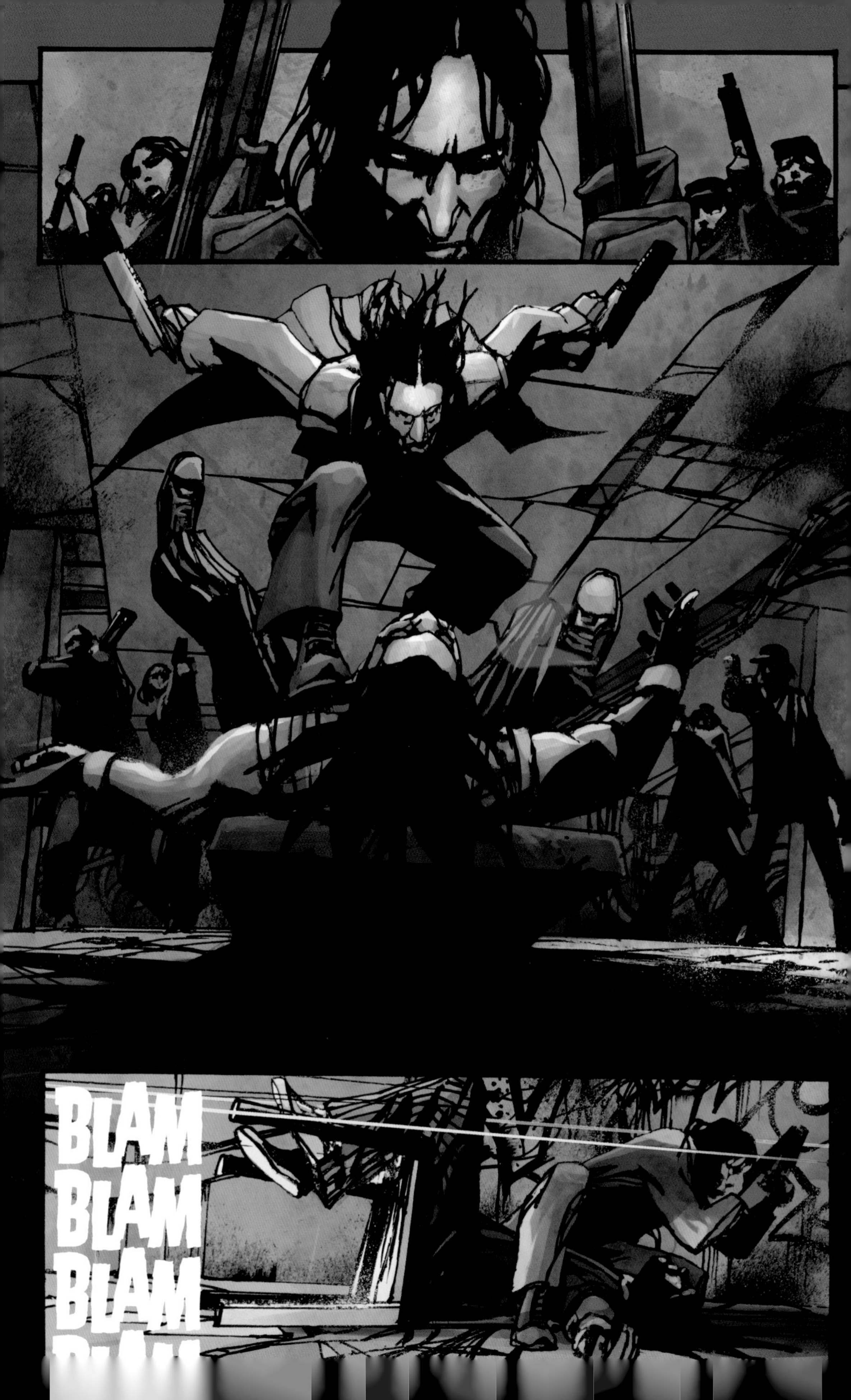
BLAM
BLAM
BLAM
BLAM

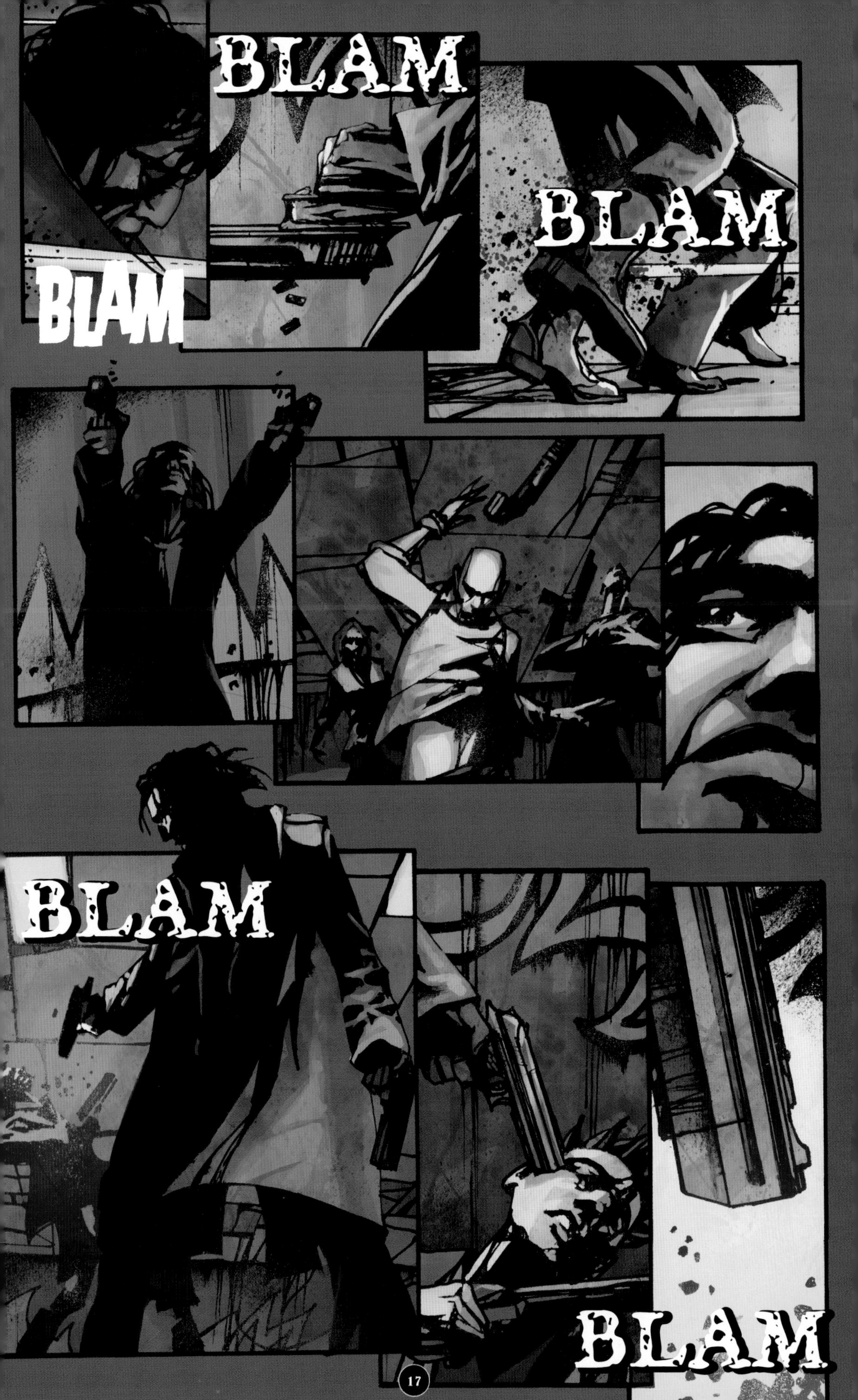
BLAM
BLAM
BLAM
BLAM
BLAM

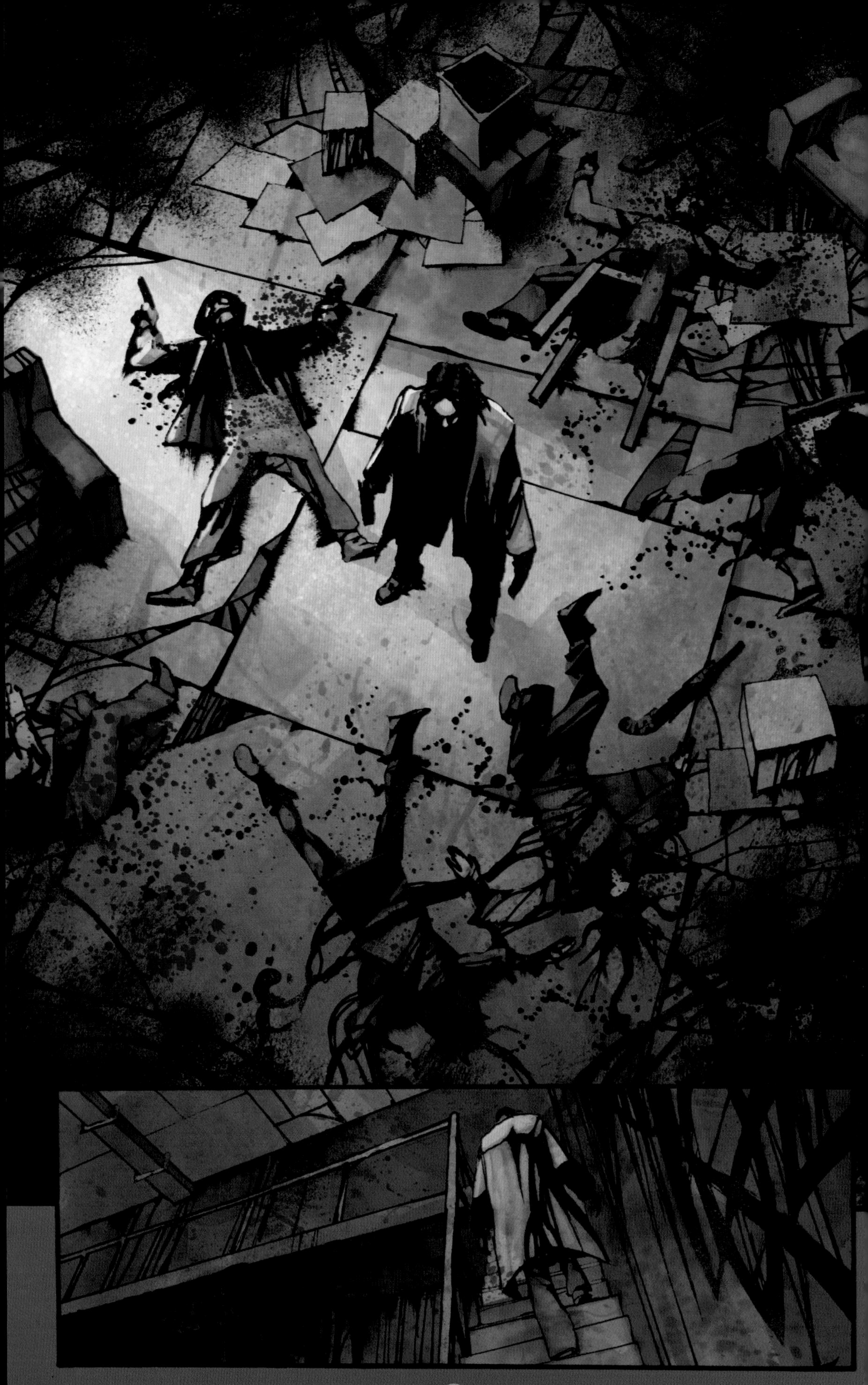

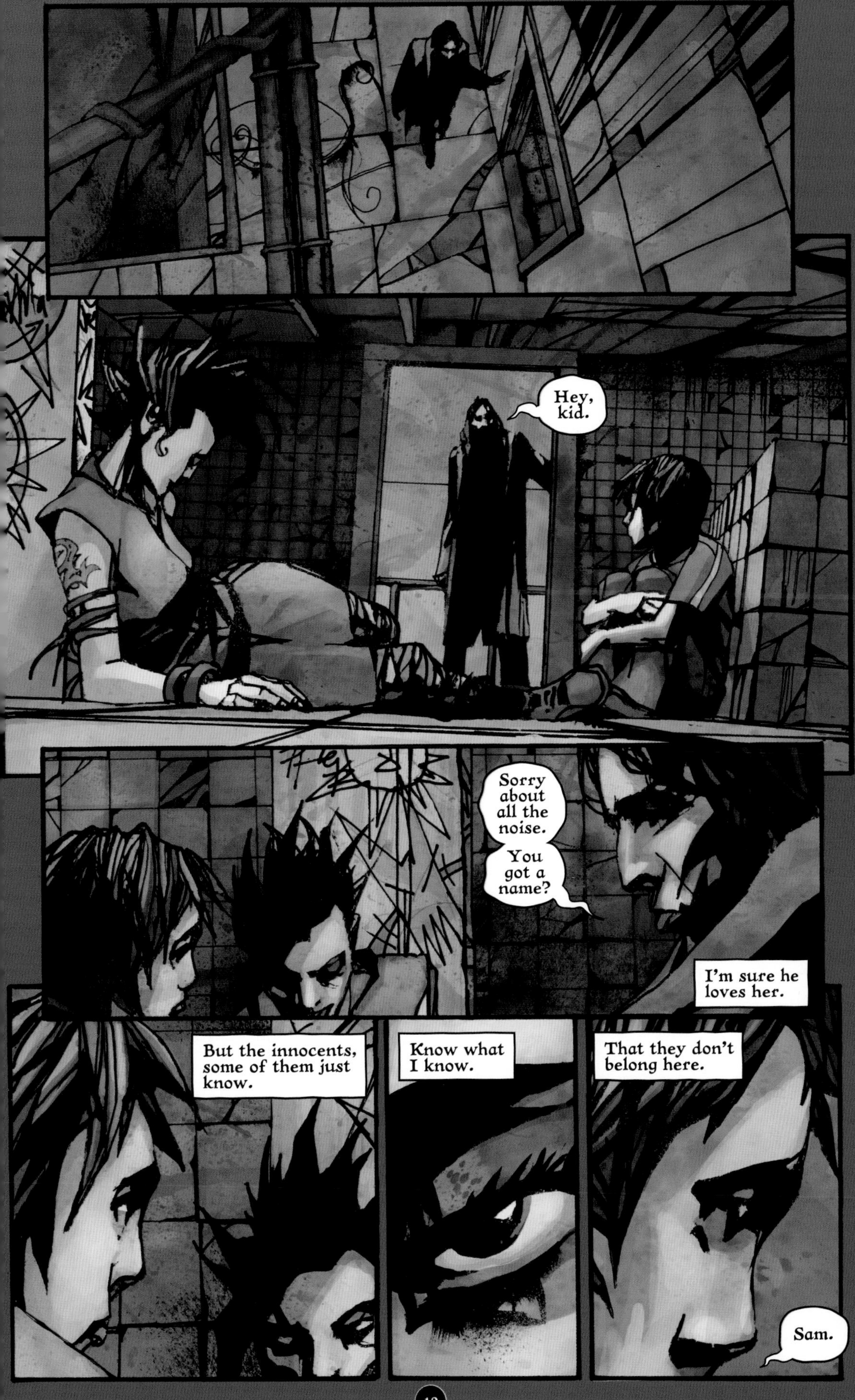
Hey, kid.
Sorry about all the noise.
You got a name?
I'm sure he loves her.
But the innocents, some of them just know.
Know what I know.
That they don't belong here.
Sam.

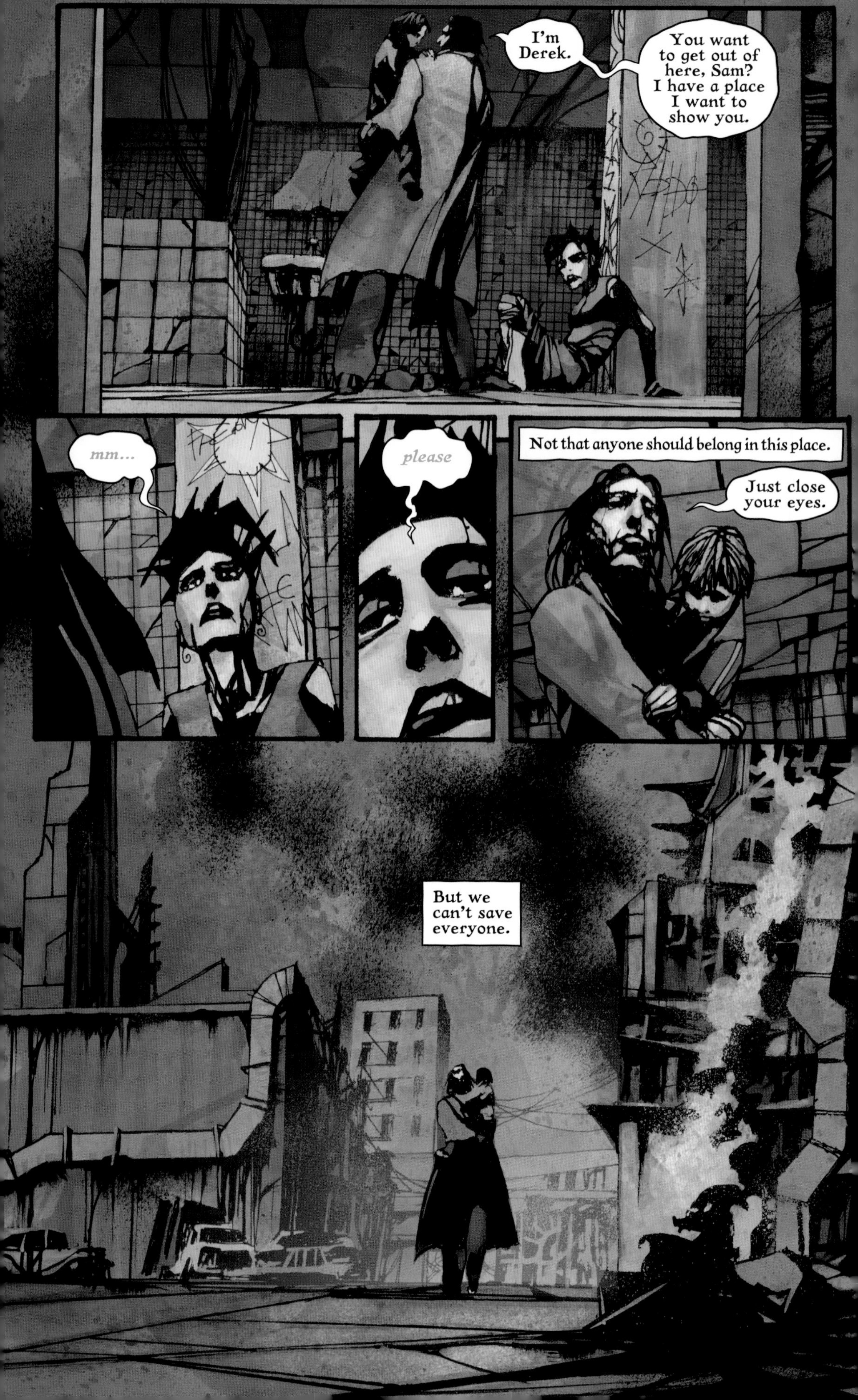
I'm Derek.
You want to get out of here, Sam? I have a place I want to show you.
mm...
please
Not that anyone should belong in this place.
Just close your eyes.
But we can't save everyone.

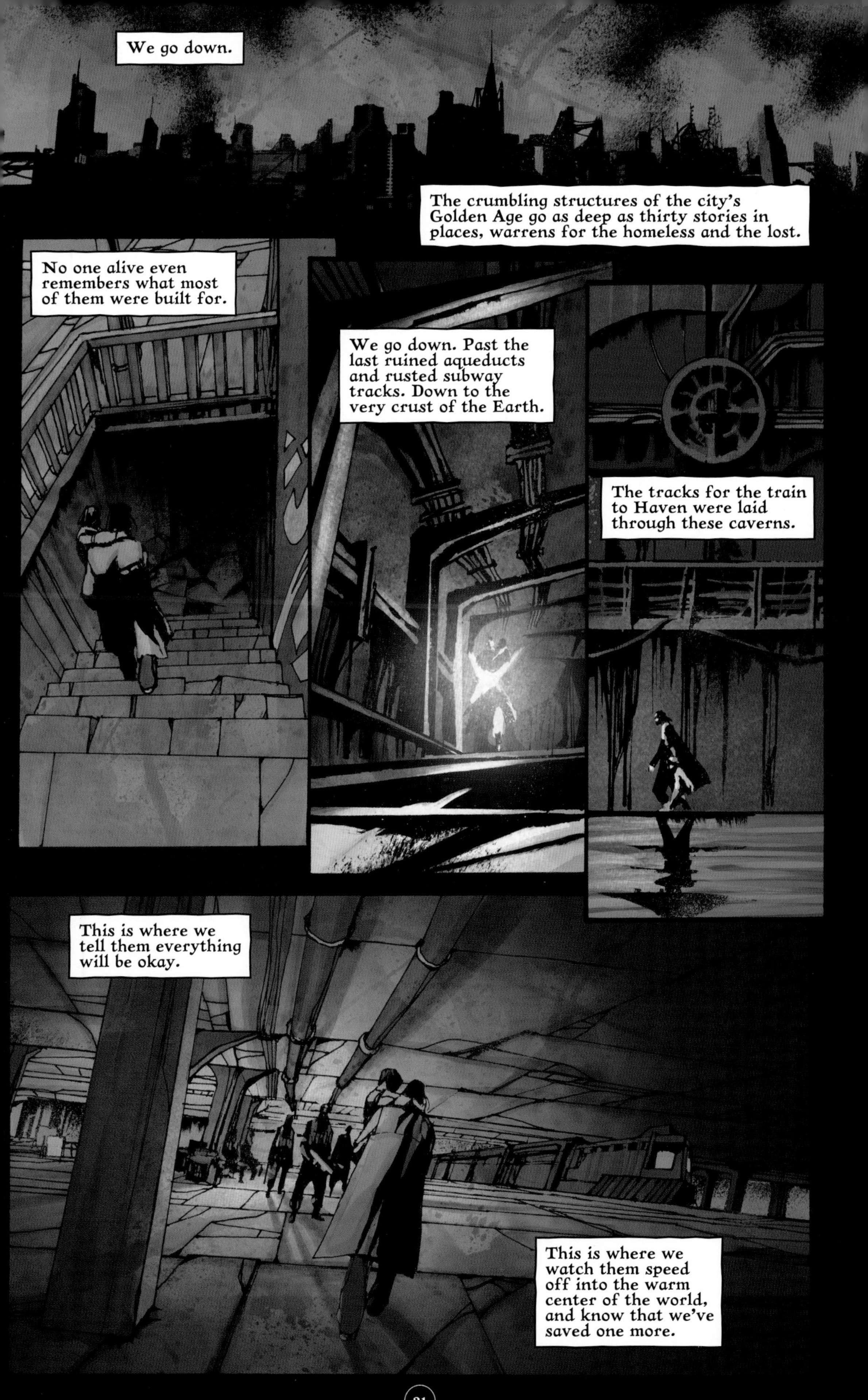
We go down.
The crumbling structures of the city's Golden Age go as deep as thirty stories in places, warrens for the homeless and the lost.
No one alive even remembers what most of them were built for.
We go down. Past the last ruined aqueducts and rusted subway tracks. Down to the very crust of the Earth.
The tracks for the train to Haven were laid through these caverns.
This is where we tell them everything will be okay.
This is where we watch them speed off into the warm center of the world, and know that we've saved one more.

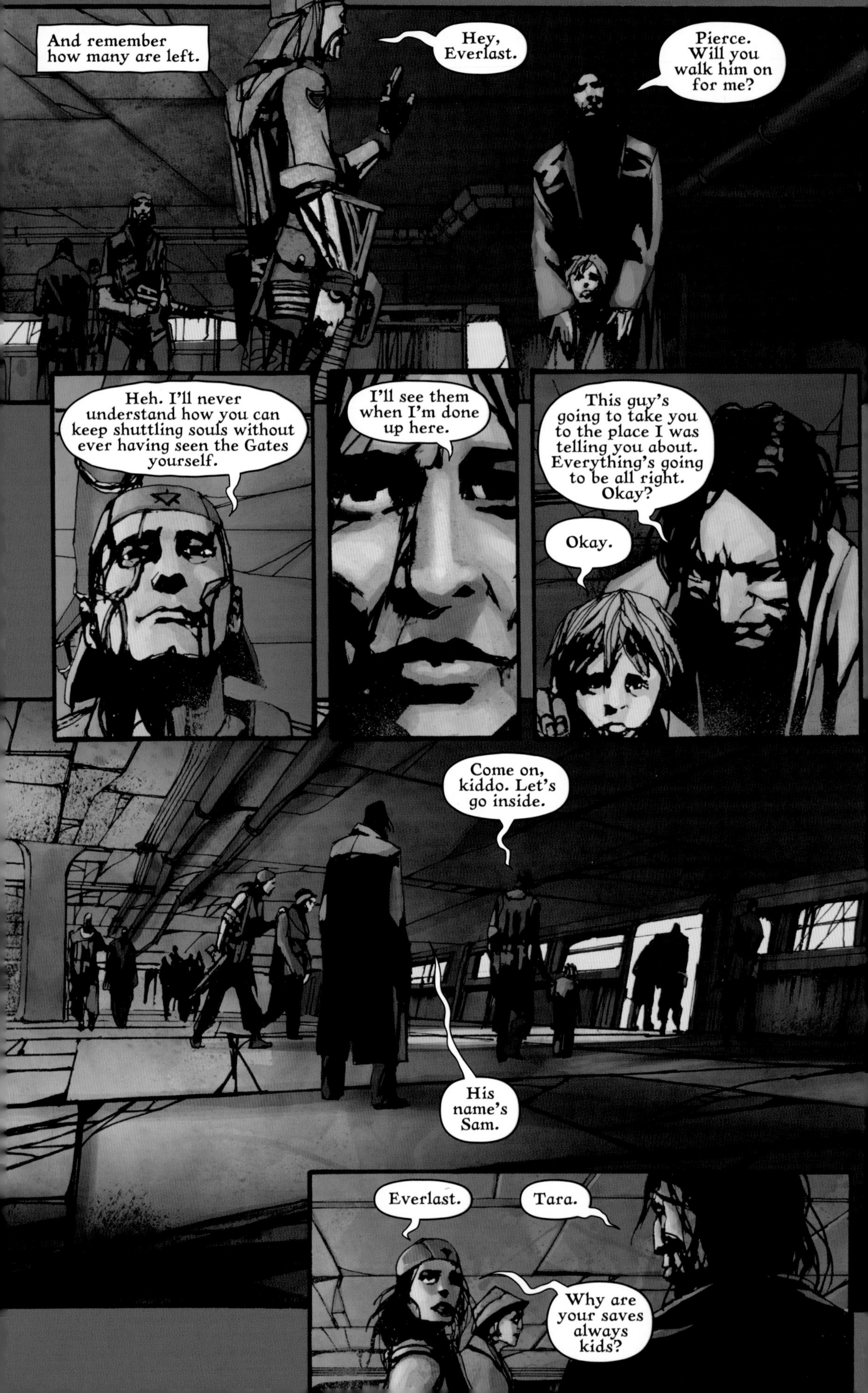
And remember how many are left.
Hey, Everlast.
Pierce. Will you walk him on for me?
Heh. I'll never understand how you can keep shuttling souls without ever having seen the Gates yourself.
I'll see them when I'm done up here.
This guy's going to take you to the place I was telling you about. Everything's going to be all right. Okay?
Okay.
Come on, kiddo. Let's go inside.
His name's Sam.
Everlast.
Tara.
Why are your saves always kids?

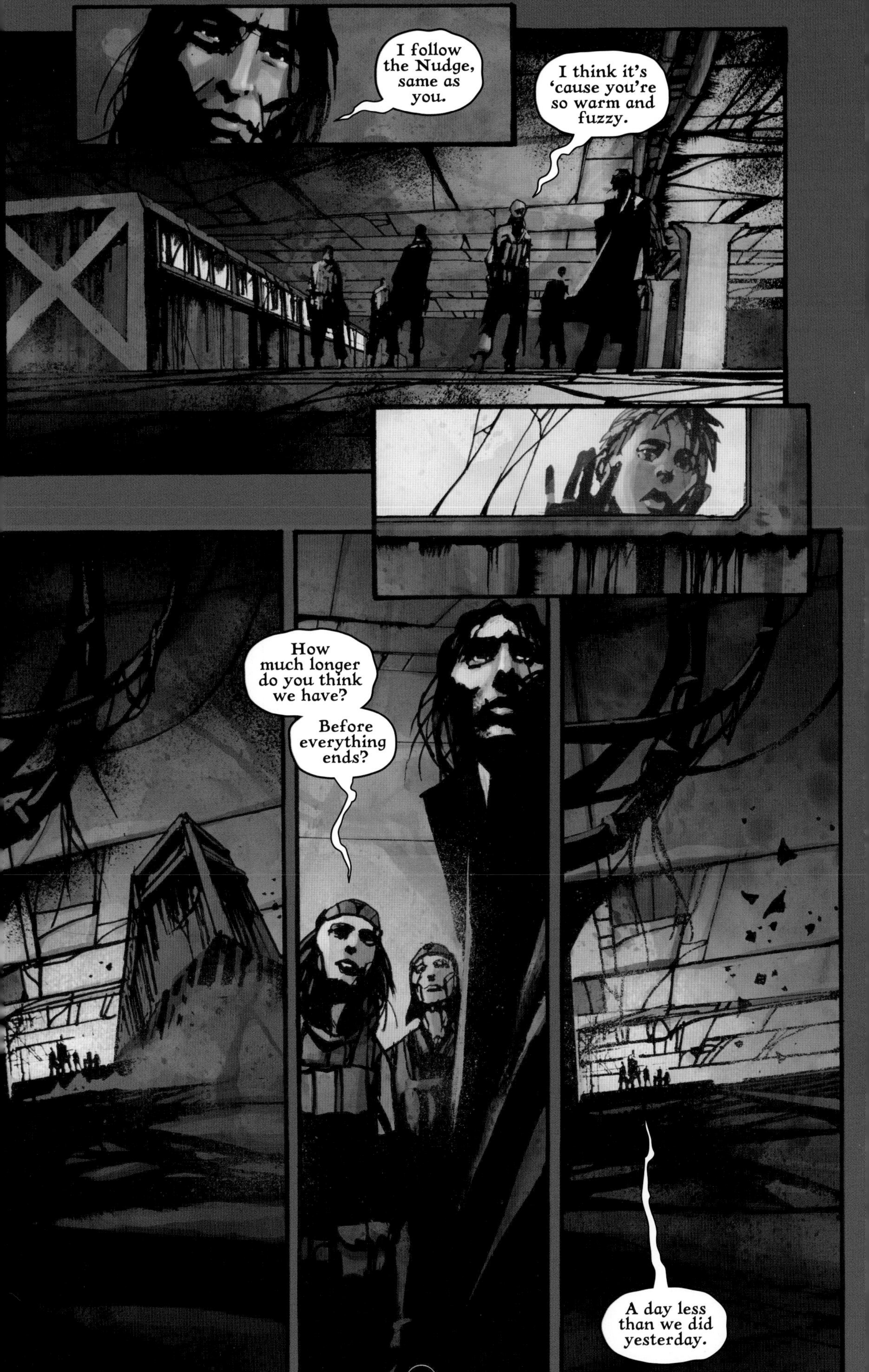
I follow the Nudge, same as you.
I think it's 'cause you're so warm and fuzzy.
How much longer do you think we have?
Before everything ends?
A day less than we did yesterday.

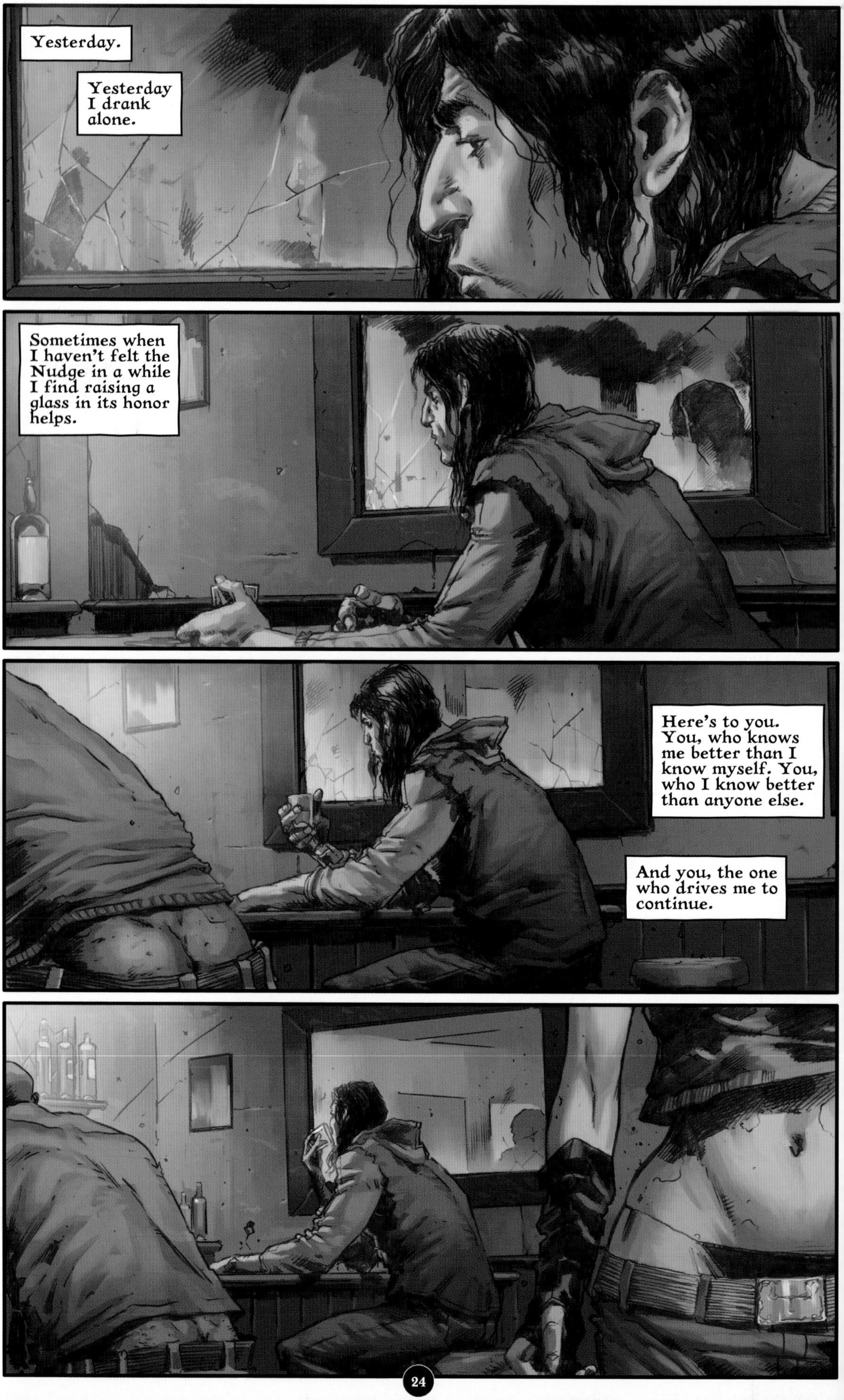
Yesterday.
Yesterday I drank alone.
Sometimes when I haven't felt the Nudge in a while I find raising a glass in its honor helps.
Here's to you. You, who knows me better than I know myself. You, who I know better than anyone else.
And you, the one who drives me to continue.

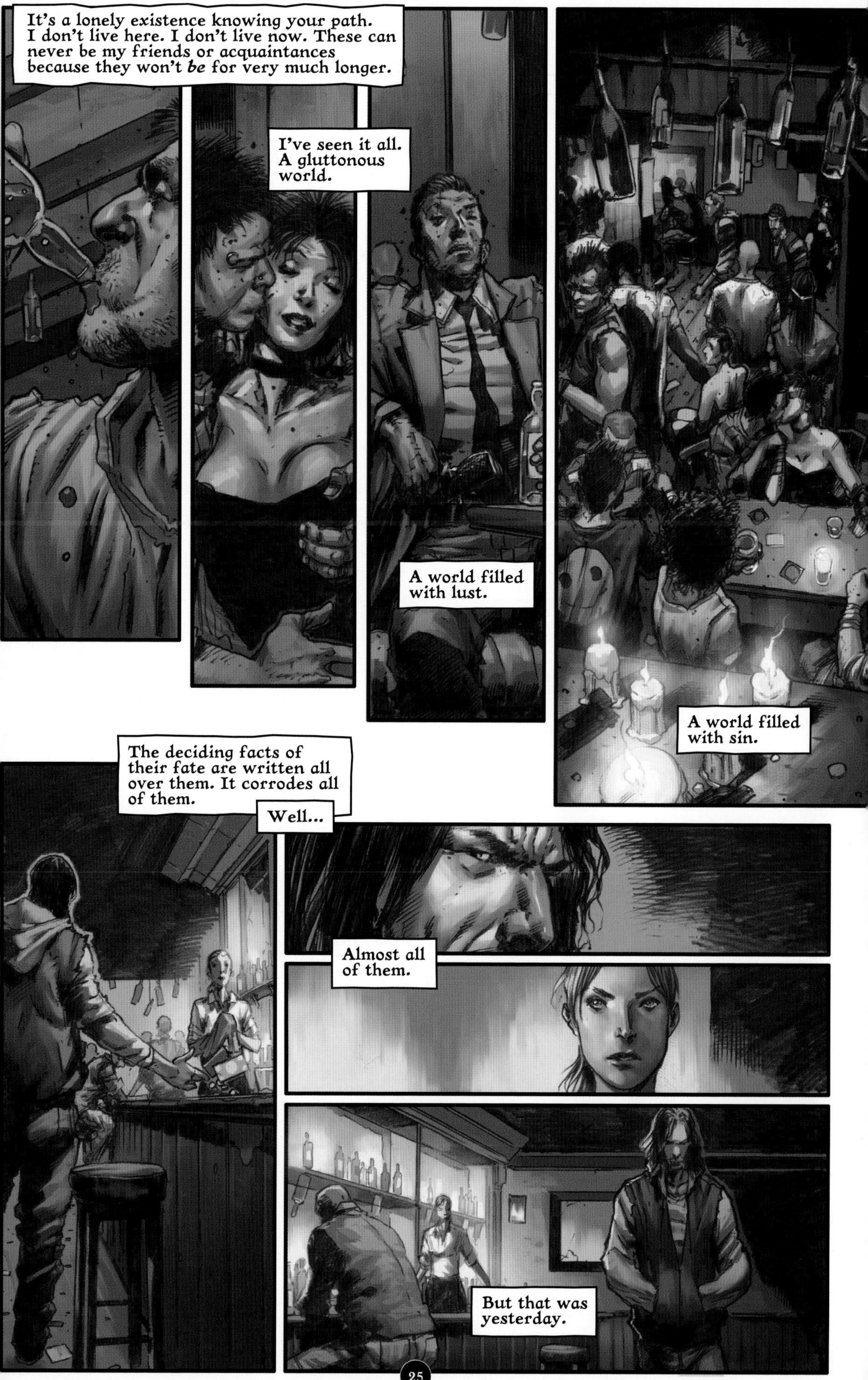
It's a lonely existence knowing your path. I don't live here. I don't live now. These can never be my friends or acquaintances because they won't *be* for very much longer.
I've seen it all. A gluttonous world.
A world filled with lust.
A world filled with sin.
The deciding facts of their fate are written all over them. It corrodes all of them.
Well...
Almost all of them.
But that was yesterday.

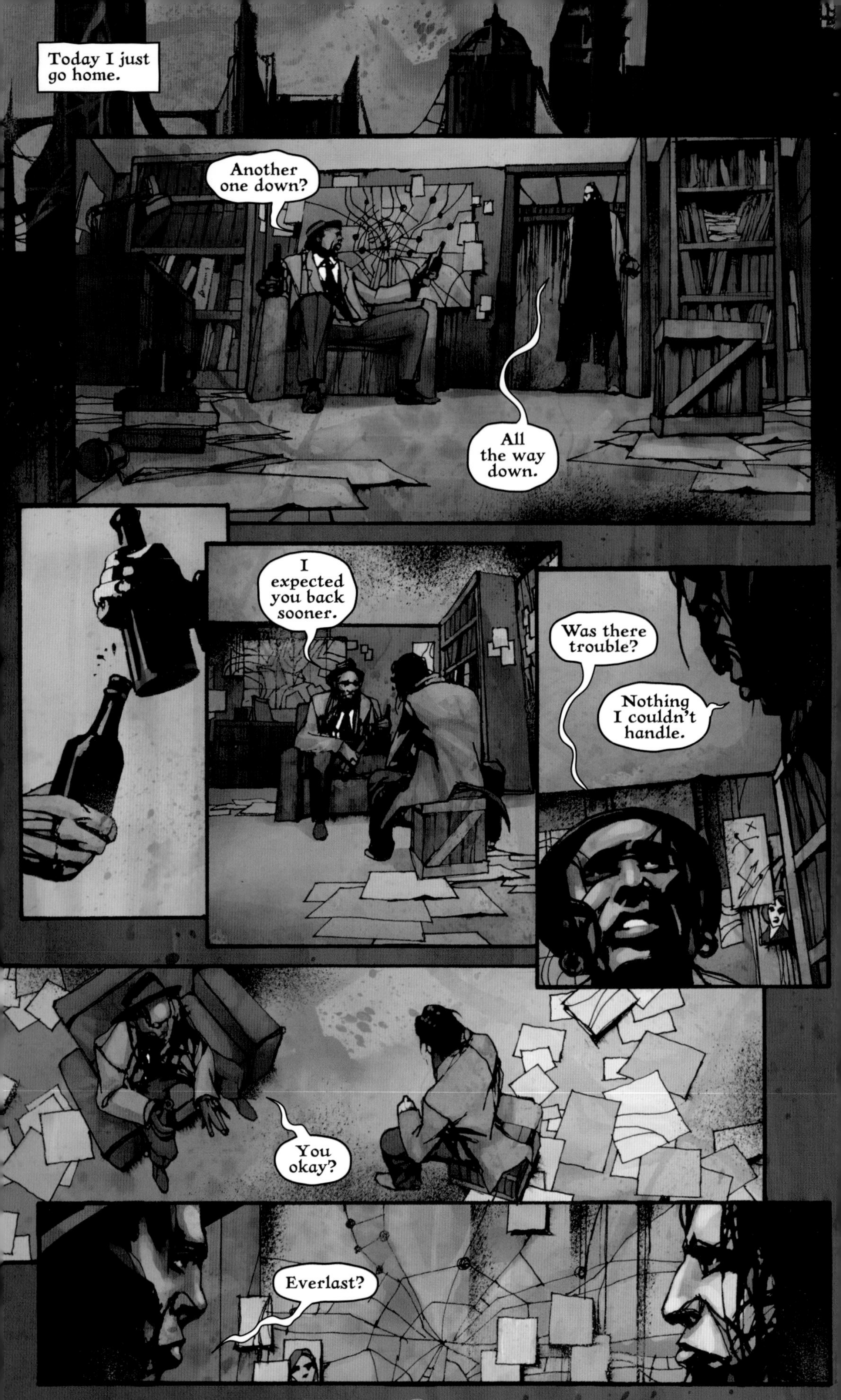
Today I just go home.
Another one down?
All the way down.
I expected you back sooner.
Was there trouble?
Nothing I couldn't handle.
You okay?
Everlast?

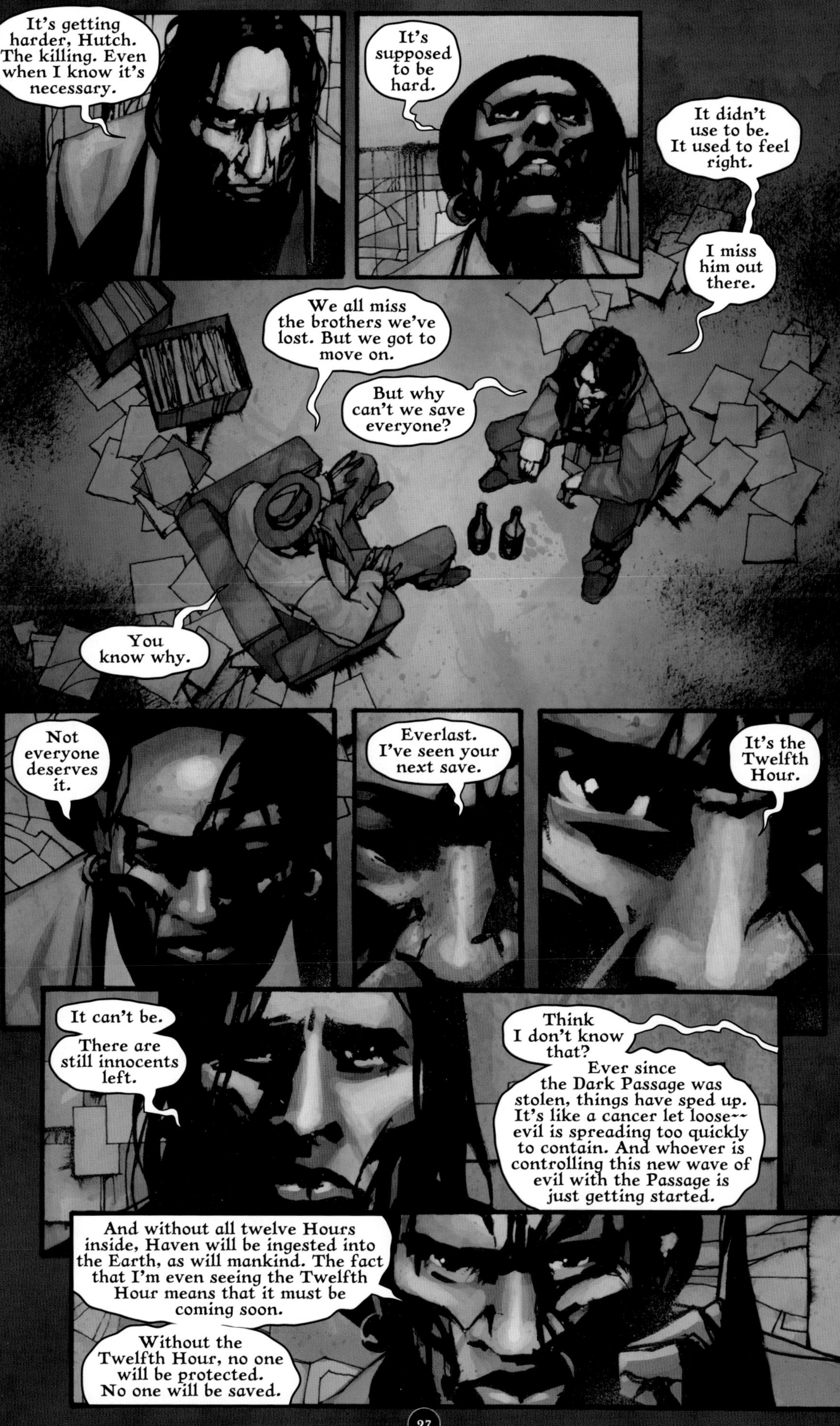

It's getting harder, Hutch. The killing. Even when I know it's necessary.
It's supposed to be hard.
It didn't use to be. It used to feel right.
I miss him out there.
We all miss the brothers we've lost. But we got to move on.
But why can't we save everyone?
You know why.
Not everyone deserves it.
Everlast. I've seen your next save.
It's the Twelfth Hour.
It can't be.
There are still innocents left.
Think I don't know that?
Ever since the Dark Passage was stolen, things have sped up. It's like a cancer let loose-- evil is spreading too quickly to contain. And whoever is controlling this new wave of evil with the Passage is just getting started.
And without all twelve Hours inside, Haven will be ingested into the Earth, as will mankind. The fact that I'm even seeing the Twelfth Hour means that it must be coming soon.
Without the Twelfth Hour, no one will be protected. No one will be saved.

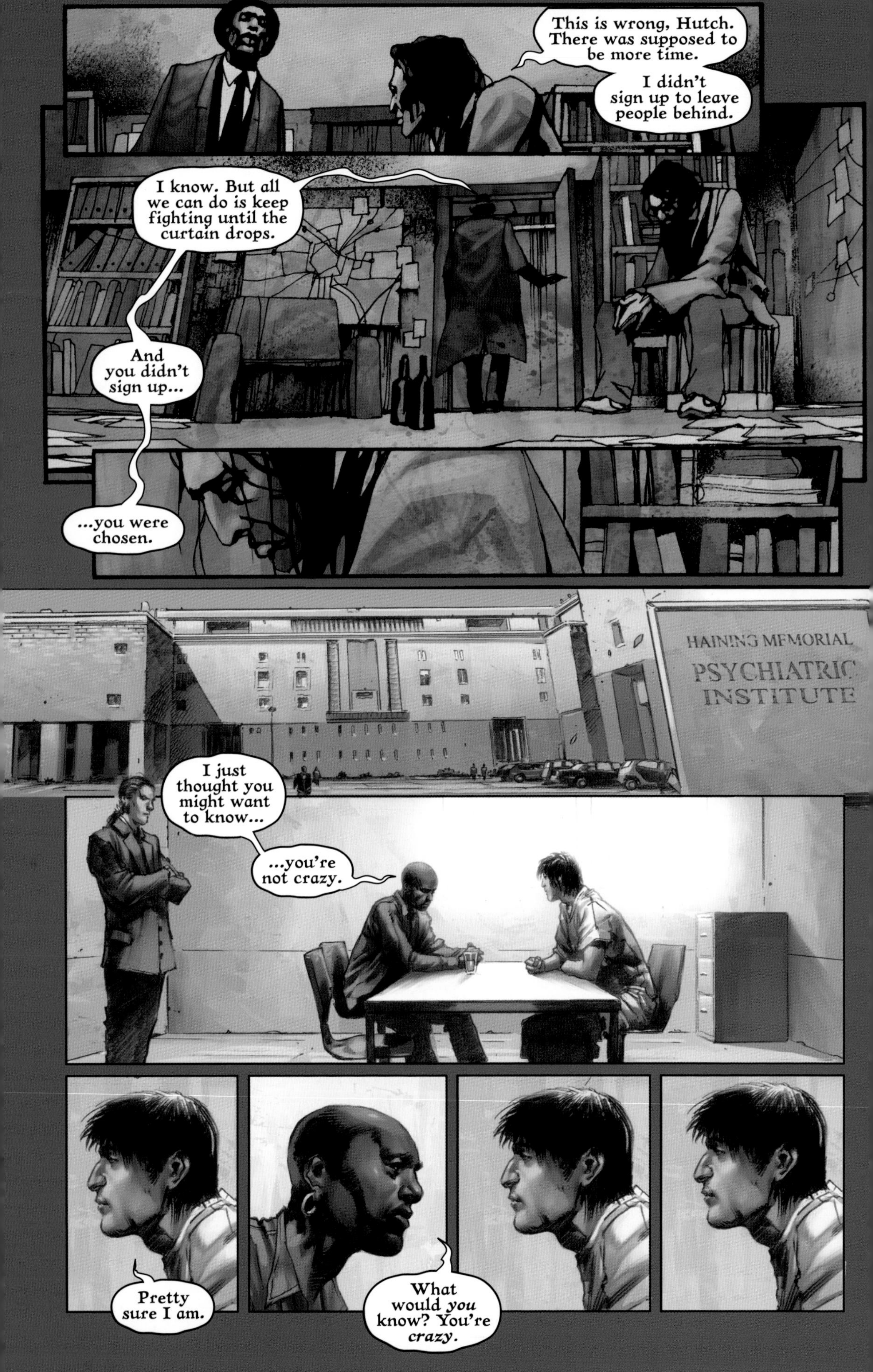
This is wrong, Hutch. There was supposed to be more time.
I didn't sign up to leave people behind.
I know. But all we can do is keep fighting until the curtain drops.
And you didn't sign up...
...you were chosen.
HAINING MEMORIAL
PSYCHIATRIC
INSTITUTE
I just thought you might want to know...
...you're not crazy.
Pretty sure I am.
What would *you* know? You're *crazy*.

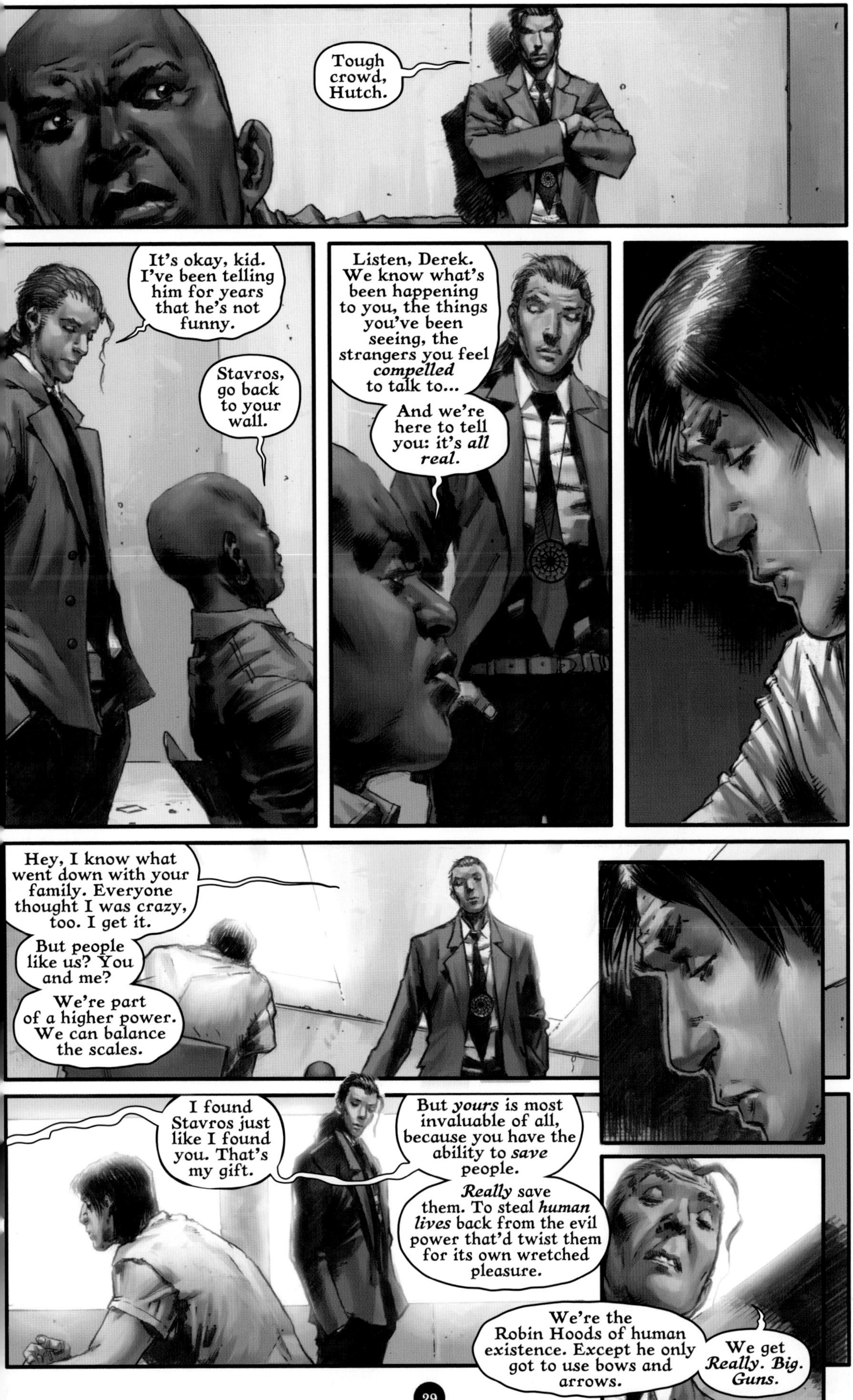

Tough crowd, Hutch.
It's okay, kid. I've been telling him for years that he's not funny.
Stavros, go back to your wall.
Listen, Derek. We know what's been happening to you, the things you've been seeing, the strangers you feel *compelled* to talk to...
And we're here to tell you: it's *all real*.
Hey, I know what went down with your family. Everyone thought I was crazy, too. I get it.
But people like us? You and me?
We're part of a higher power. We can balance the scales.
I found Stavros just like I found you. That's my gift.
But *yours* is most invaluable of all, because you have the ability to *save* people.
Really save them. To steal *human lives* back from the evil power that'd twist them for its own wretched pleasure.
We're the Robin Hoods of human existence. Except he only got to use bows and arrows.
We get *Really. Big. Guns.*

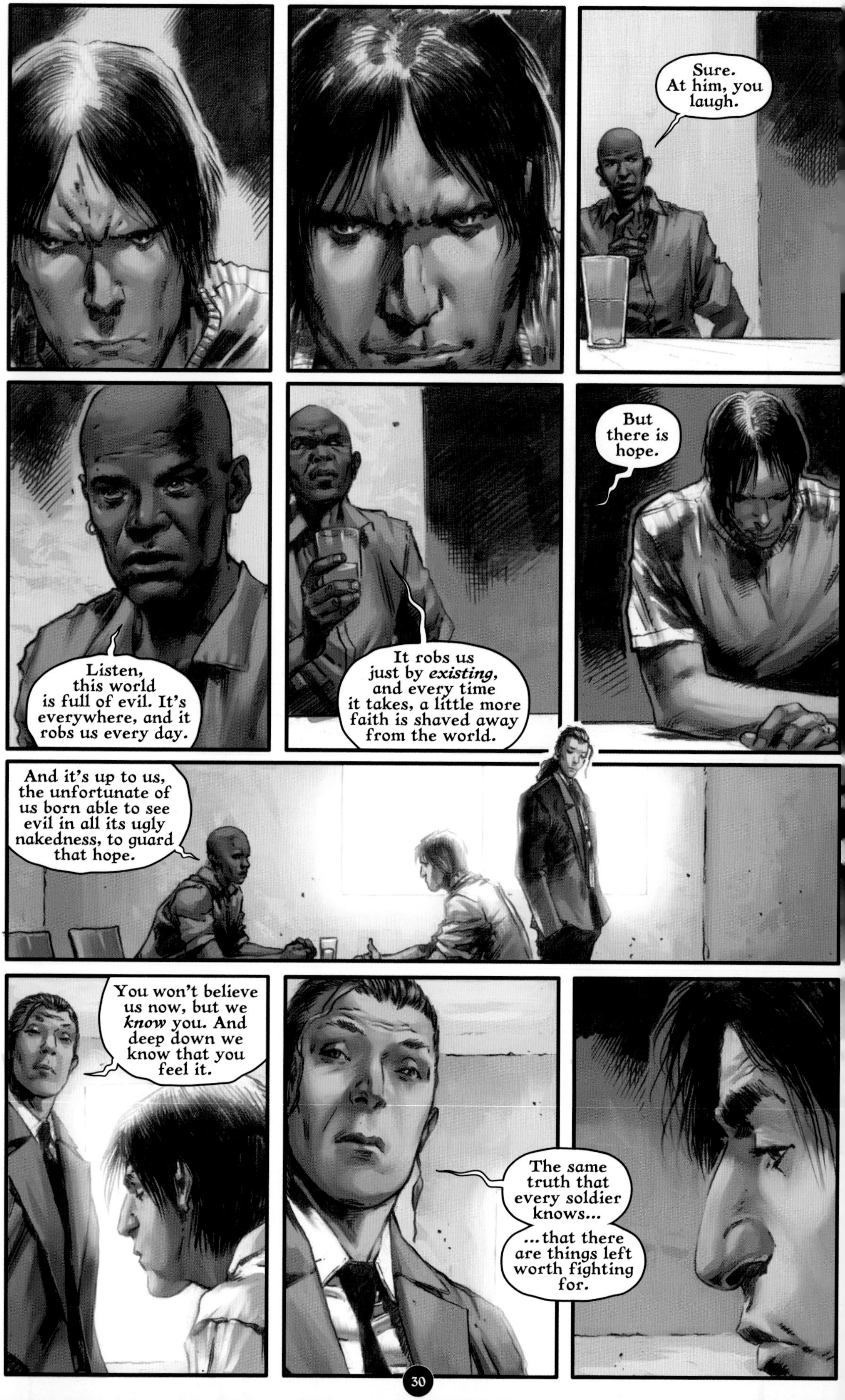
Sure. At him, you laugh.
Listen, this world is full of evil. It's everywhere, and it robs us every day.
It robs us just by *existing*, and every time it takes, a little more faith is shaved away from the world.
But there is hope.
And it's up to us, the unfortunate of us born able to see evil in all its ugly nakedness, to guard that hope.
You won't believe us now, but we *know* you. And deep down we know that you feel it.
The same truth that every soldier knows...
...that there are things left worth fighting for.

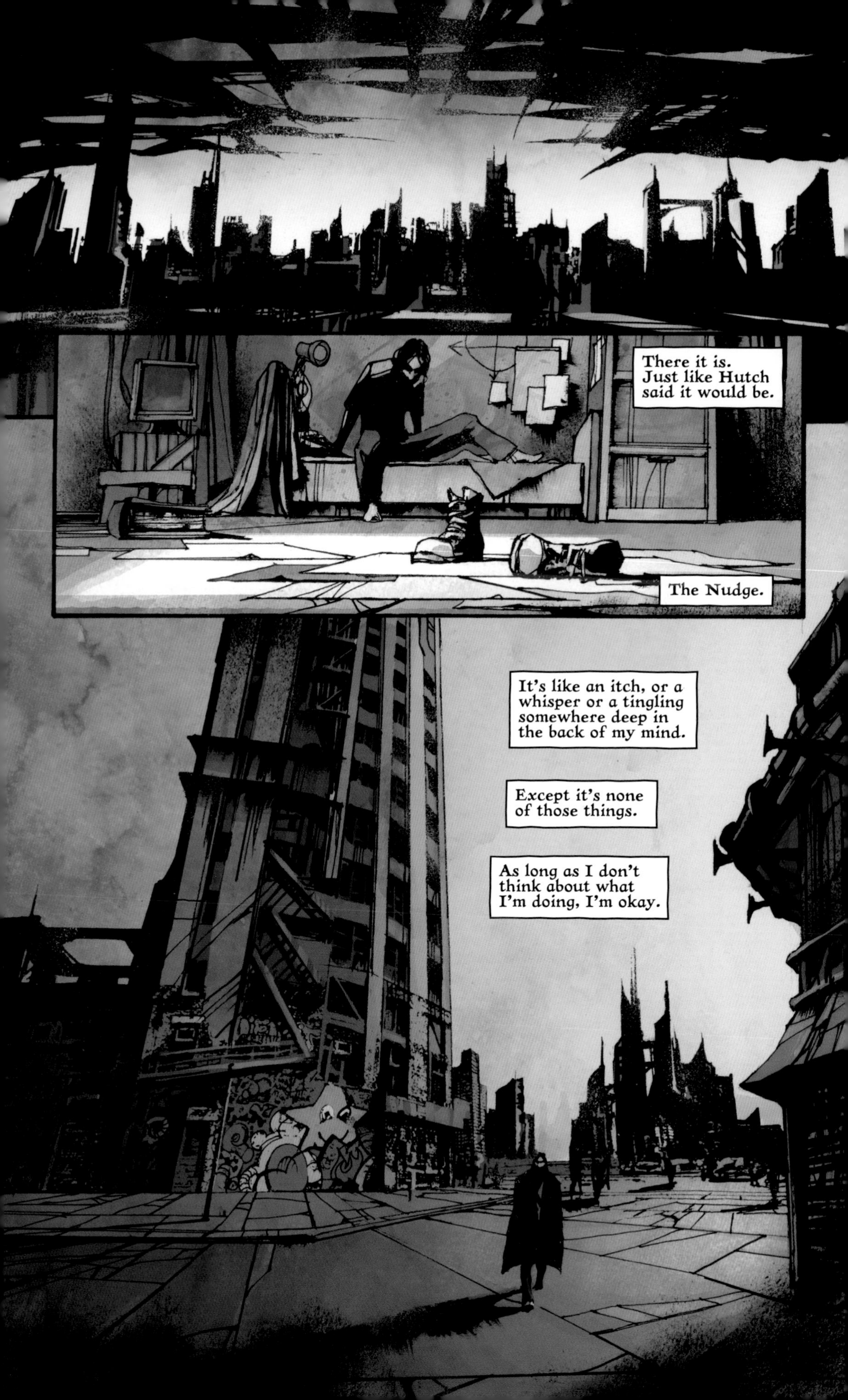
There it is. Just like Hutch said it would be.
The Nudge.
It's like an itch, or a whisper or a tingling somewhere deep in the back of my mind.
Except it's none of those things.
As long as I don't think about what I'm doing, I'm okay.

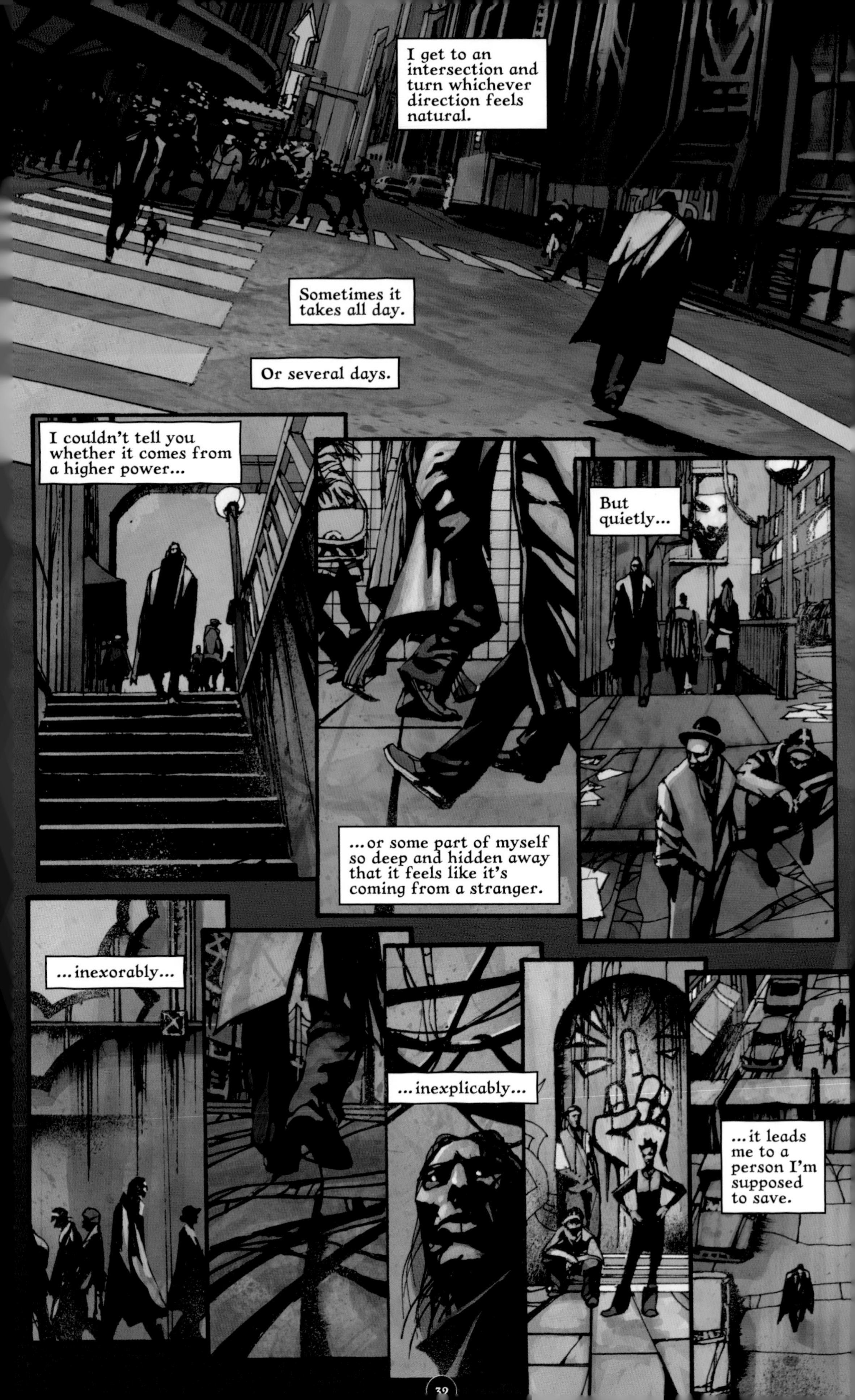
I get to an intersection and turn whichever direction feels natural.
Sometimes it takes all day.
Or several days.
I couldn't tell you whether it comes from a higher power...
...or some part of myself so deep and hidden away that it feels like it's coming from a stranger.
But quietly...
...inexorably...
...inexplicably...
...it leads me to a person I'm supposed to save.

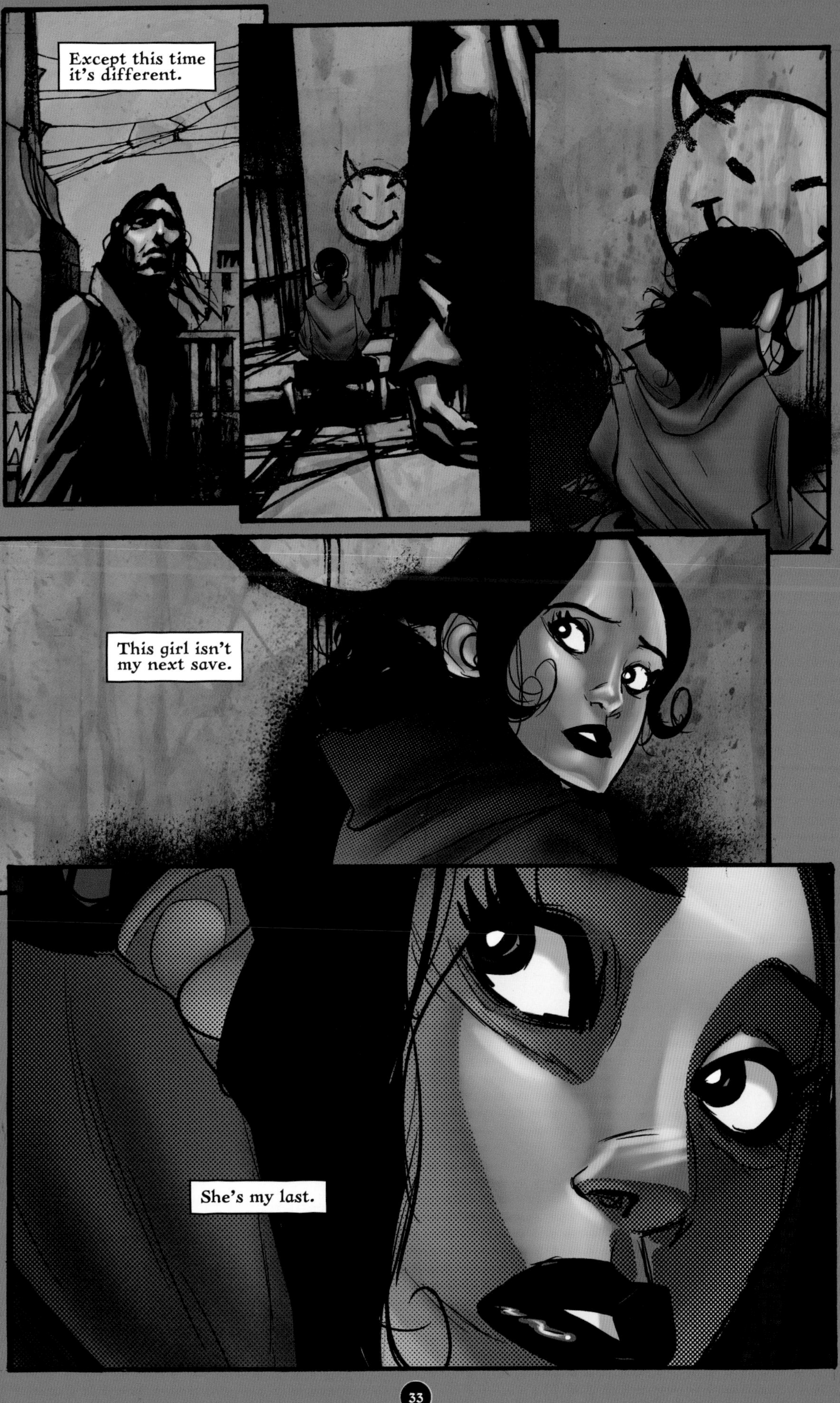
Except this time it's different.
This girl isn't my next save.
She's my last.

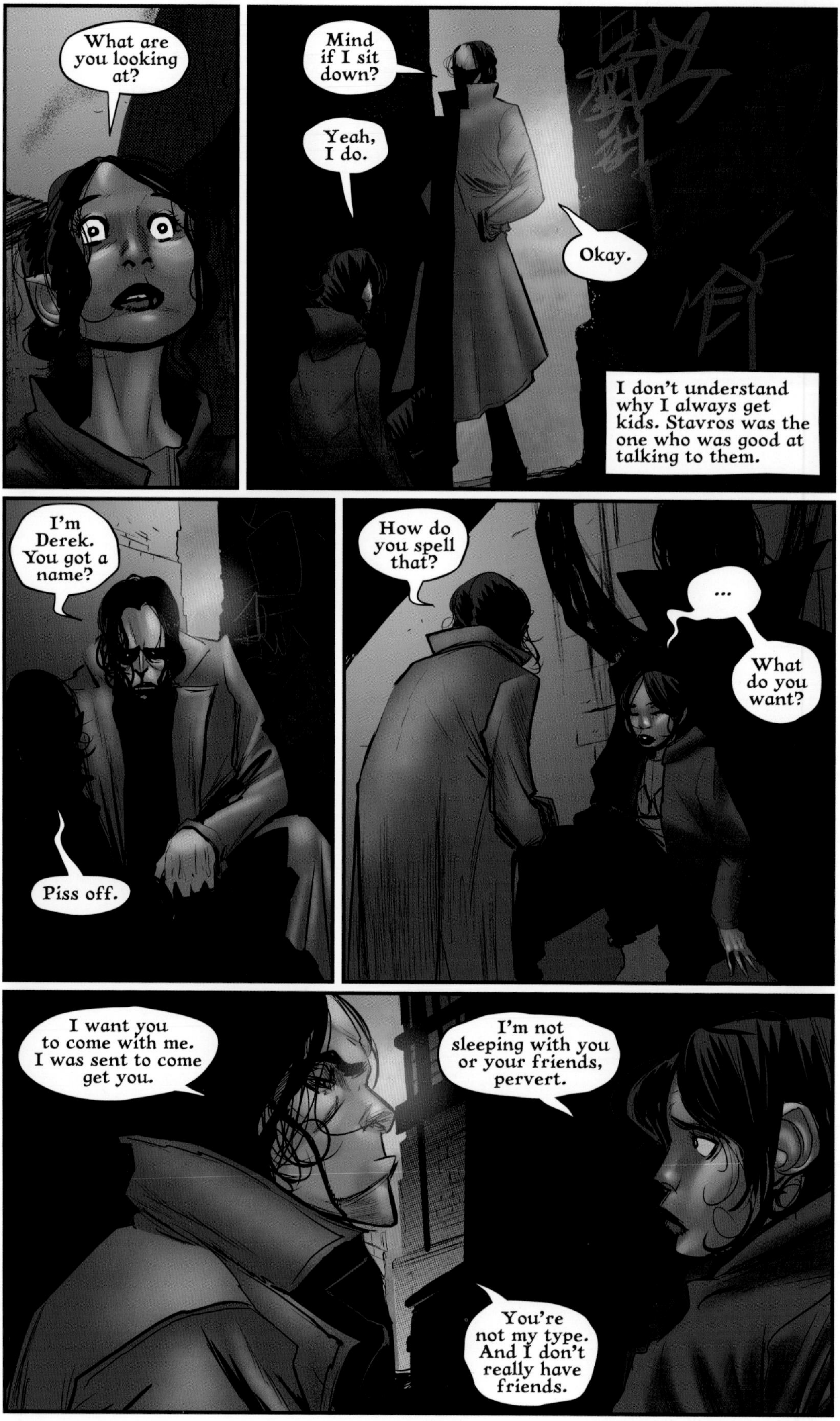
What are you looking at?
Mind if I sit down?
Yeah, I do.
Okay.
I don't understand why I always get kids. Stavros was the one who was good at talking to them.
I'm Derek. You got a name?
Piss off.
How do you spell that?
...
What do you want?
I want you to come with me. I was sent to come get you.
I'm not sleeping with you or your friends, pervert.
You're not my type. And I don't really have friends.

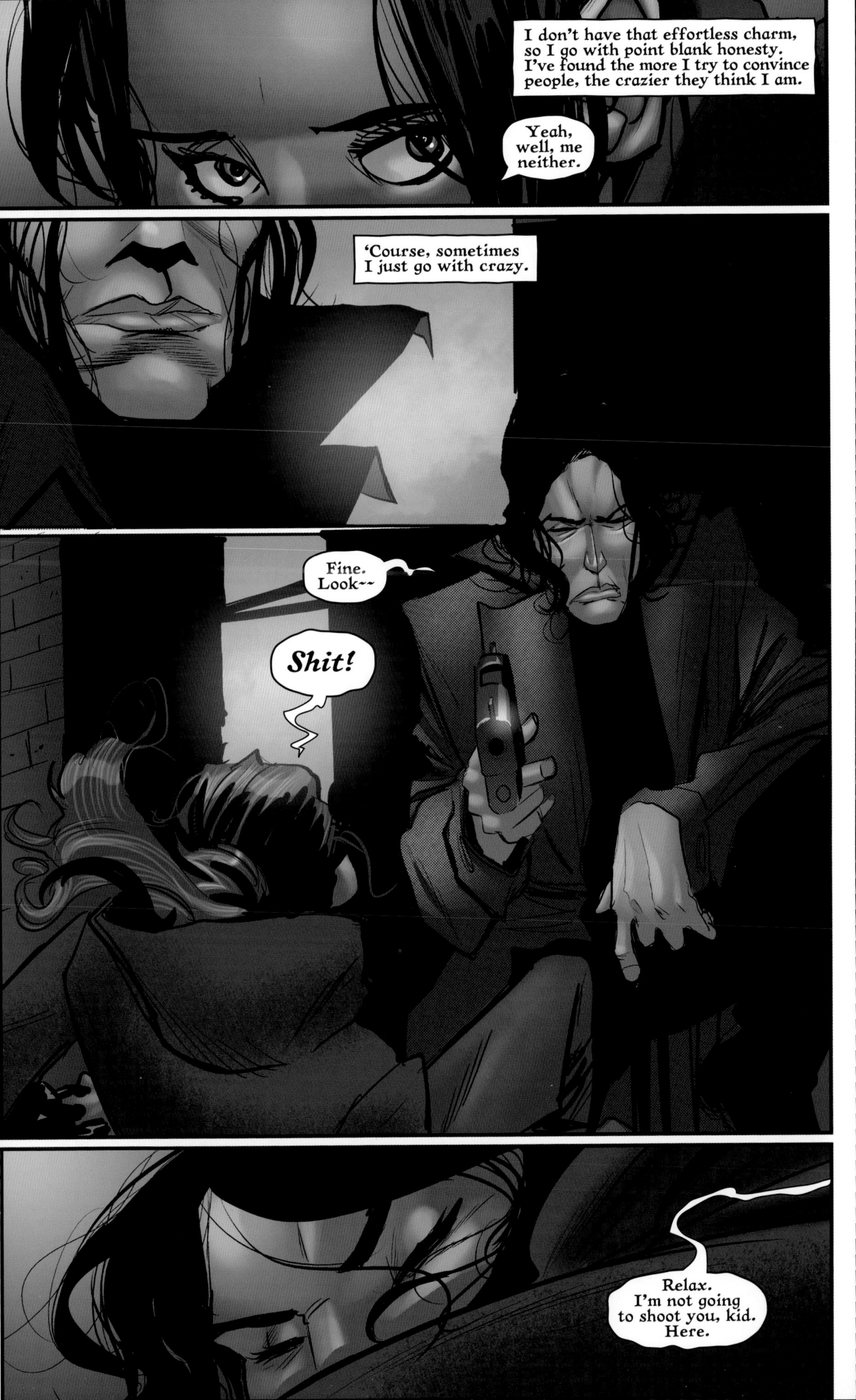
I don't have that effortless charm, so I go with point blank honesty. I've found the more I try to convince people, the crazier they think I am.
Yeah, well, me neither.
'Course, sometimes I just go with crazy.
Fine. Look--
Shit!
Relax. I'm not going to shoot you, kid. Here.

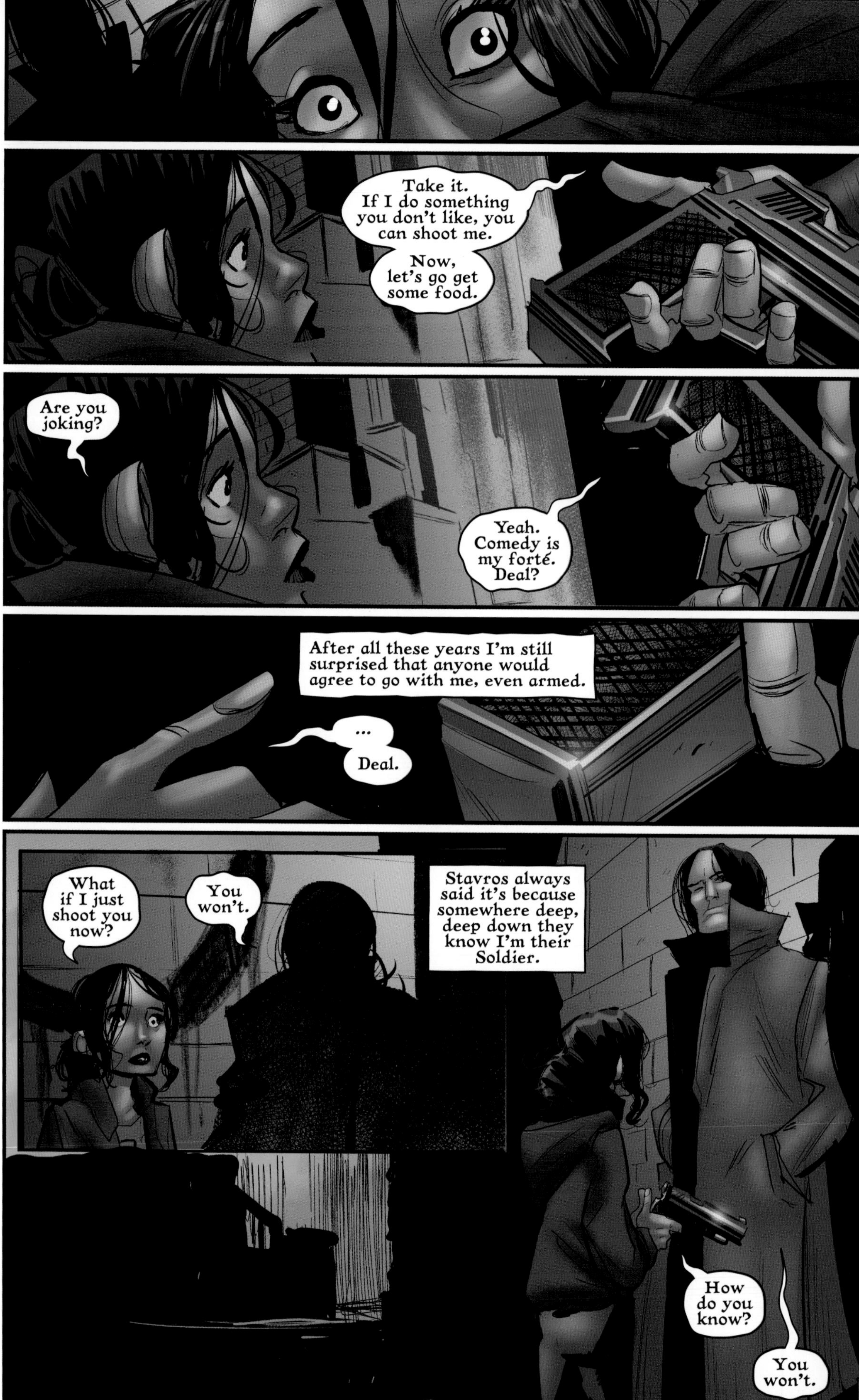
Take it.
If I do something you don't like, you can shoot me.
Now, let's go get some food.
Are you joking?
Yeah. Comedy is my forté. Deal?
After all these years I'm still surprised that anyone would agree to go with me, even armed.
...
Deal.
What if I just shoot you now?
You won't.
Stavros always said it's because somewhere deep, deep down they know I'm their Soldier.
How do you know?
You won't.

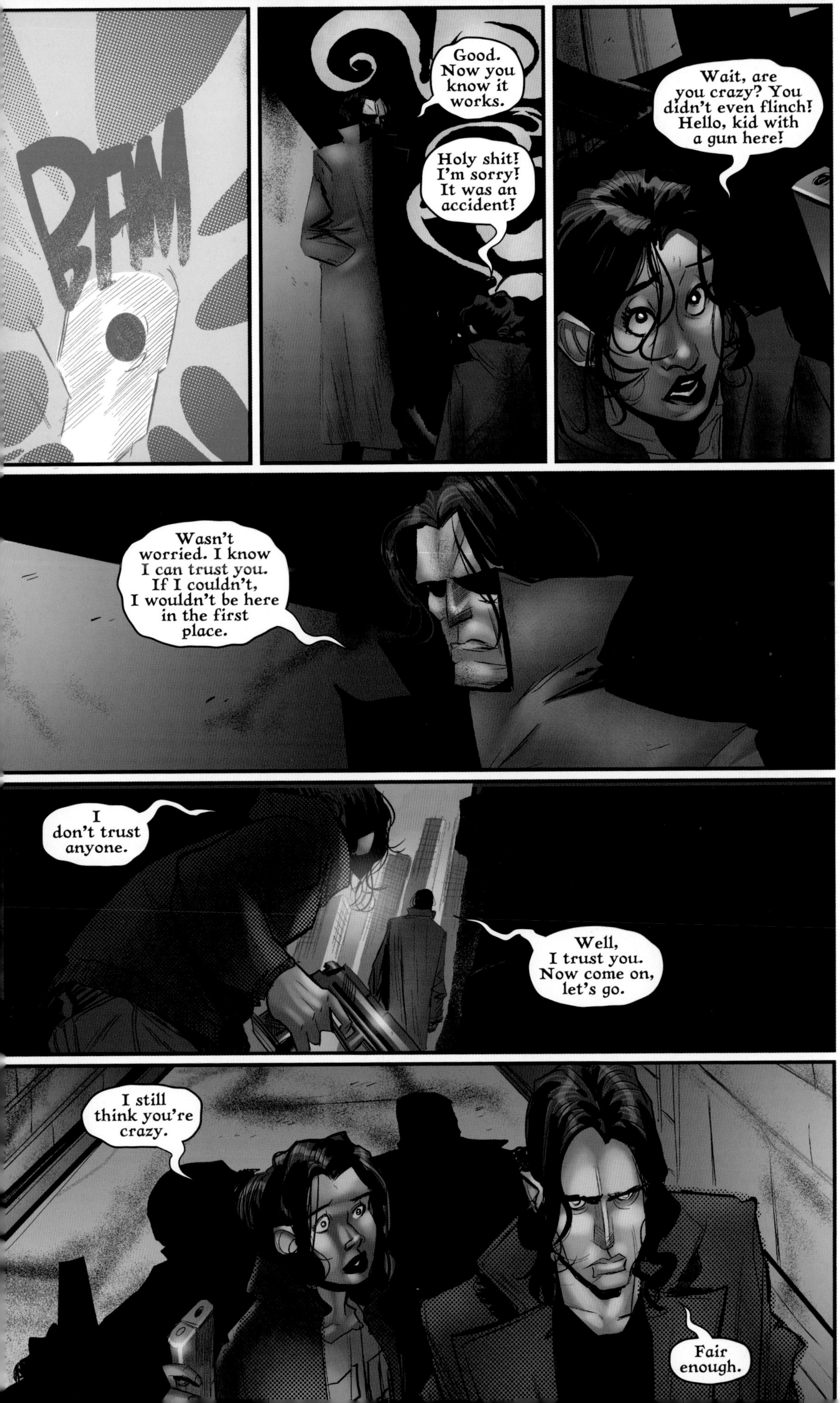
BAM
Good. Now you know it works.
Holy shit! I'm sorry! It was an accident!
Wait, are you crazy? You didn't even flinch! Hello, kid with a gun here!
Wasn't worried. I know I can trust you. If I couldn't, I wouldn't be here in the first place.
I don't trust anyone.
Well, I trust you. Now come on, let's go.
I still think you're crazy.
Fair enough.

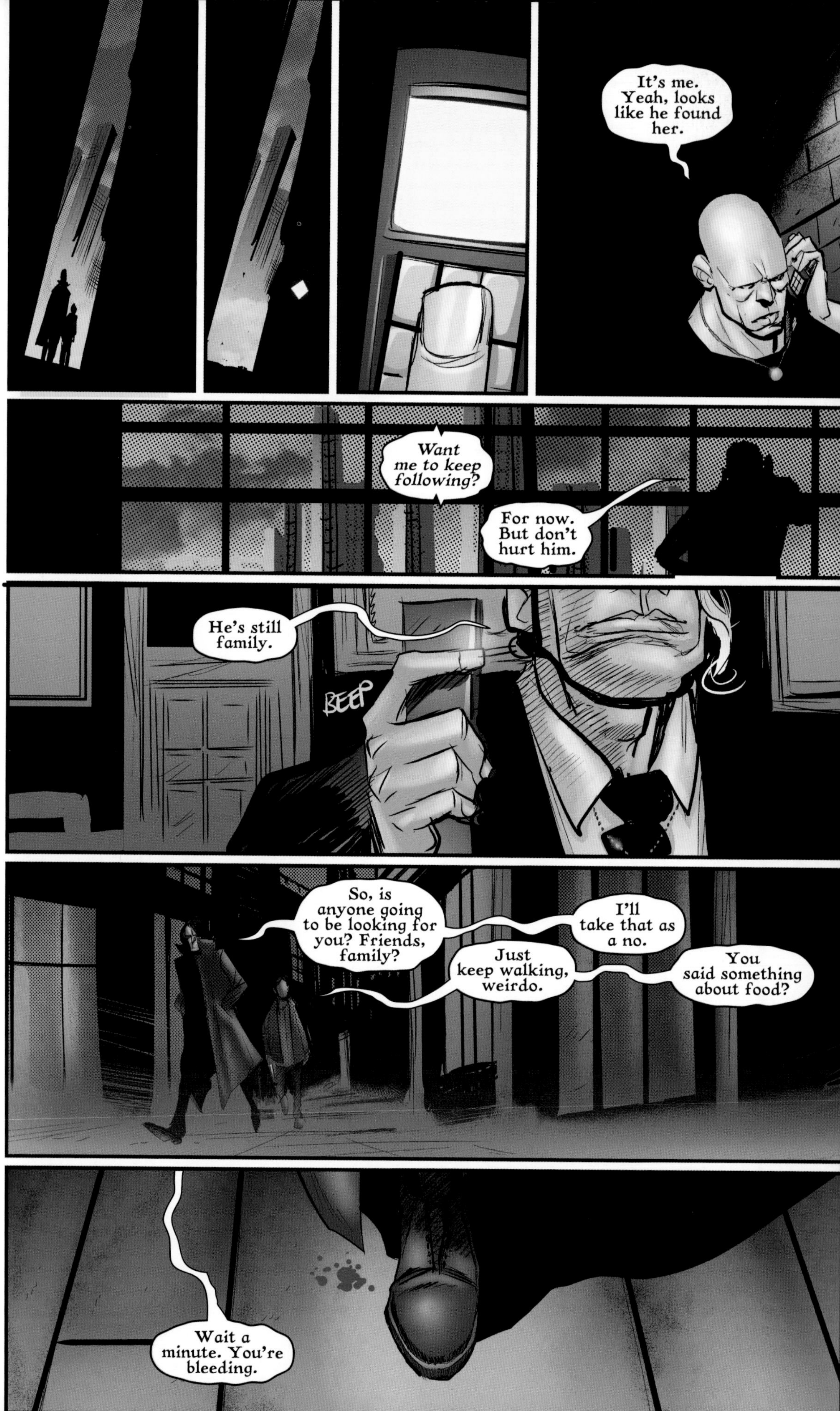
It's me. Yeah, looks like he found her.
Want me to keep following?
For now. But don't hurt him.
He's still family.
BEEP
So, is anyone going to be looking for you? Friends, family?
I'll take that as a no.
Just keep walking, weirdo.
You said something about food?
Wait a minute. You're bleeding.

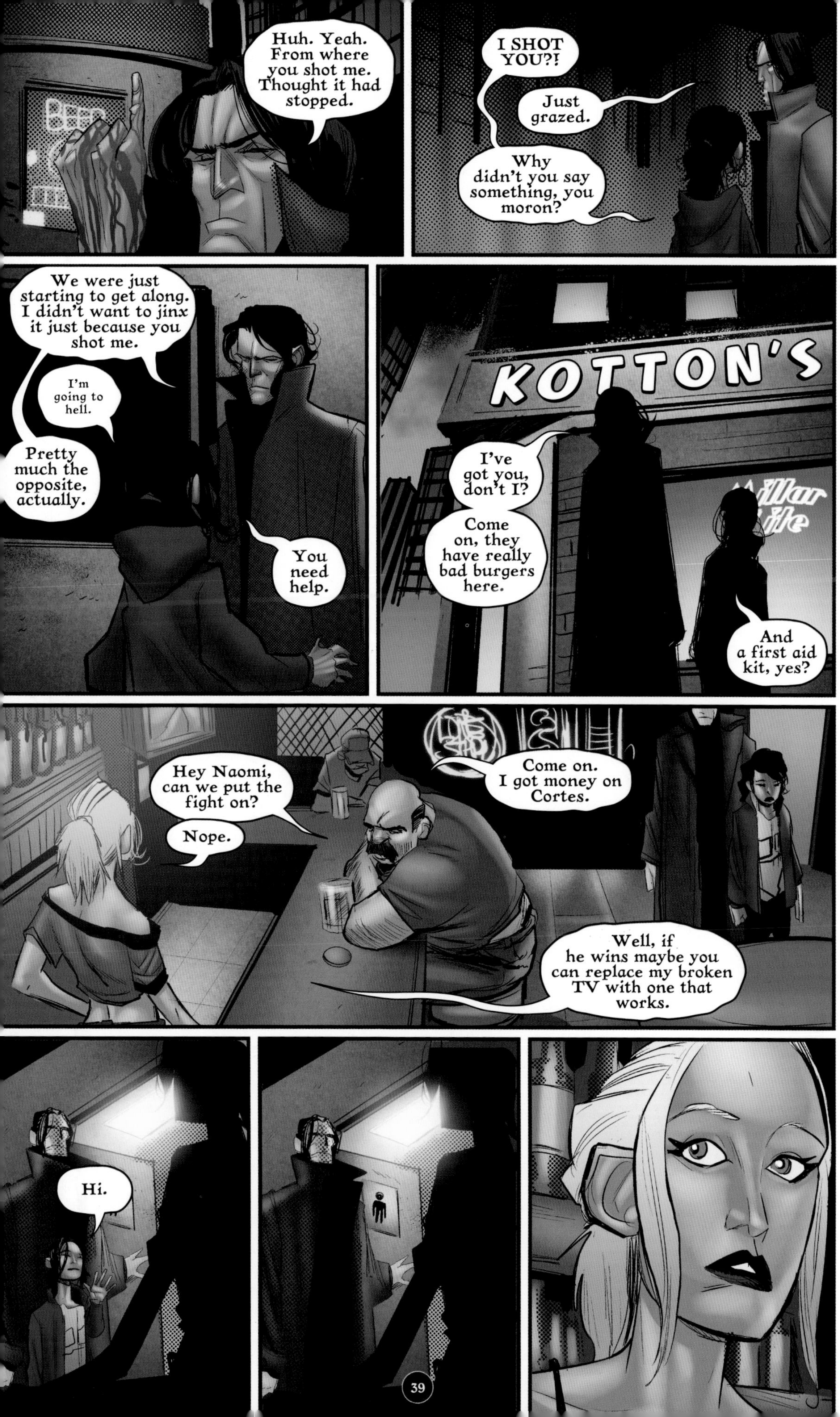
Huh. Yeah. From where you shot me. Thought it had stopped.
I SHOT YOU?!
Just grazed.
Why didn't you say something, you moron?
We were just starting to get along. I didn't want to jinx it just because you shot me.
I'm going to hell.
Pretty much the opposite, actually.
You need help.
KOTTON'S
I've got you, don't I?
Come on, they have really bad burgers here.
And a first aid kit, yes?
Hey Naomi, can we put the fight on?
Nope.
Come on. I got money on Cortes.
Well, if he wins maybe you can replace my broken TV with one that works.
Hi.

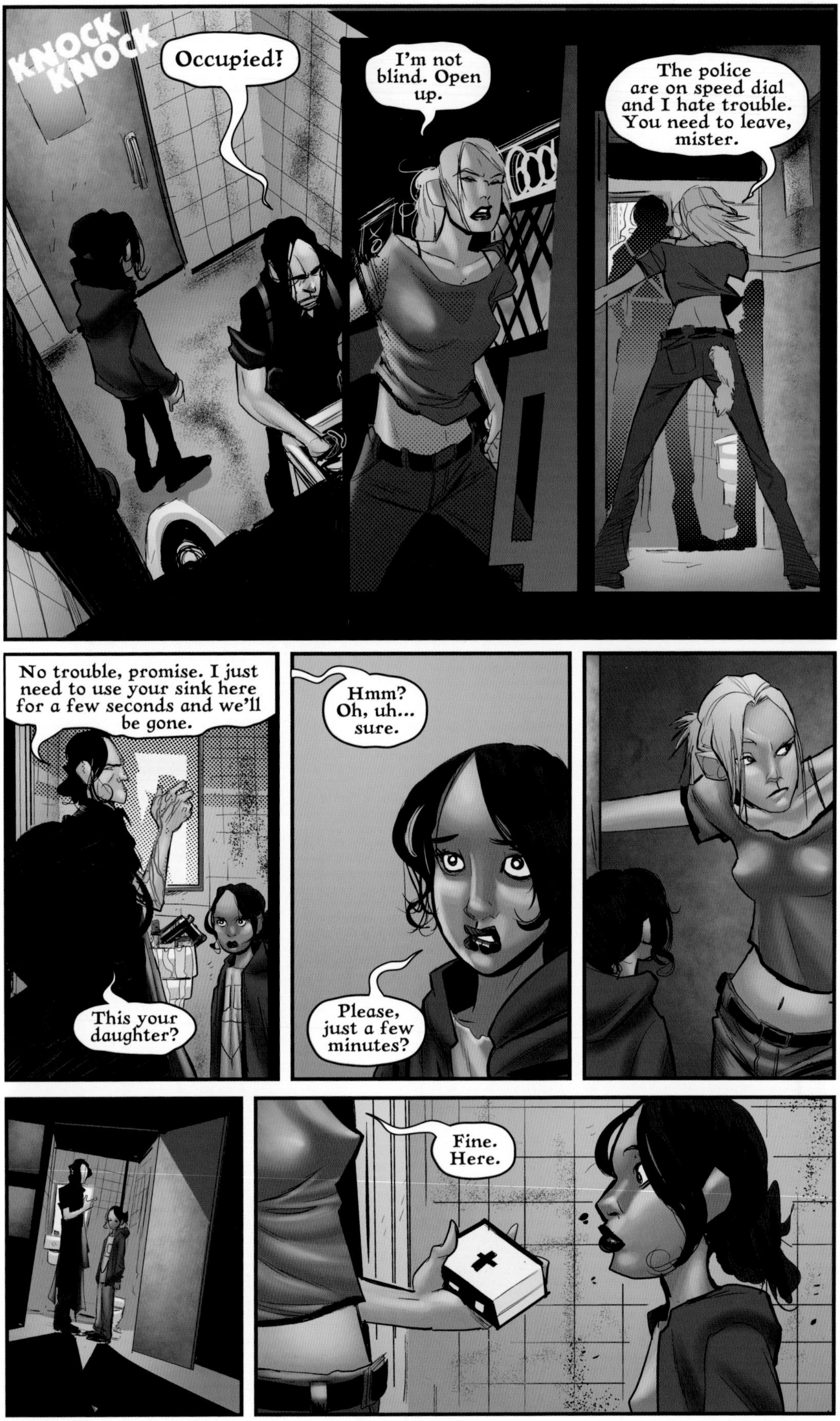
KNOCK KNOCK
Occupied!
I'm not blind. Open up.
The police are on speed dial and I hate trouble. You need to leave, mister.
No trouble, promise. I just need to use your sink here for a few seconds and we'll be gone.
This your daughter?
Hmm? Oh, uh... sure.
Please, just a few minutes?
Fine. Here.

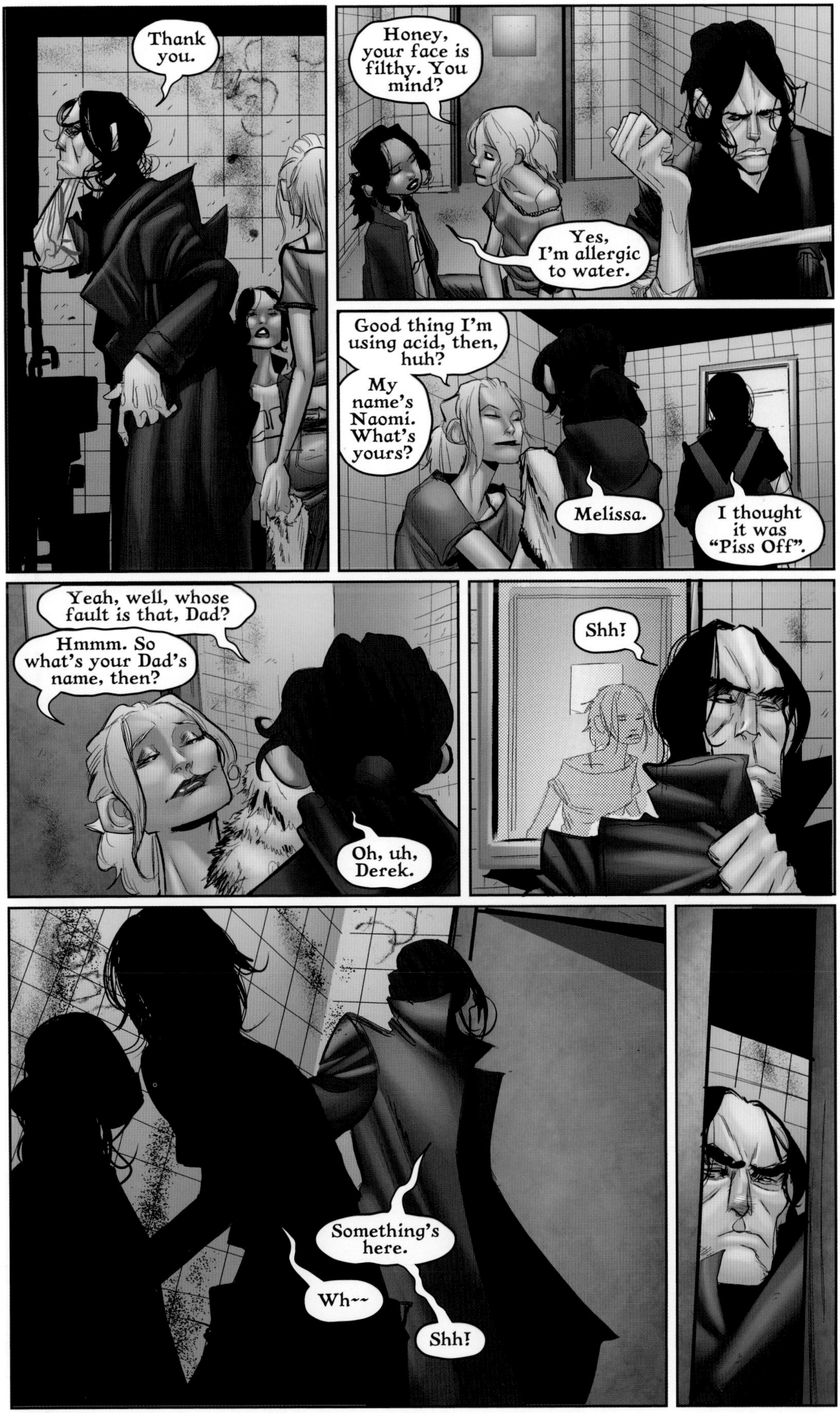
Thank you.
Honey, your face is filthy. You mind?
Yes, I'm allergic to water.
Good thing I'm using acid, then, huh?
My name's Naomi. What's yours?
Melissa.
I thought it was "Piss Off".
Yeah, well, whose fault is that, Dad?
Hmmm. So what's your Dad's name, then?
Oh, uh, Derek.
Shh!
Something's here.
Wh--
Shh!

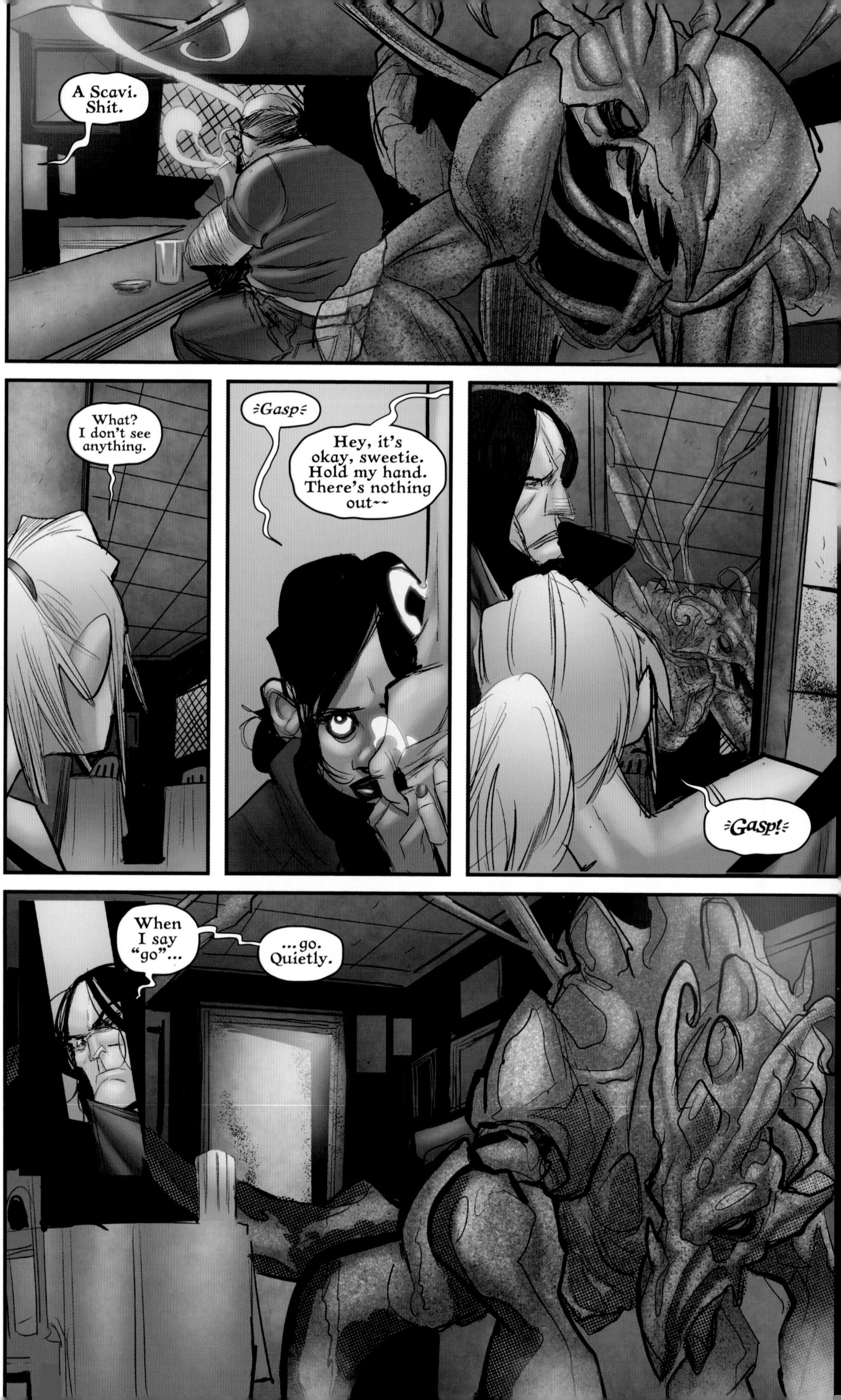
A Scavi. Shit.
What? I don't see anything.
Gasp
Hey, it's okay, sweetie. Hold my hand. There's nothing out~~
Gasp!
When I say "go"...
...go. Quietly.

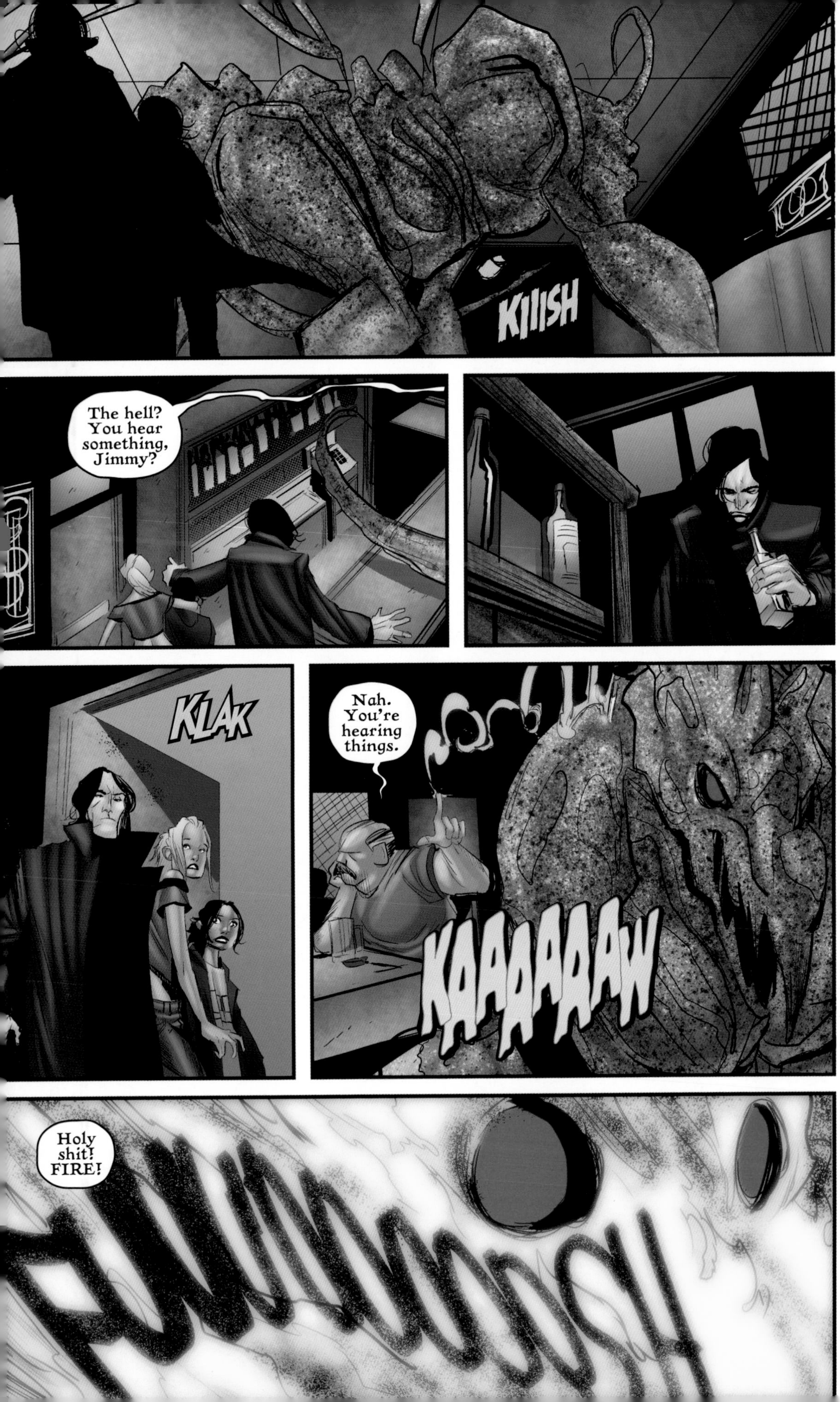
KIIISH
The hell? You hear something, Jimmy?
KLAK
Nah. You're hearing things.
KAAAAAAW
Holy shit! FIRE!
FWOOOOOSH

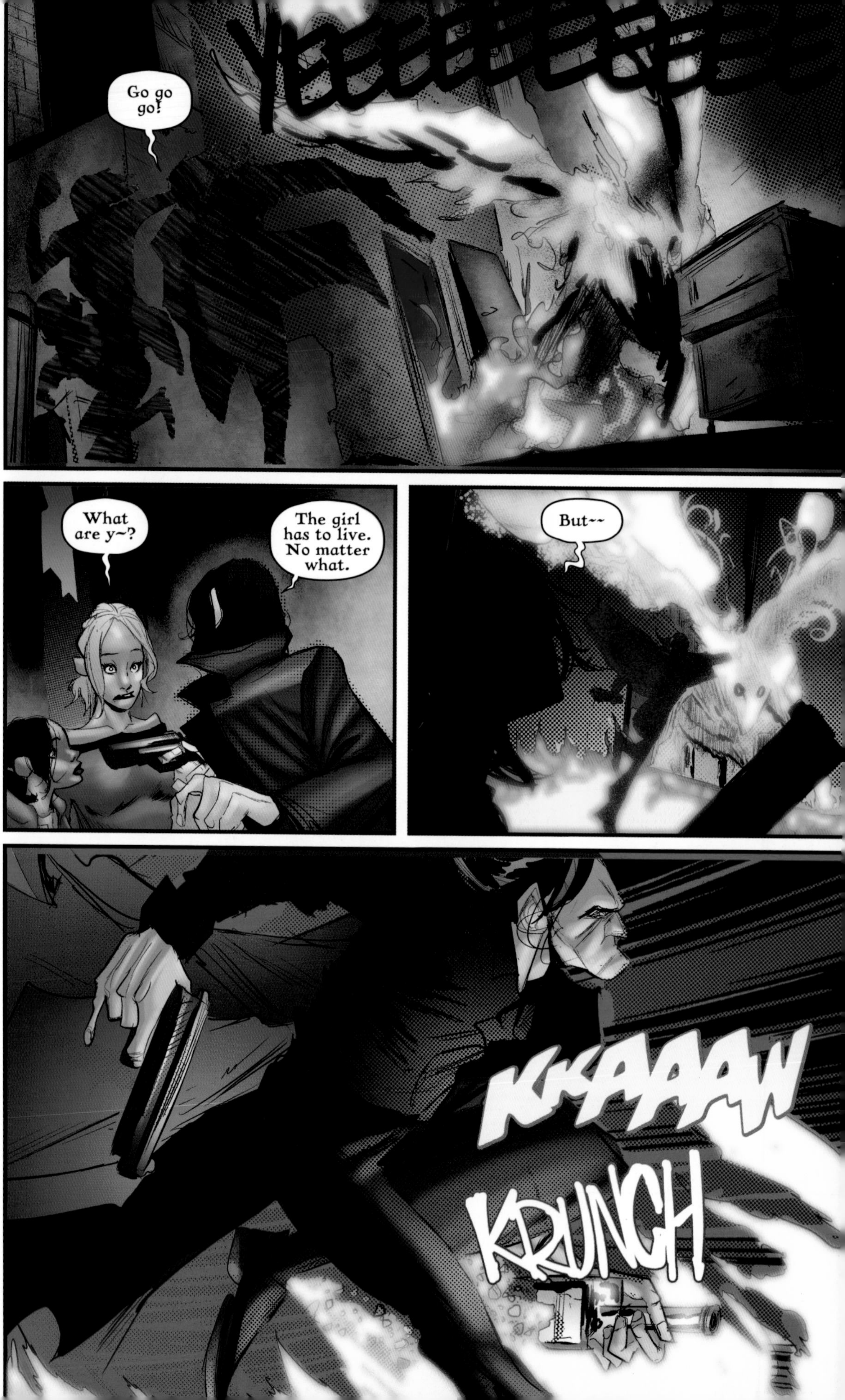
YEEEEEEEEEEE
Go go go!
What are y~?
The girl has to live. No matter what.
But~~
KKAAAAW
KRUNCH

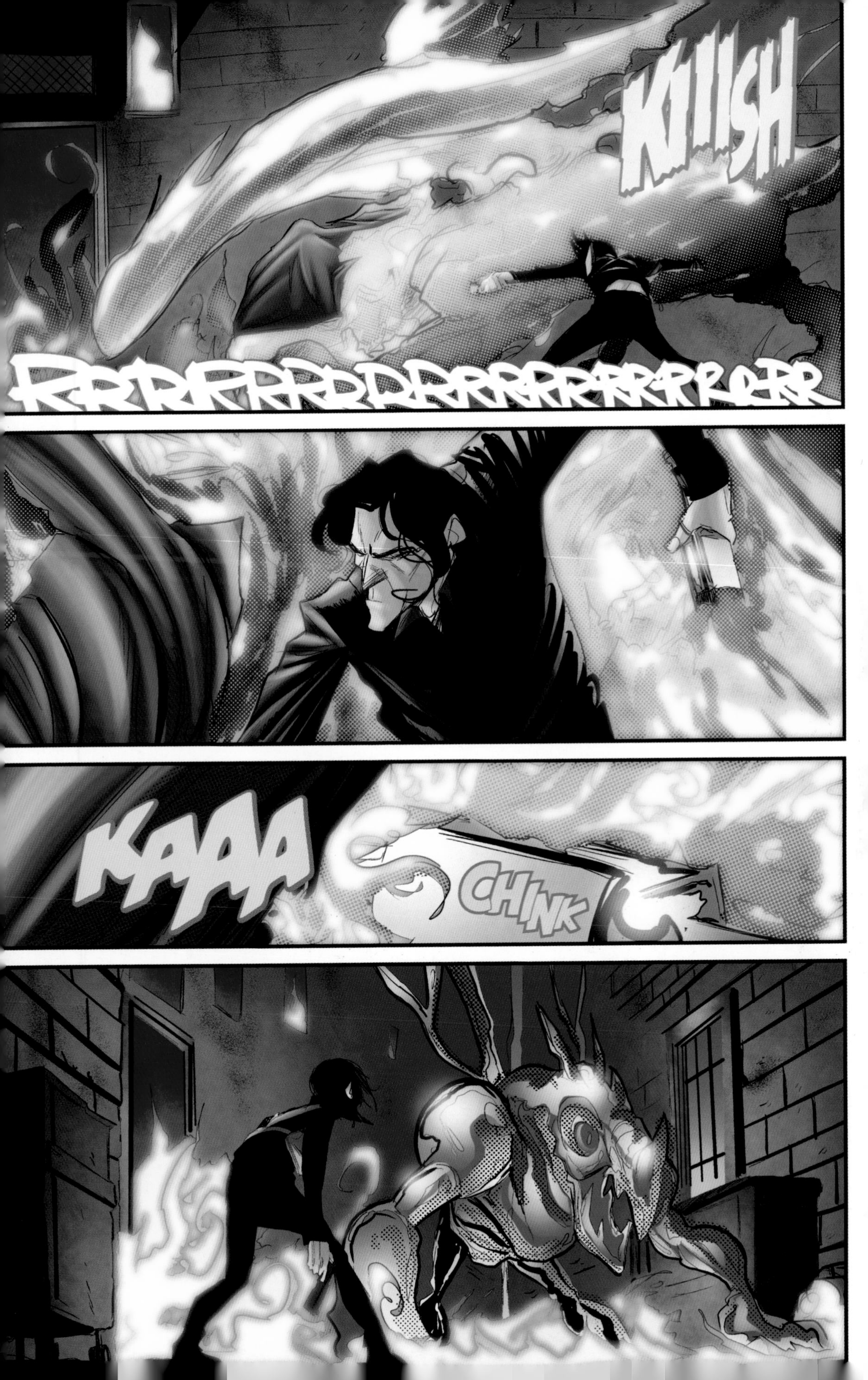
KIISH
RRRRRRRRRRRRRRRRRRRR
KAAA
CHINK

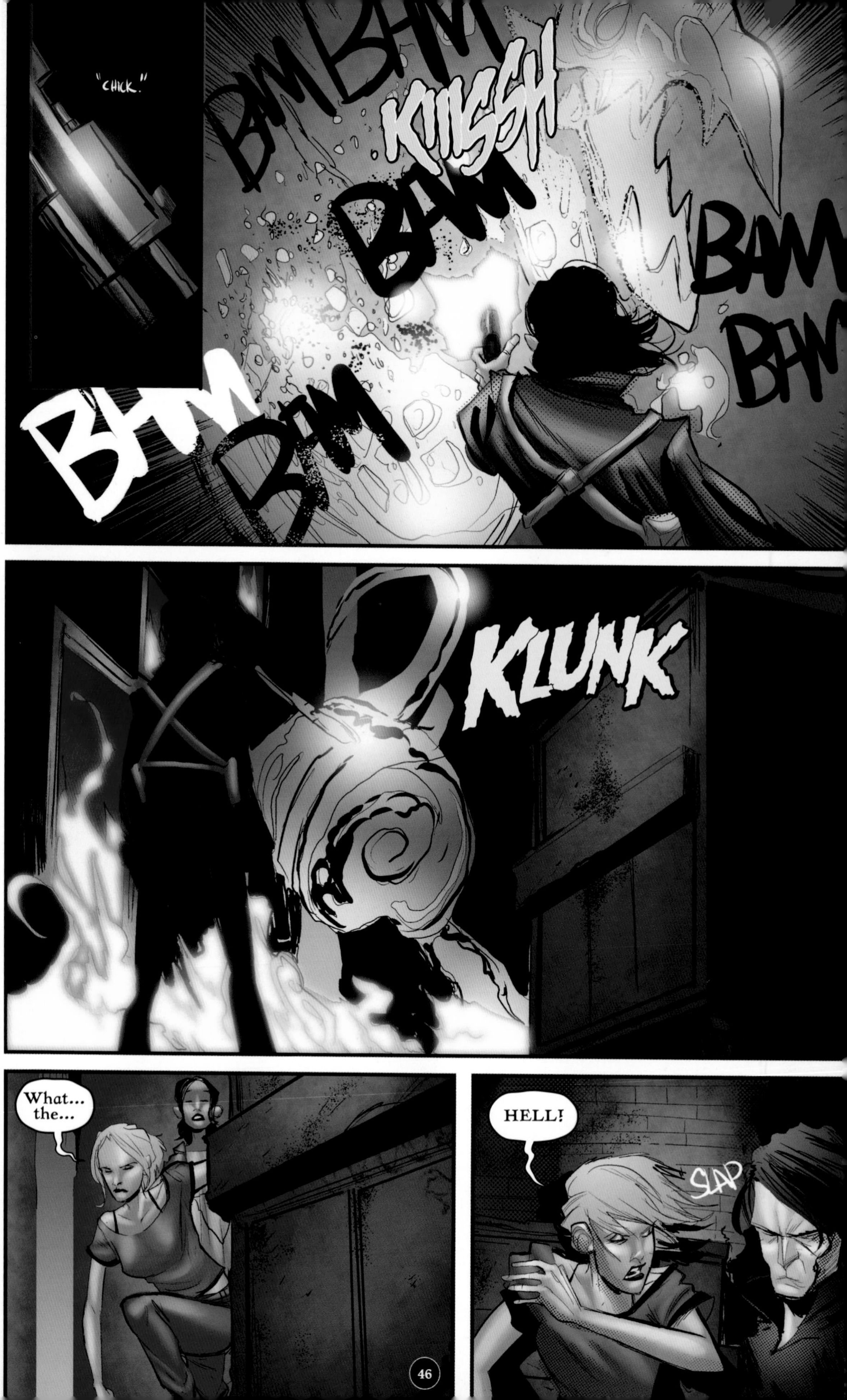
"CHICK."
BAM BAM
KRISSH
BAM
BAM
BAM
BAM
BAM
KLUNK
What... the...
HELL!
SLAP

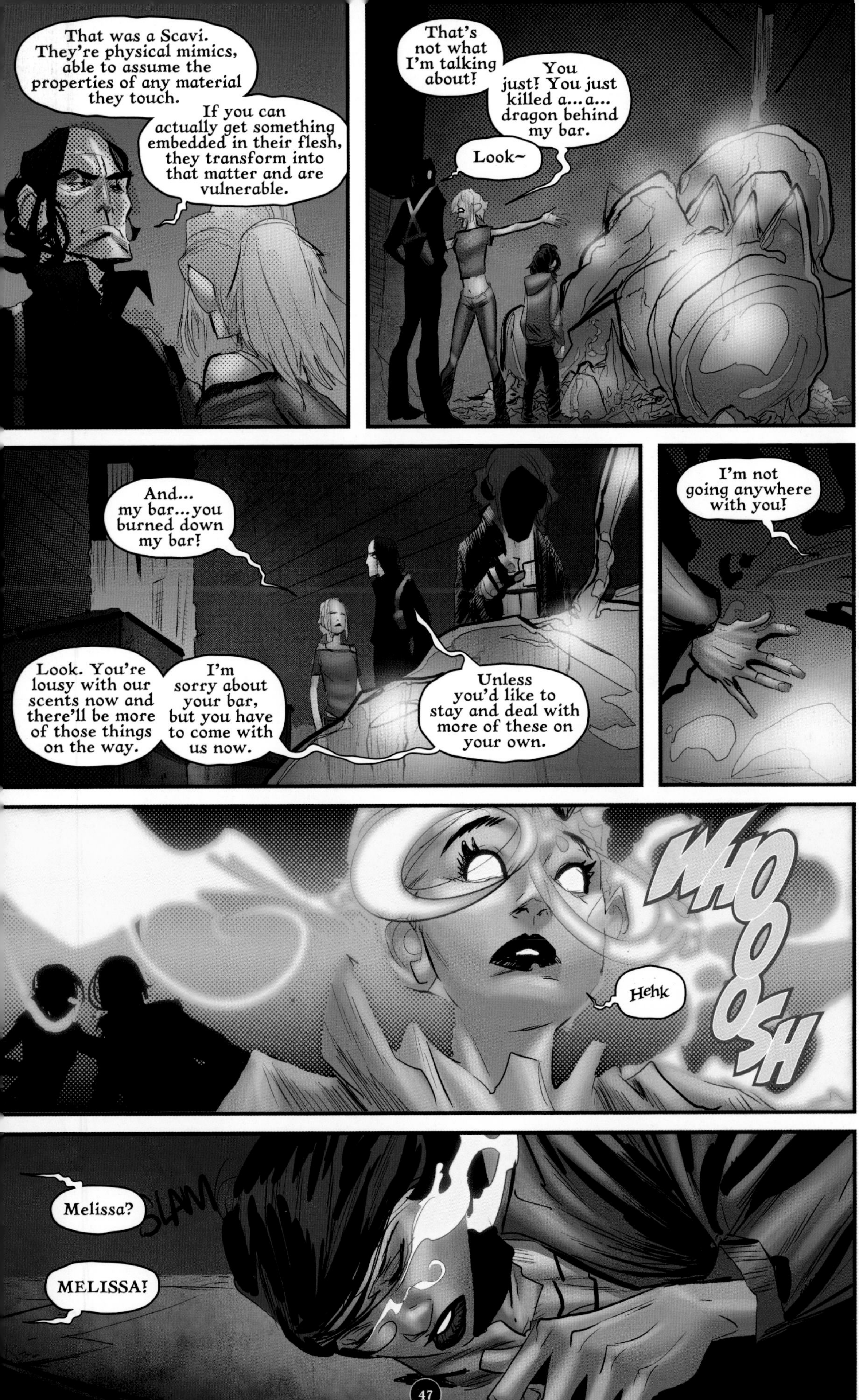
That was a Scavi. They're physical mimics, able to assume the properties of any material they touch.
If you can actually get something embedded in their flesh, they transform into that matter and are vulnerable.
That's not what I'm talking about!
You just! You just killed a...a... dragon behind my bar.
Look~
And... my bar...you burned down my bar!
Look. You're lousy with our scents now and there'll be more of those things on the way.
I'm sorry about your bar, but you have to come with us now.
Unless you'd like to stay and deal with more of these on your own.
I'm not going anywhere with you!
WHOOOOSH
Hehk
Melissa?
SLAM
MELISSA!

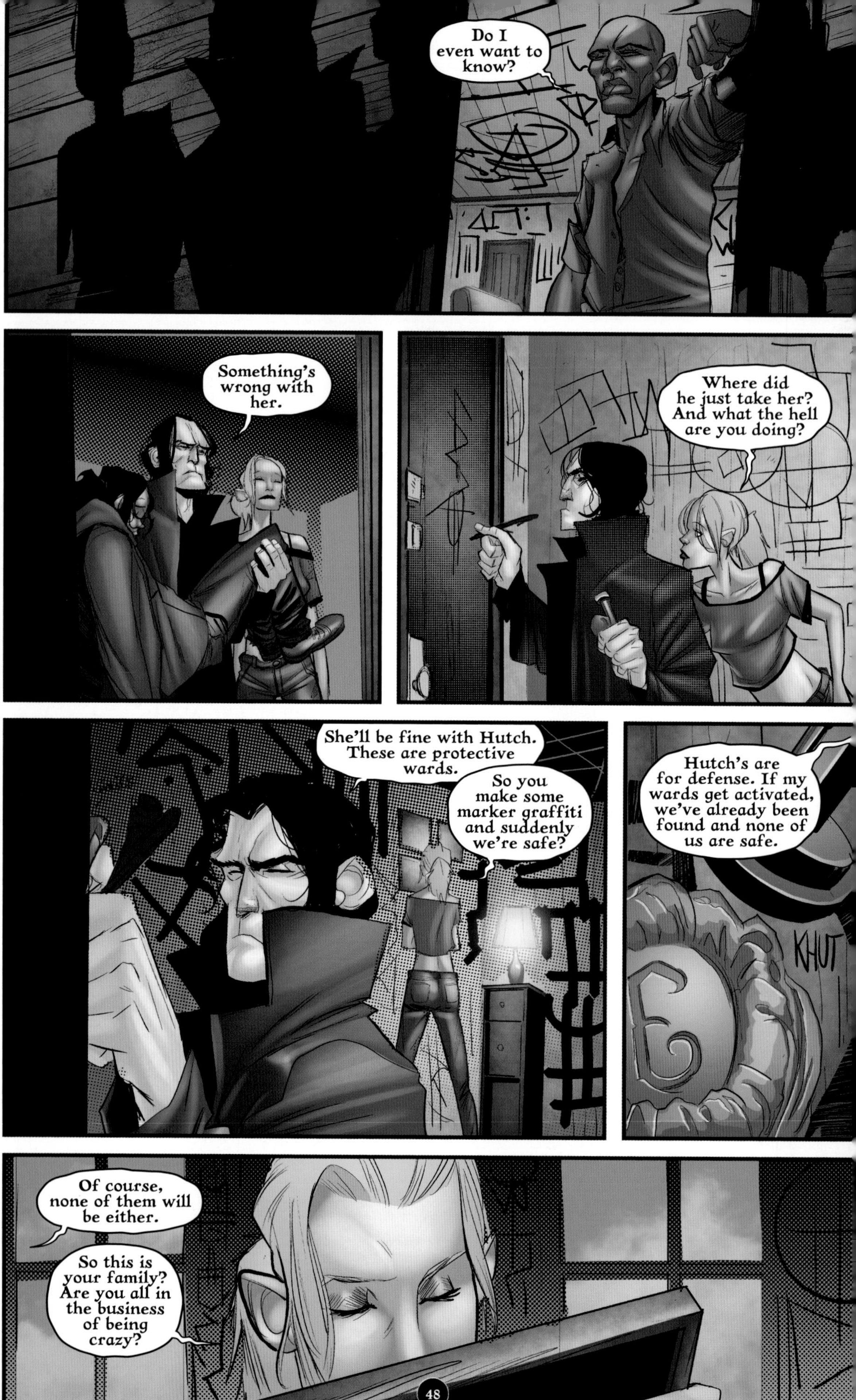

Do I even want to know?
Something's wrong with her.
Where did he just take her? And what the hell are you doing?
She'll be fine with Hutch. These are protective wards.
So you make some marker graffiti and suddenly we're safe?
Hutch's are for defense. If my wards get activated, we've already been found and none of us are safe.
KHUT
Of course, none of them will be either.
So this is your family? Are you all in the business of being crazy?

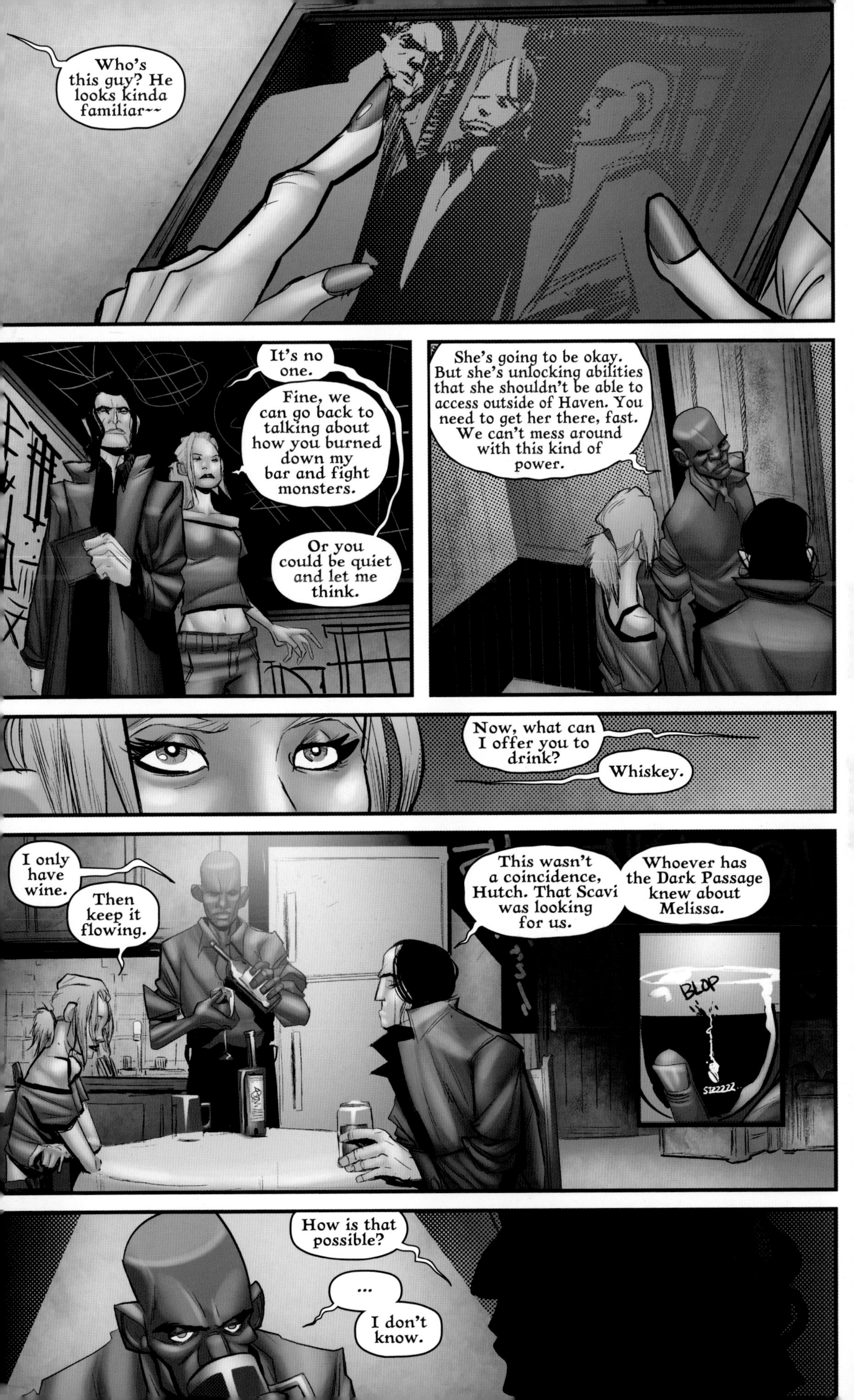
Who's this guy? He looks kinda familiar~~
It's no one.
Fine, we can go back to talking about how you burned down my bar and fight monsters.
Or you could be quiet and let me think.
She's going to be okay. But she's unlocking abilities that she shouldn't be able to access outside of Haven. You need to get her there, fast. We can't mess around with this kind of power.
Now, what can I offer you to drink?
Whiskey.
I only have wine.
Then keep it flowing.
This wasn't a coincidence, Hutch. That Scavi was looking for us.
Whoever has the Dark Passage knew about Melissa.
BLOP
SIZZZZZ...
How is that possible?
...
I don't know.

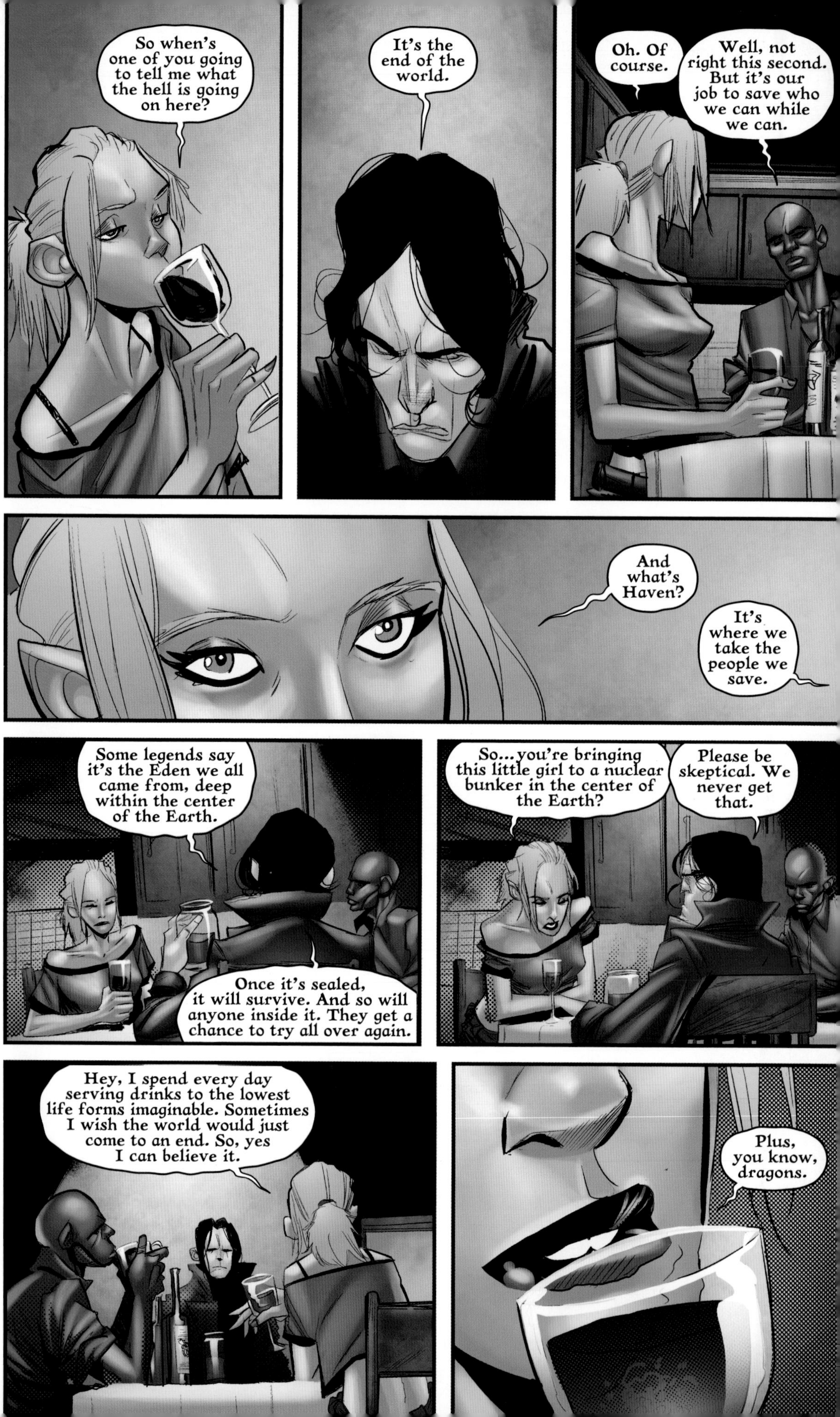
So when's one of you going to tell me what the hell is going on here?
It's the end of the world.
Oh. Of course.
Well, not right this second. But it's our job to save who we can while we can.
And what's Haven?
It's where we take the people we save.
Some legends say it's the Eden we all came from, deep within the center of the Earth.
Once it's sealed, it will survive. And so will anyone inside it. They get a chance to try all over again.
So...you're bringing this little girl to a nuclear bunker in the center of the Earth?
Please be skeptical. We never get that.
Hey, I spend every day serving drinks to the lowest life forms imaginable. Sometimes I wish the world would just come to an end. So, yes I can believe it.
Plus, you know, dragons.

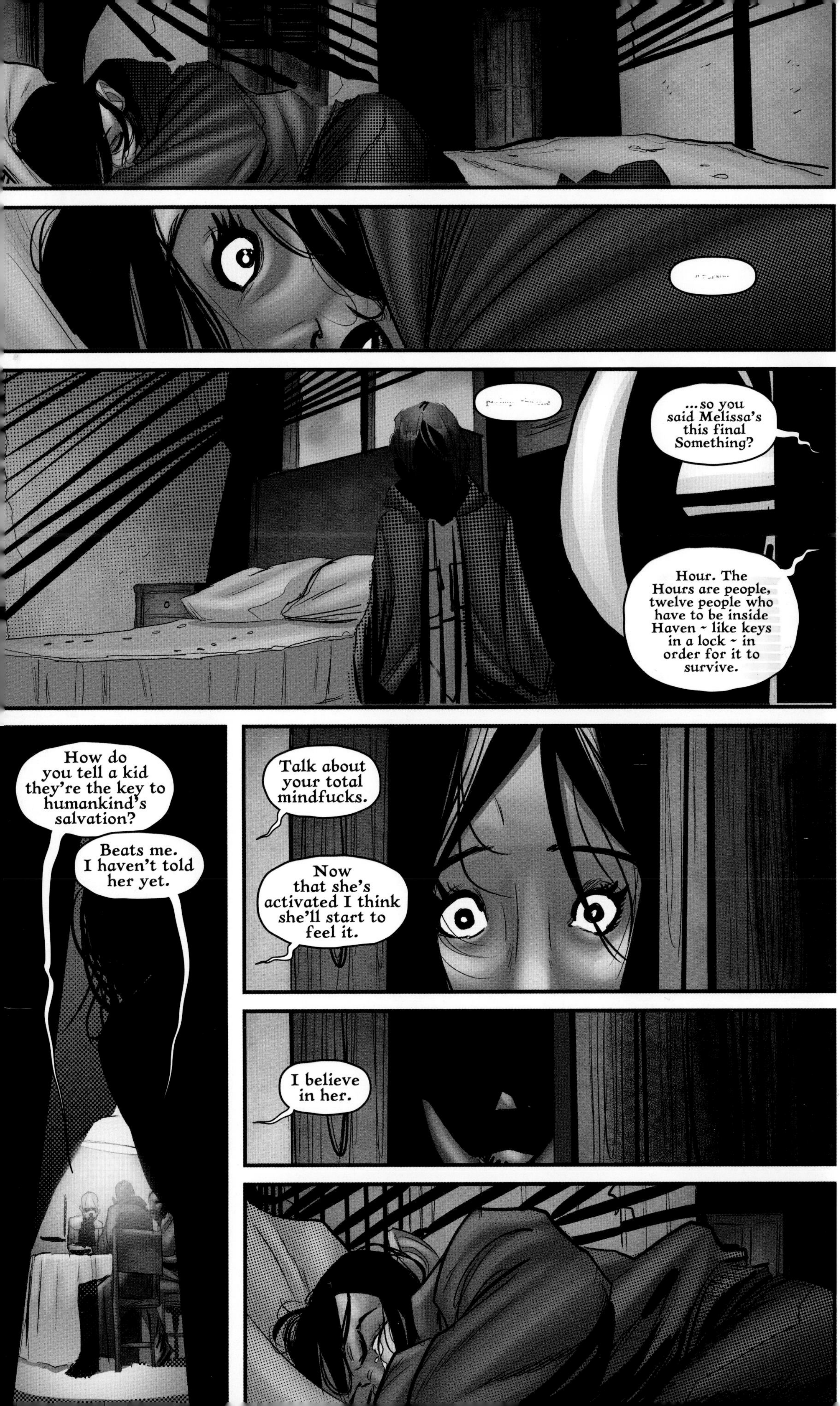

...so you said Melissa's this final Something?
Hour. The Hours are people, twelve people who have to be inside Haven ~ like keys in a lock ~ in order for it to survive.
How do you tell a kid they're the key to humankind's salvation?
Beats me. I haven't told her yet.
Talk about your total mindfucks.
Now that she's activated I think she'll start to feel it.
I believe in her.

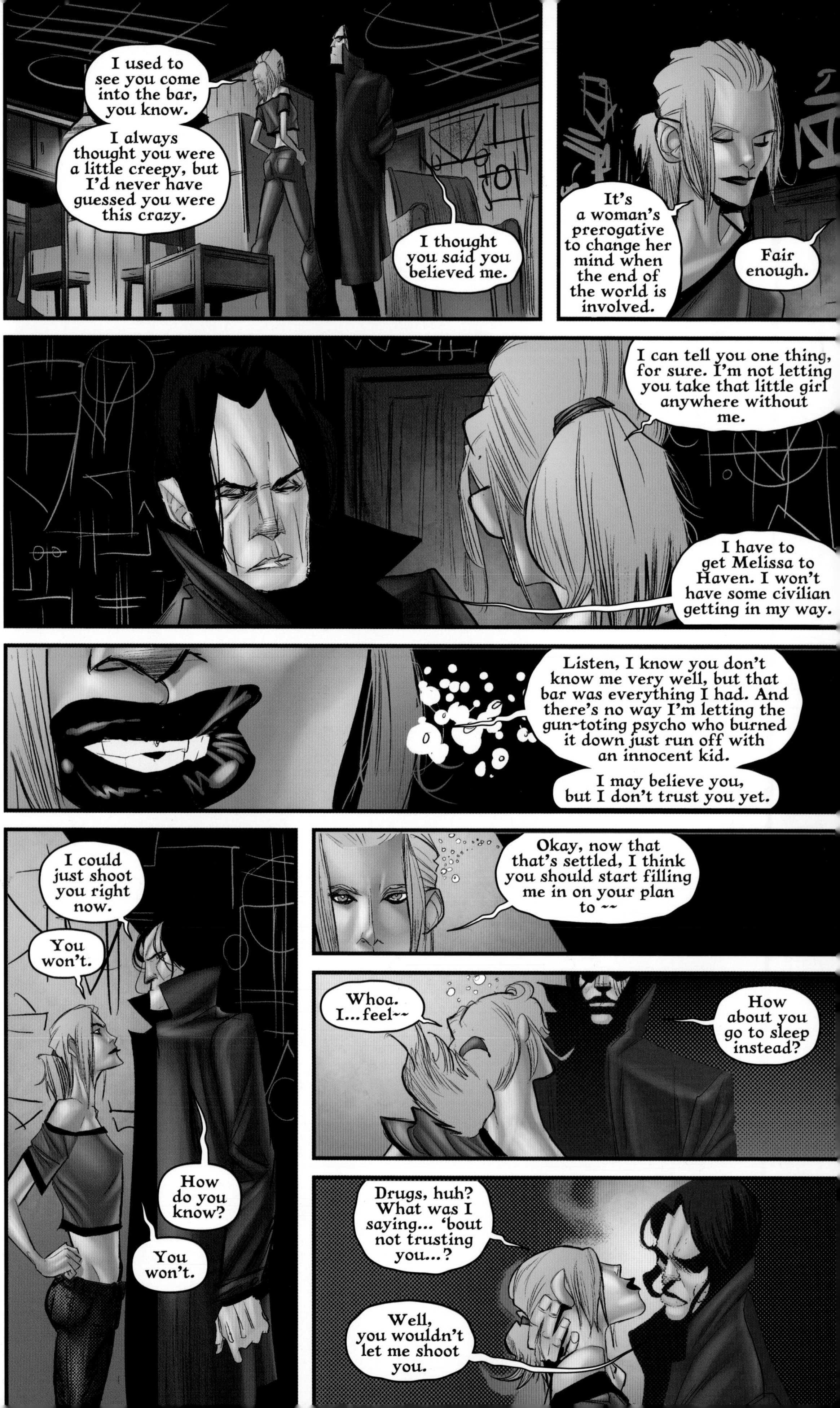
I used to see you come into the bar, you know.
I always thought you were a little creepy, but I'd never have guessed you were this crazy.
I thought you said you believed me.
It's a woman's prerogative to change her mind when the end of the world is involved.
Fair enough.
I can tell you one thing, for sure. I'm not letting you take that little girl anywhere without me.
I have to get Melissa to Haven. I won't have some civilian getting in my way.
Listen, I know you don't know me very well, but that bar was everything I had. And there's no way I'm letting the gun~toting psycho who burned it down just run off with an innocent kid.
I may believe you, but I don't trust you yet.
I could just shoot you right now.
You won't.
How do you know?
You won't.
Okay, now that that's settled, I think you should start filling me in on your plan to ~~
Whoa. I...feel~~
How about you go to sleep instead?
Drugs, huh? What was I saying... 'bout not trusting you...?
Well, you wouldn't let me shoot you.

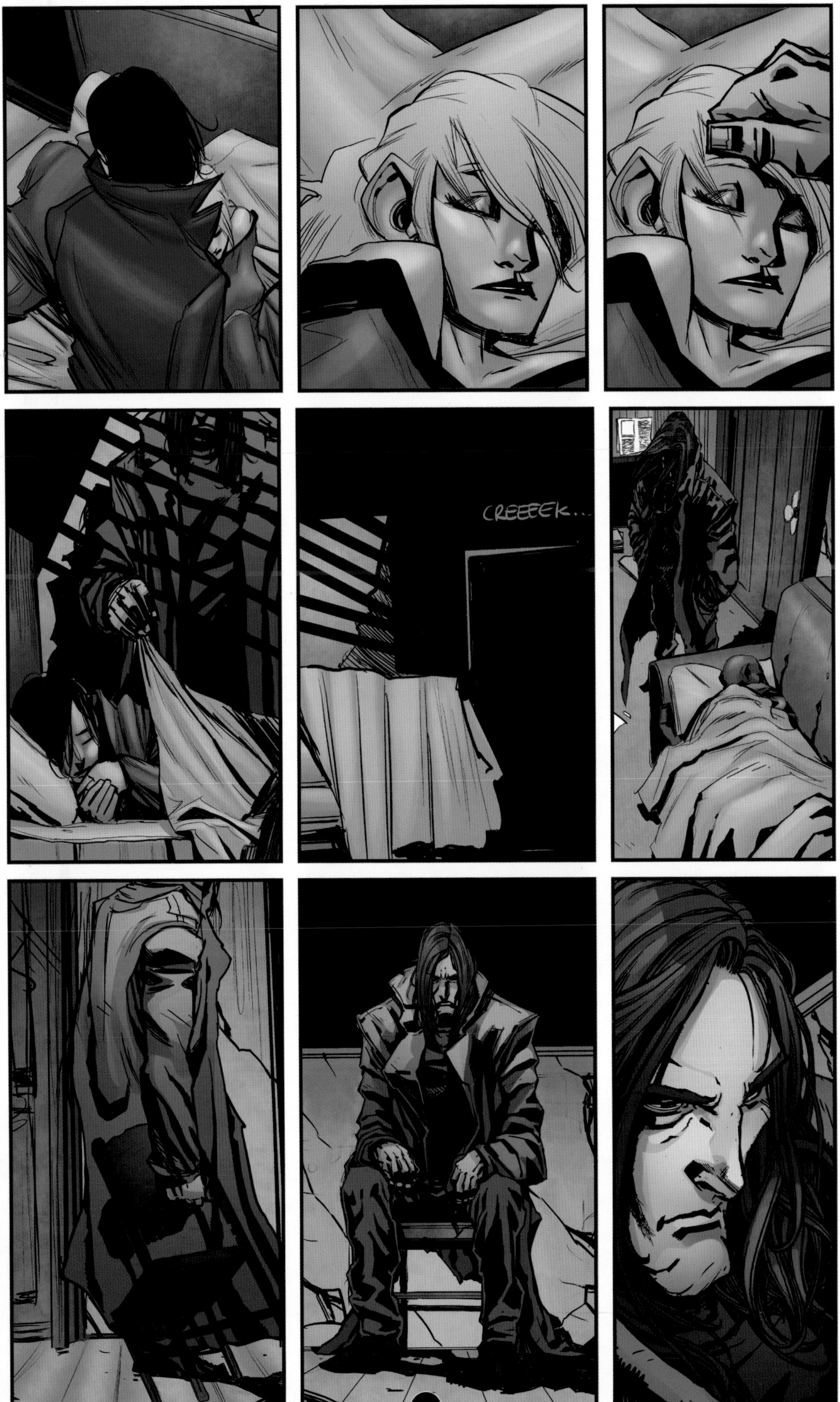
CREEEEK...

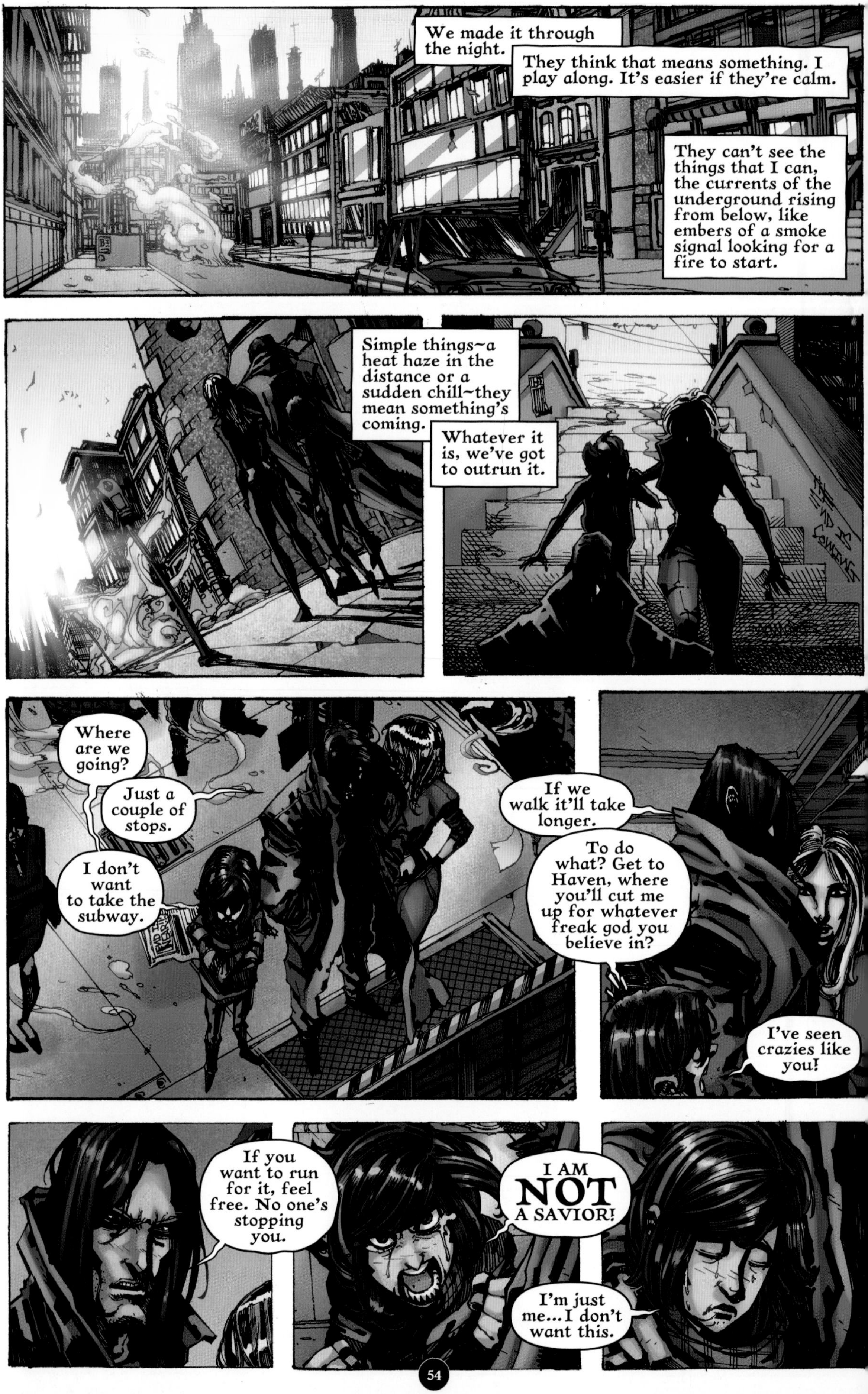

We made it through the night.
They think that means something. I play along. It's easier if they're calm.
They can't see the things that I can, the currents of the underground rising from below, like embers of a smoke signal looking for a fire to start.
Simple things~a heat haze in the distance or a sudden chill~they mean something's coming.
Whatever it is, we've got to outrun it.
Where are we going?
Just a couple of stops.
I don't want to take the subway.
If we walk it'll take longer.
To do what? Get to Haven, where you'll cut me up for whatever freak god you believe in?
I've seen crazies like you!
If you want to run for it, feel free. No one's stopping you.
I AM NOT A SAVIOR!
I'm just me...I don't want this.

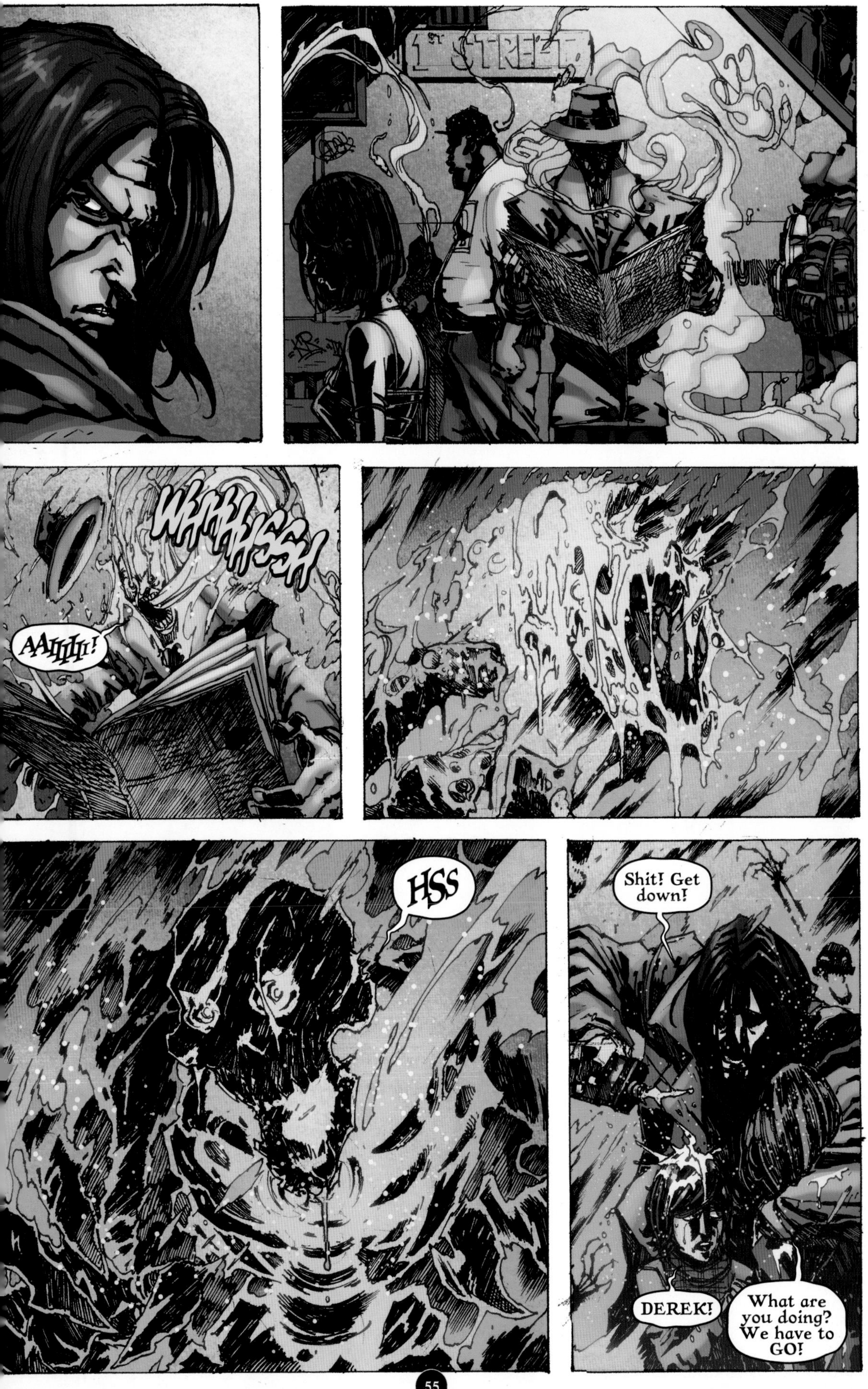
1ST STREET
WHHHSSH
AAIIIIII!
HSS
Shit! Get down!
DEREK!
What are you doing? We have to GO!

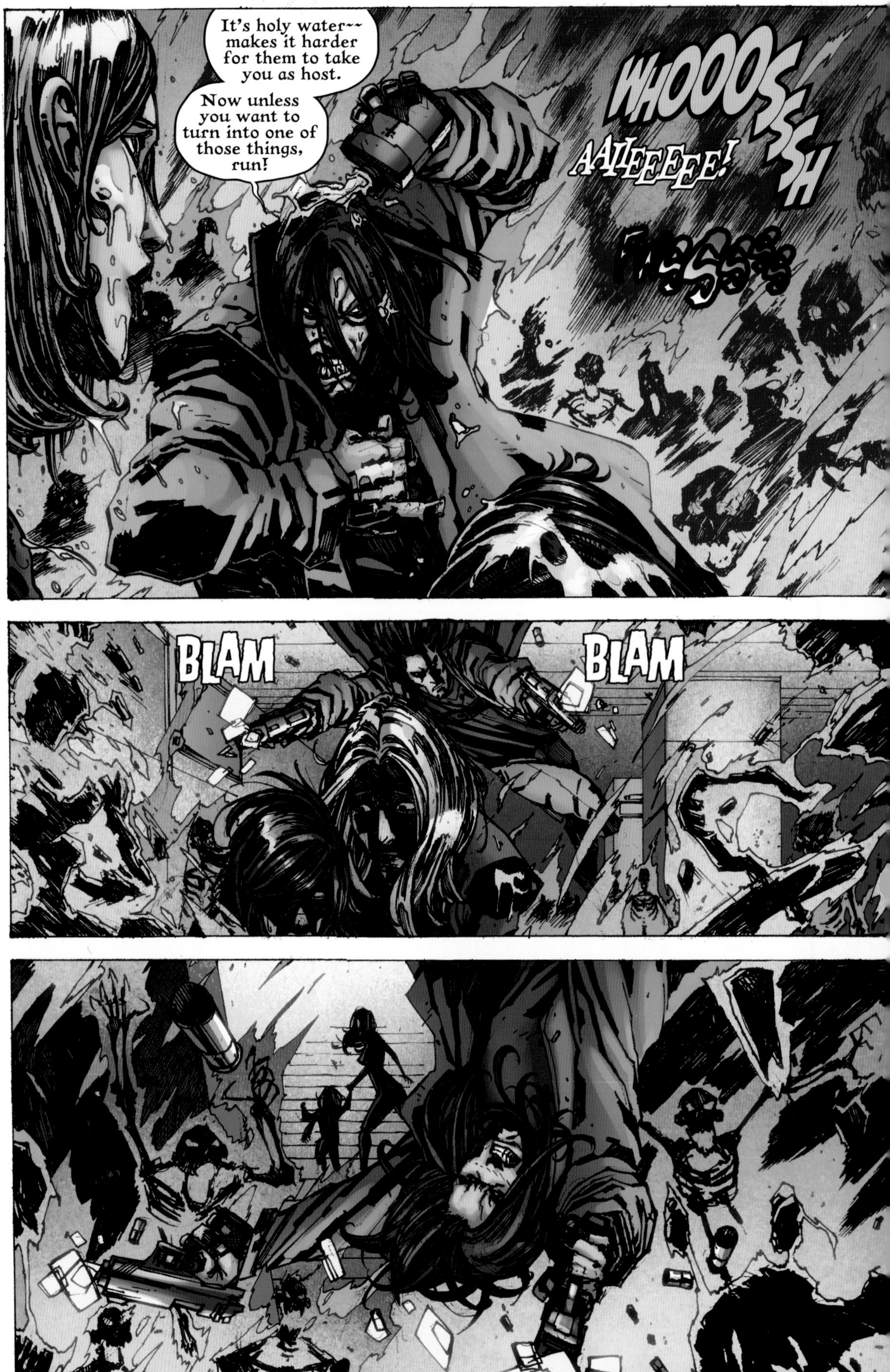
It's holy water-- makes it harder for them to take you as host.
Now unless you want to turn into one of those things, run!
WHOOOSSSH
AAIEEEEEE!
BLAM
BLAM

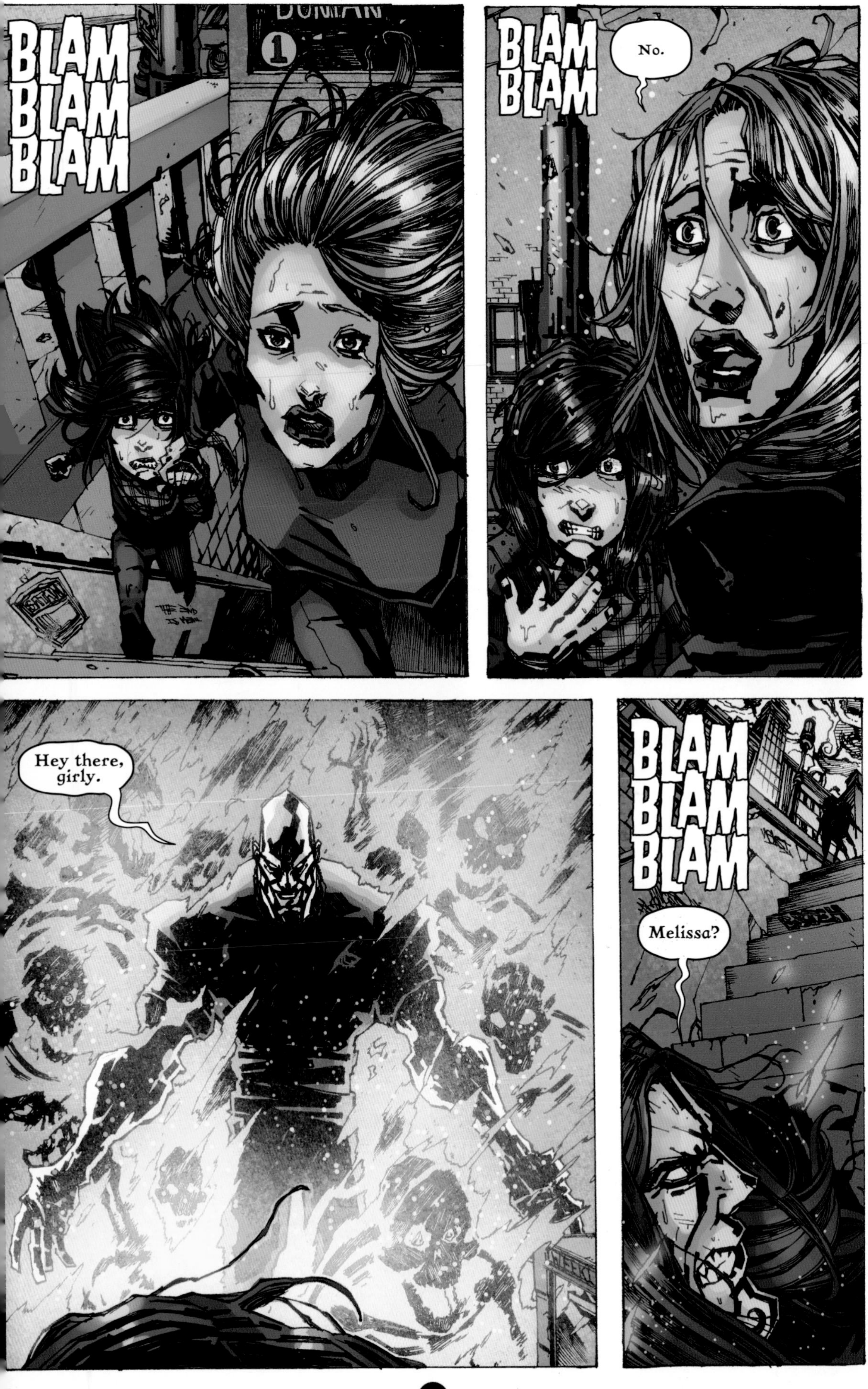
BLAM
BLAM
BLAM
BLAM
BLAM
No.
Hey there, girly.
BLAM
BLAM
BLAM
Melissa?

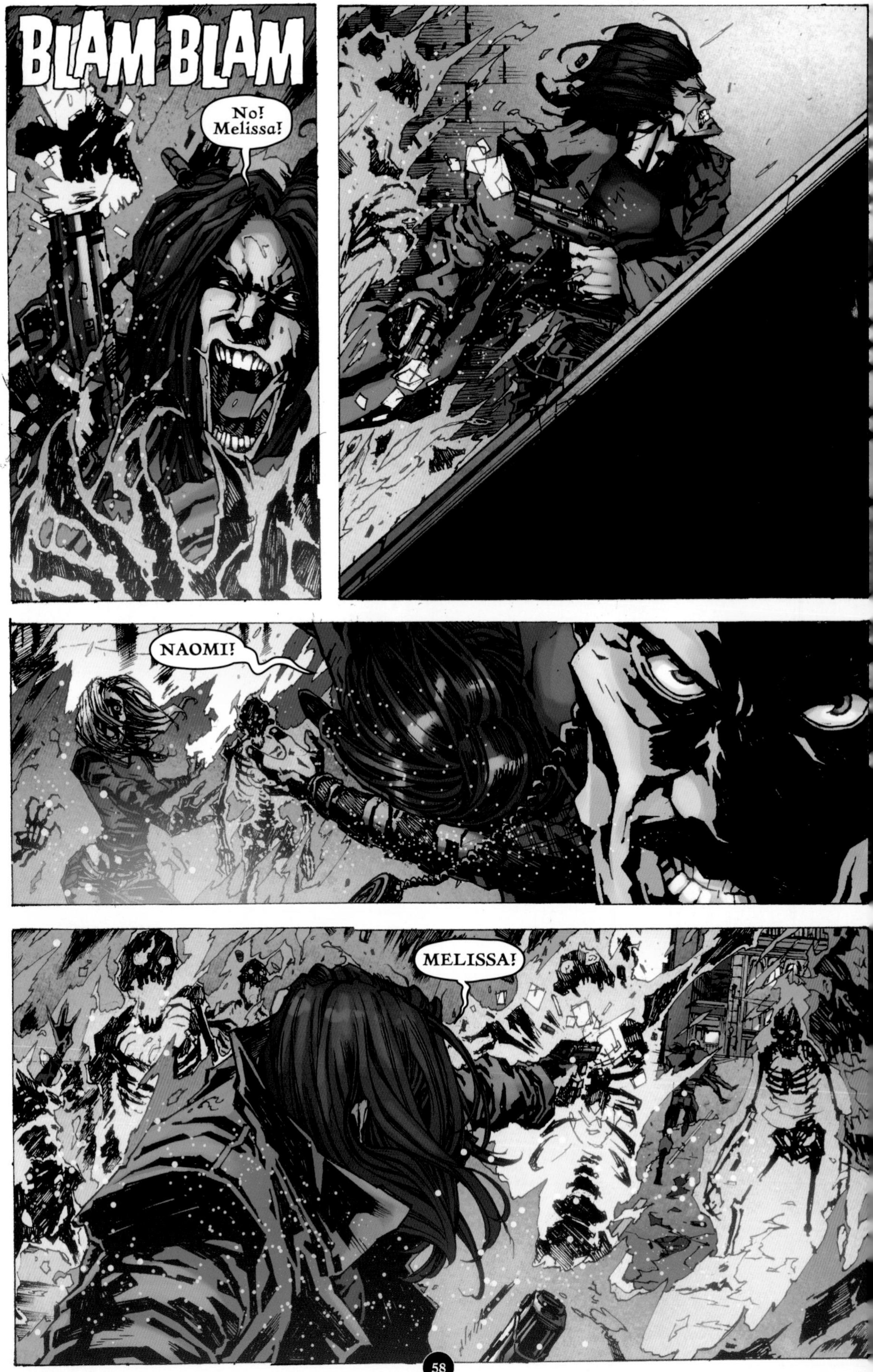
BLAM BLAM
No! Melissa!
NAOMI!
MELISSA!

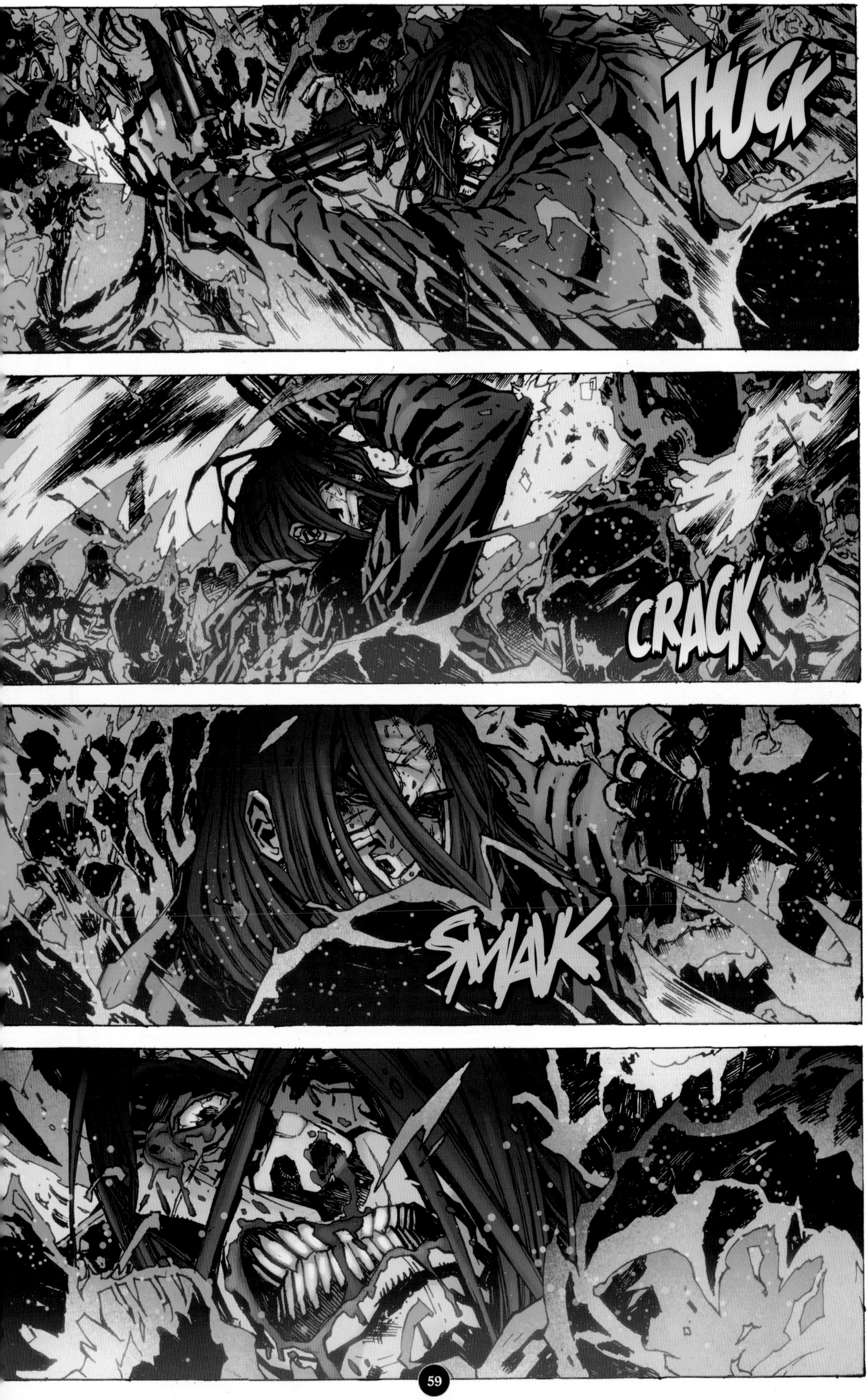
THUCK
CRACK
SMAK

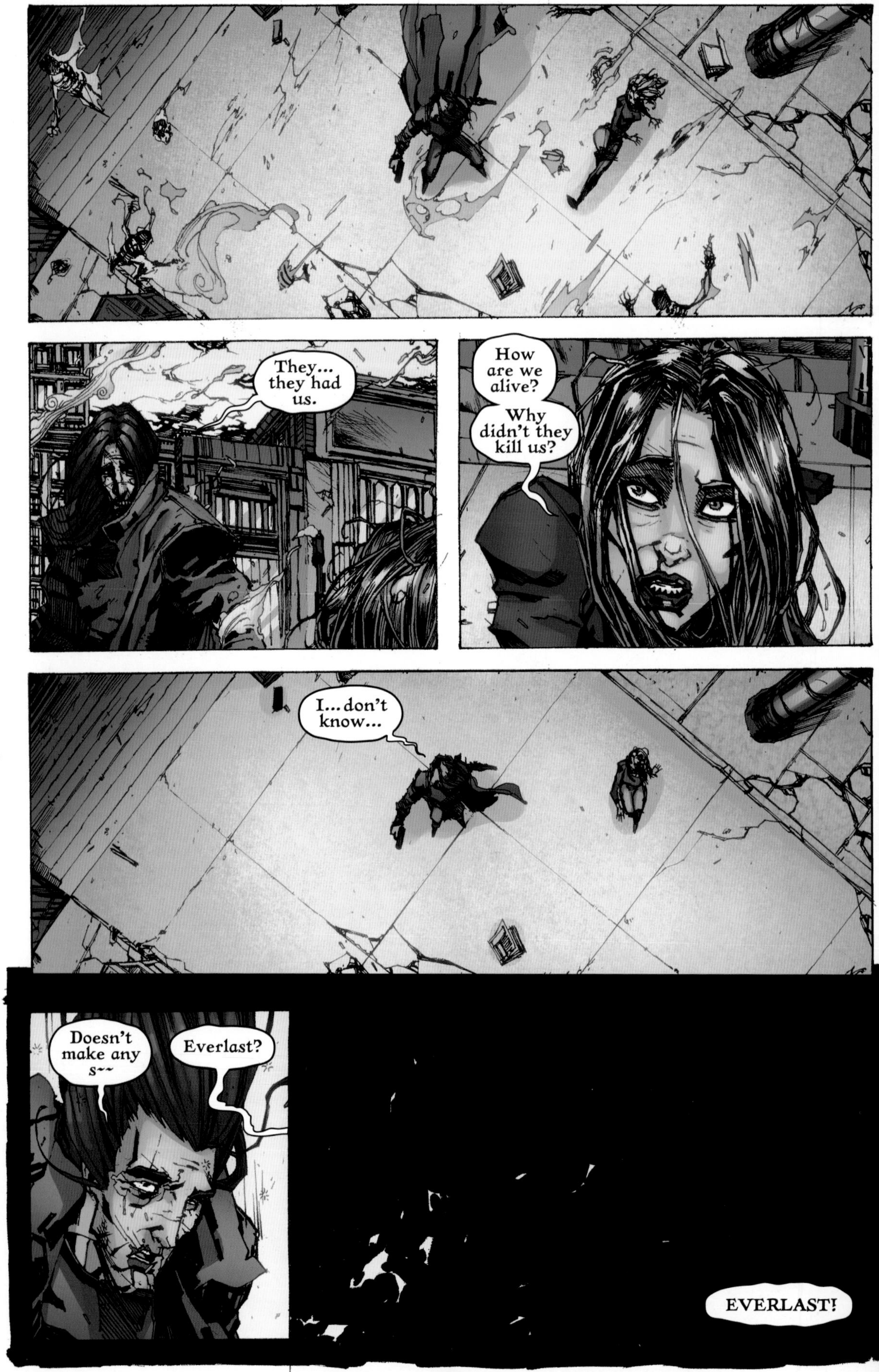
They... they had us.
How are we alive?
Why didn't they kill us?
I...don't know...
Doesn't make any s~~
Everlast?
EVERLAST!

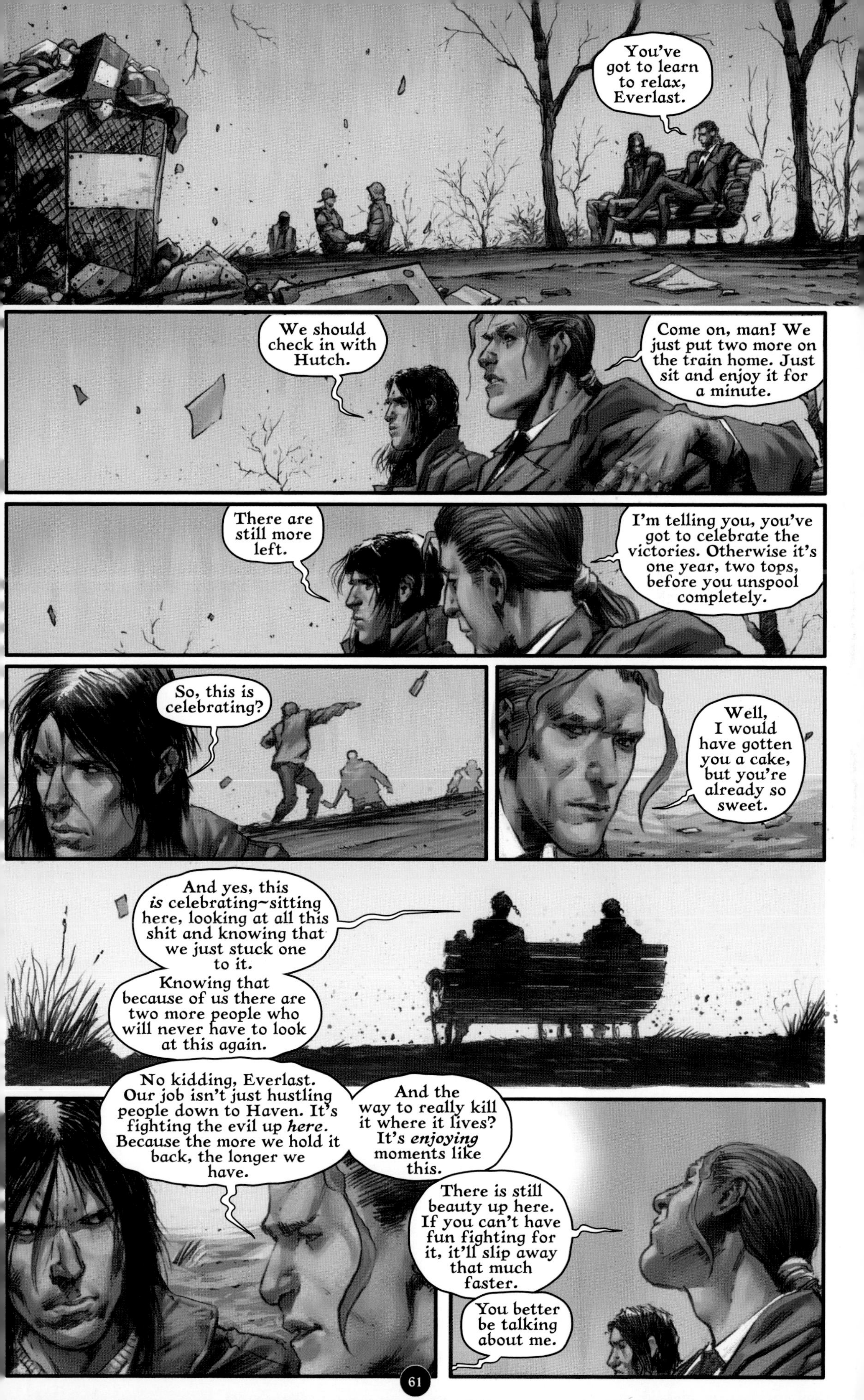

You've got to learn to relax, Everlast.
We should check in with Hutch.
Come on, man! We just put two more on the train home. Just sit and enjoy it for a minute.
There are still more left.
I'm telling you, you've got to celebrate the victories. Otherwise it's one year, two tops, before you unspool completely.
So, this is celebrating?
Well, I would have gotten you a cake, but you're already so sweet.
And yes, this *is* celebrating~sitting here, looking at all this shit and knowing that we just stuck one to it.
Knowing that because of us there are two more people who will never have to look at this again.
No kidding, Everlast. Our job isn't just hustling people down to Haven. It's fighting the evil up *here*. Because the more we hold it back, the longer we have.
And the way to really kill it where it lives? It's *enjoying* moments like this.
There is still beauty up here. If you can't have fun fighting for it, it'll slip away that much faster.
You better be talking about me.

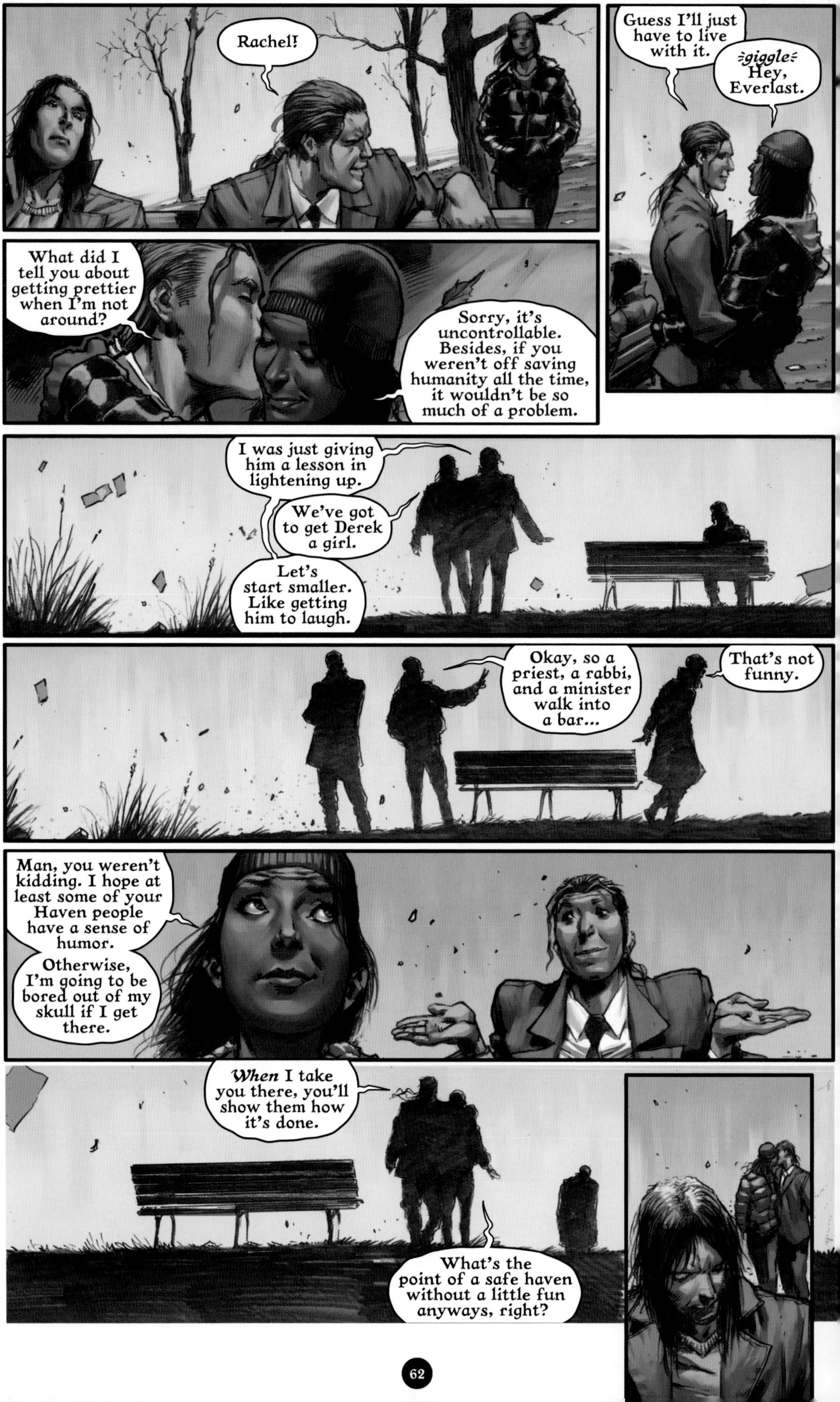
Rachel!
Guess I'll just have to live with it.
giggle Hey, Everlast.
What did I tell you about getting prettier when I'm not around?
Sorry, it's uncontrollable. Besides, if you weren't off saving humanity all the time, it wouldn't be so much of a problem.
I was just giving him a lesson in lightening up.
We've got to get Derek a girl.
Let's start smaller. Like getting him to laugh.
Okay, so a priest, a rabbi, and a minister walk into a bar...
That's not funny.
Man, you weren't kidding. I hope at least some of your Haven people have a sense of humor.
Otherwise, I'm going to be bored out of my skull if I get there.
When I take you there, you'll show them how it's done.
What's the point of a safe haven without a little fun anyways, right?

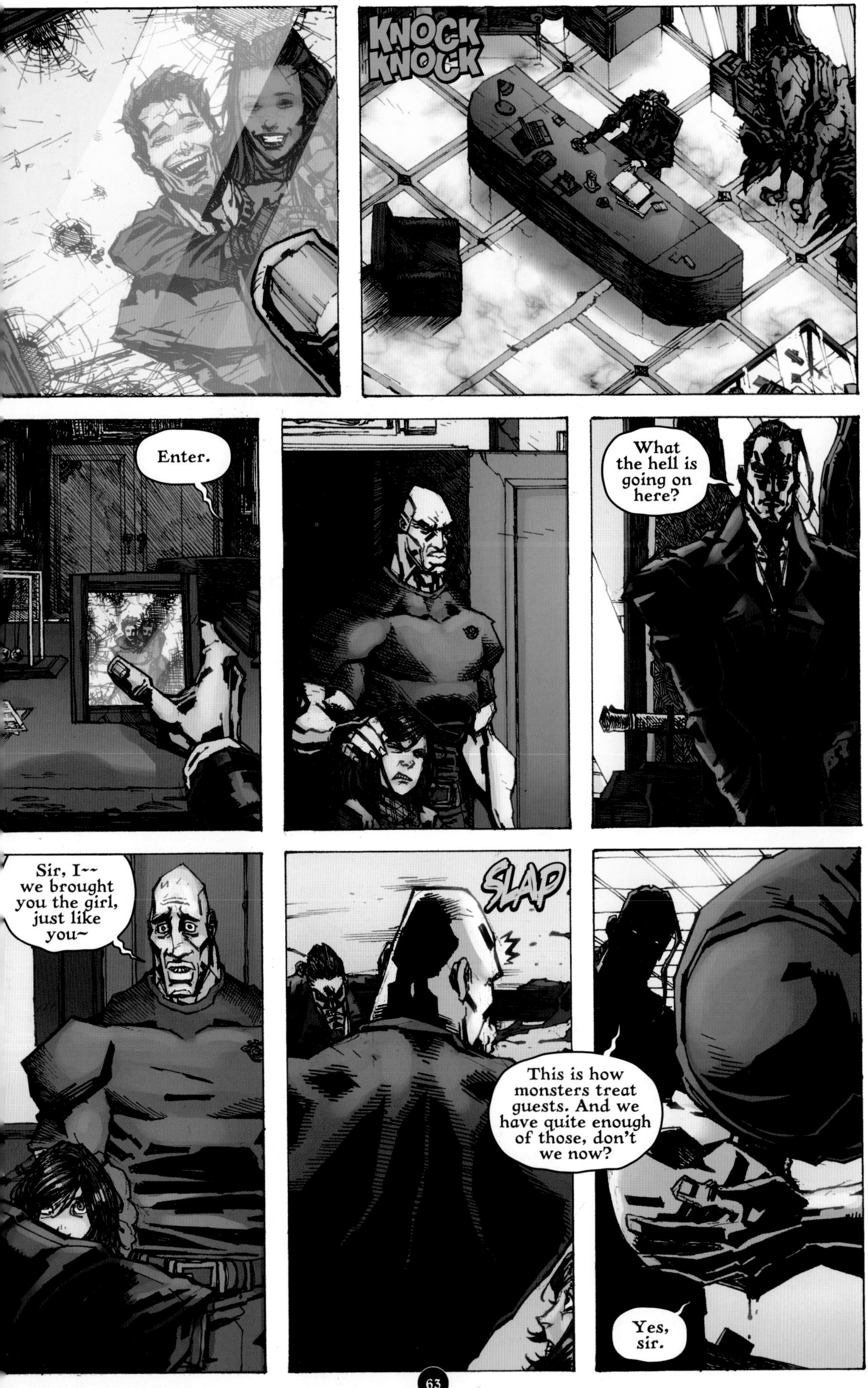
KNOCK KNOCK
Enter.
What the hell is going on here?
Sir, I-- we brought you the girl, just like you~
SLAP
This is how monsters treat guests. And we have quite enough of those, don't we now?
Yes, sir.

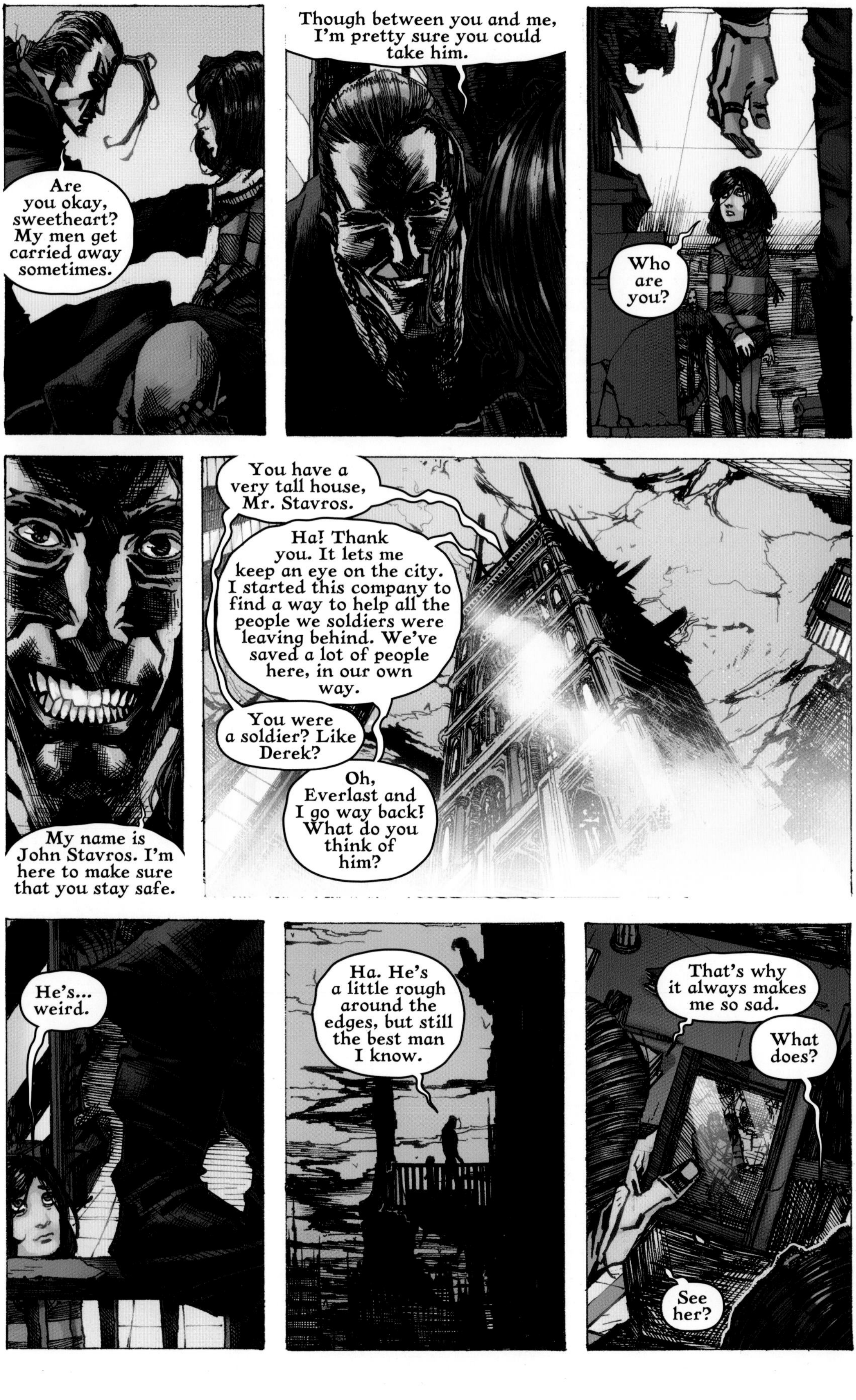
Are you okay, sweetheart? My men get carried away sometimes.
Though between you and me, I'm pretty sure you could take him.
Who are you?
My name is John Stavros. I'm here to make sure that you stay safe.
You have a very tall house, Mr. Stavros.
Ha! Thank you. It lets me keep an eye on the city. I started this company to find a way to help all the people we soldiers were leaving behind. We've saved a lot of people here, in our own way.
You were a soldier? Like Derek?
Oh, Everlast and I go way back! What do you think of him?
He's... weird.
Ha. He's a little rough around the edges, but still the best man I know.
That's why it always makes me so sad.
What does?
See her?

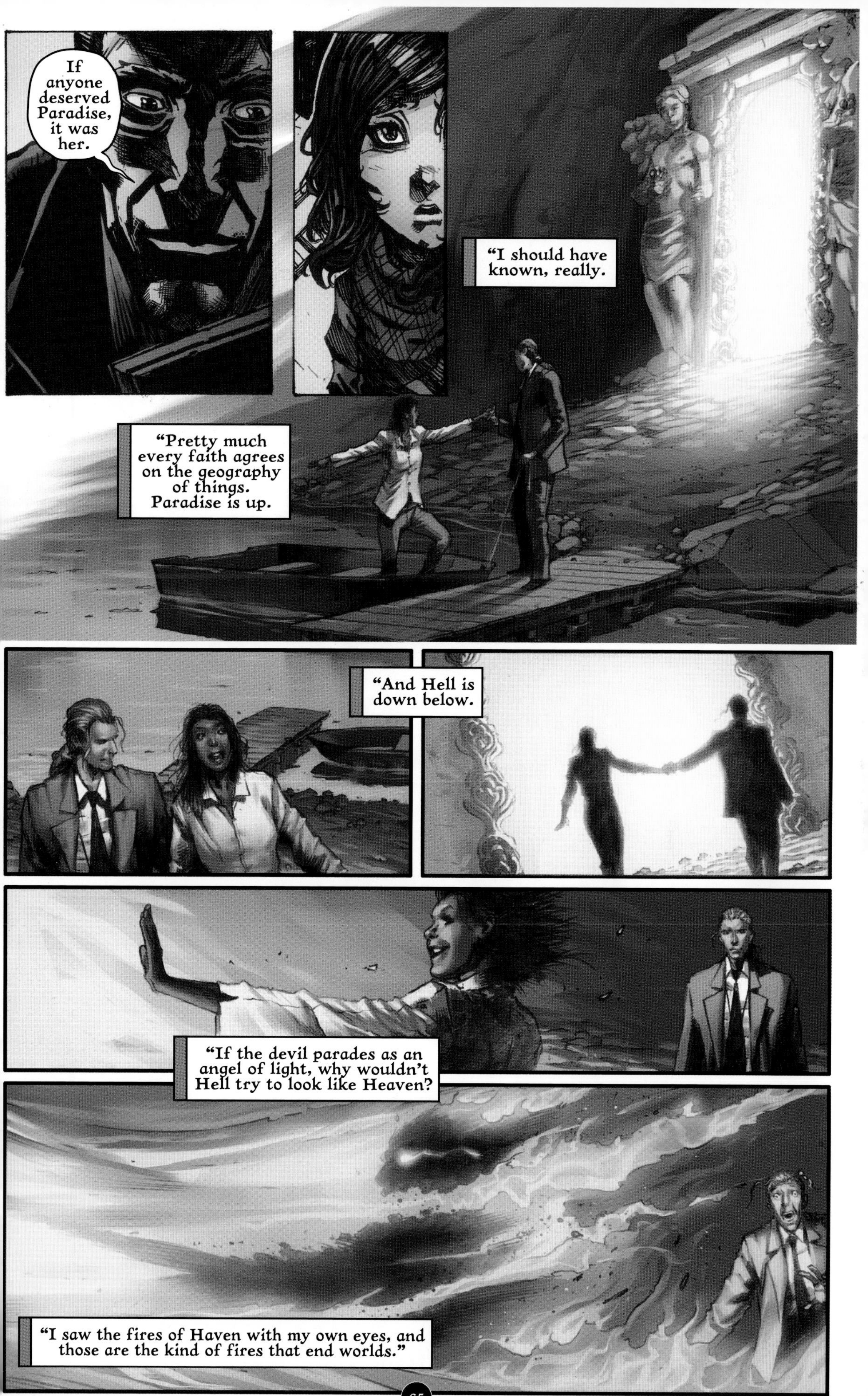
If anyone deserved Paradise, it was her.
"I should have known, really.
"Pretty much every faith agrees on the geography of things. Paradise is up.
"And Hell is down below.
"If the devil parades as an angel of light, why wouldn't Hell try to look like Heaven?
"I saw the fires of Haven with my own eyes, and those are the kind of fires that end worlds."

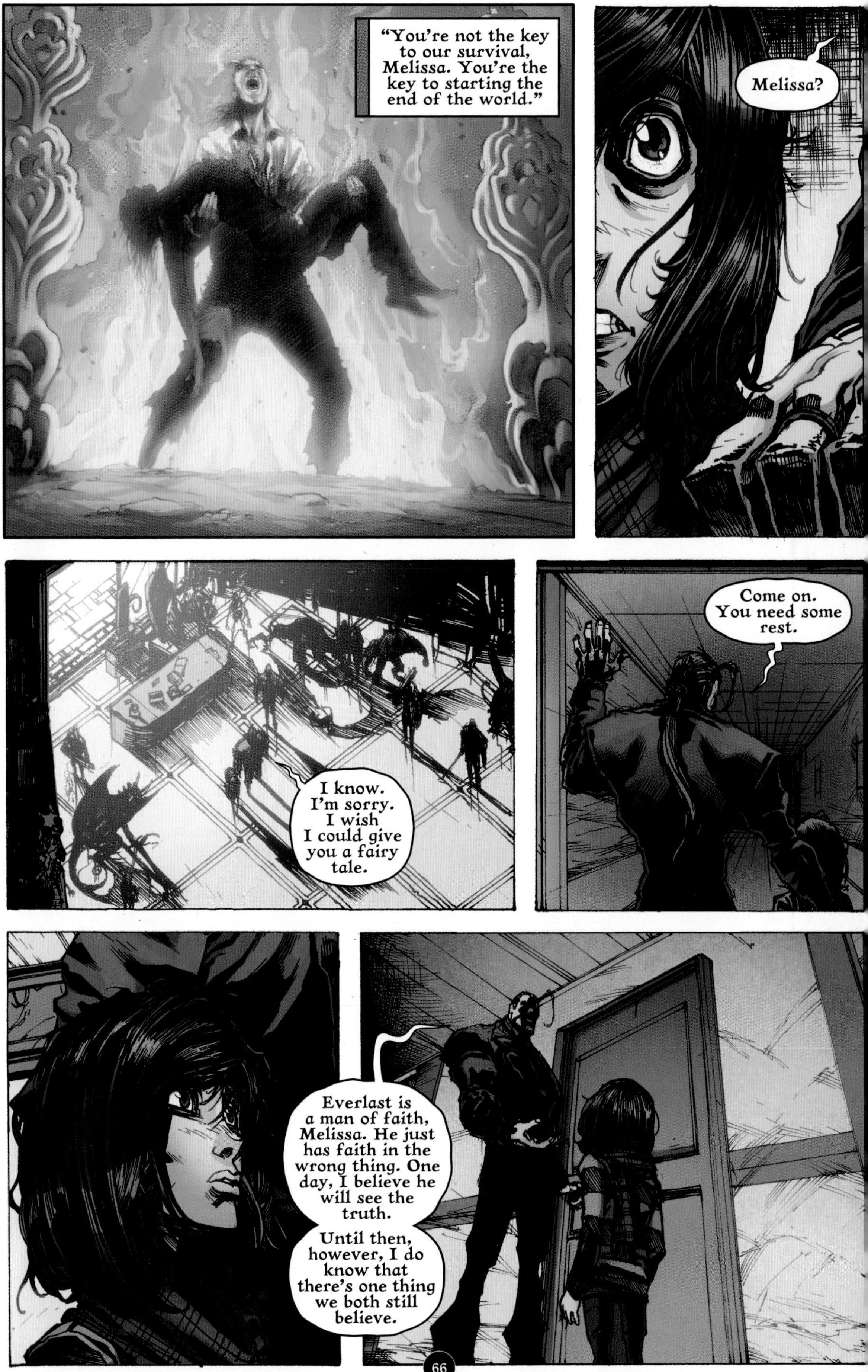
"You're not the key to our survival, Melissa. You're the key to starting the end of the world."
Melissa?
I know. I'm sorry. I wish I could give you a fairy tale.
Come on. You need some rest.
Everlast is a man of faith, Melissa. He just has faith in the wrong thing. One day, I believe he will see the truth.
Until then, however, I do know that there's one thing we both still believe.

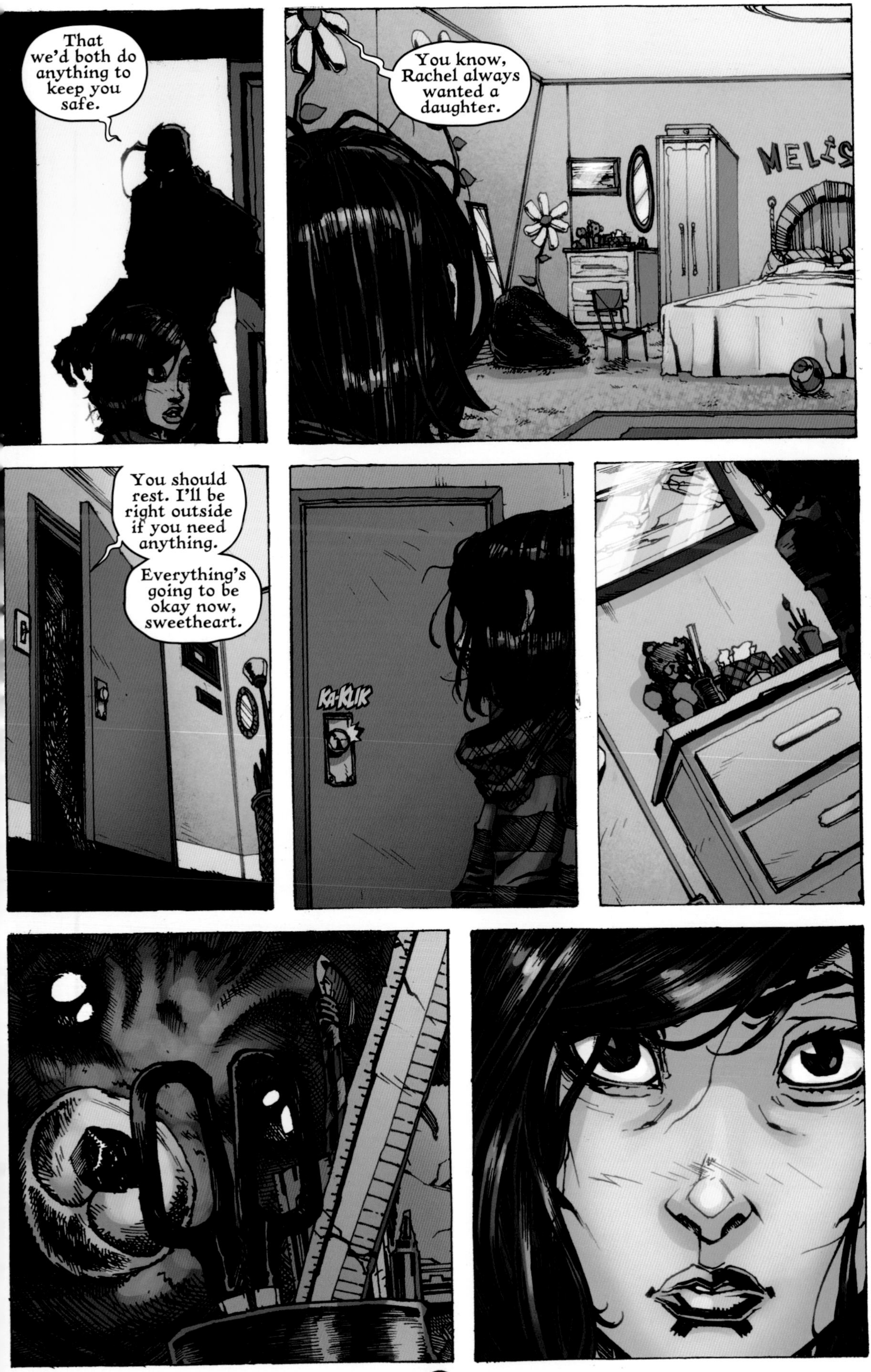
That we'd both do anything to keep you safe.
You know, Rachel always wanted a daughter.
MELIS
You should rest. I'll be right outside if you need anything.
Everything's going to be okay now, sweetheart.
KA-KLIK

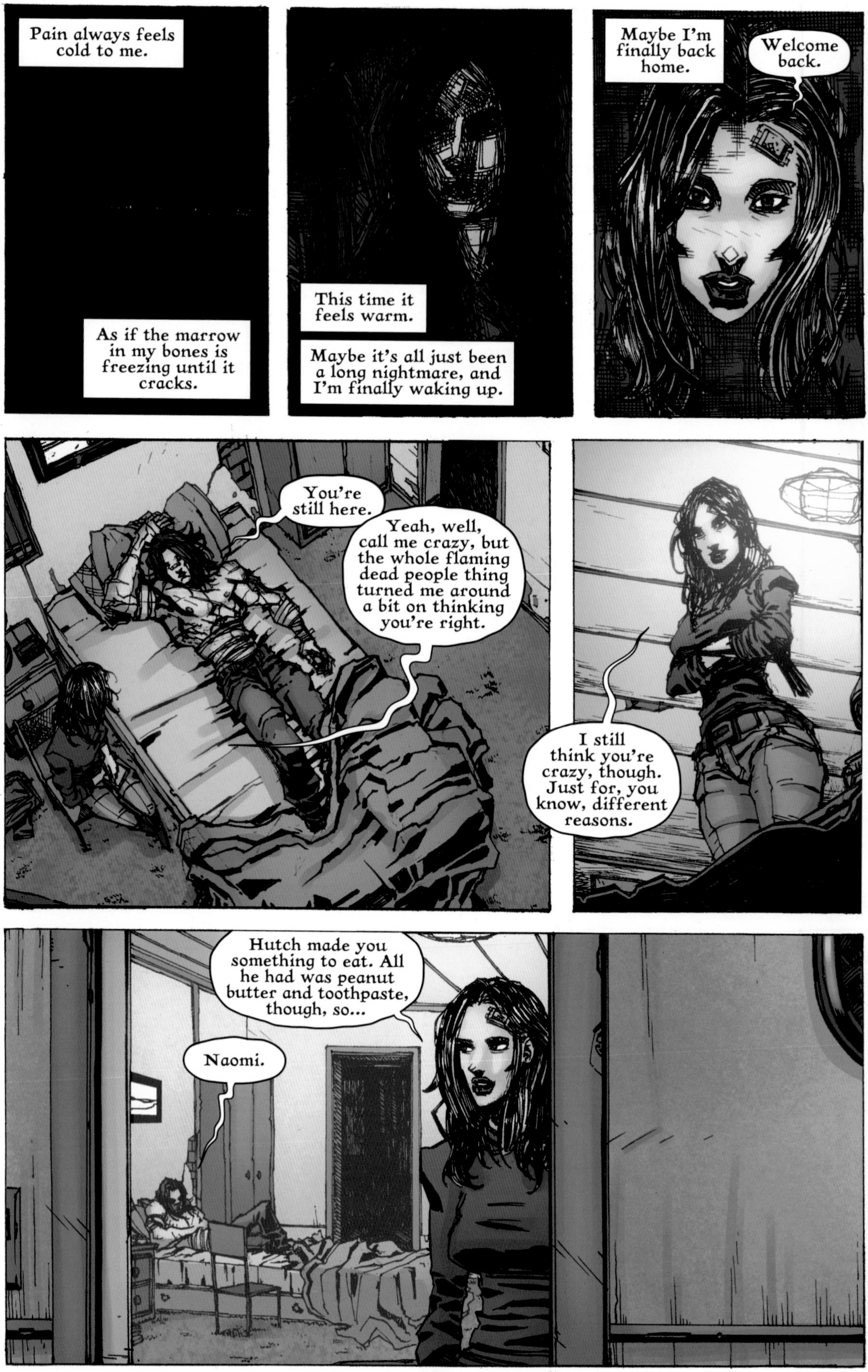

Pain always feels cold to me.
As if the marrow in my bones is freezing until it cracks.
This time it feels warm.
Maybe it's all just been a long nightmare, and I'm finally waking up.
Maybe I'm finally back home.
Welcome back.
You're still here.
Yeah, well, call me crazy, but the whole flaming dead people thing turned me around a bit on thinking you're right.
I still think you're crazy, though. Just for, you know, different reasons.
Hutch made you something to eat. All he had was peanut butter and toothpaste, though, so...
Naomi.

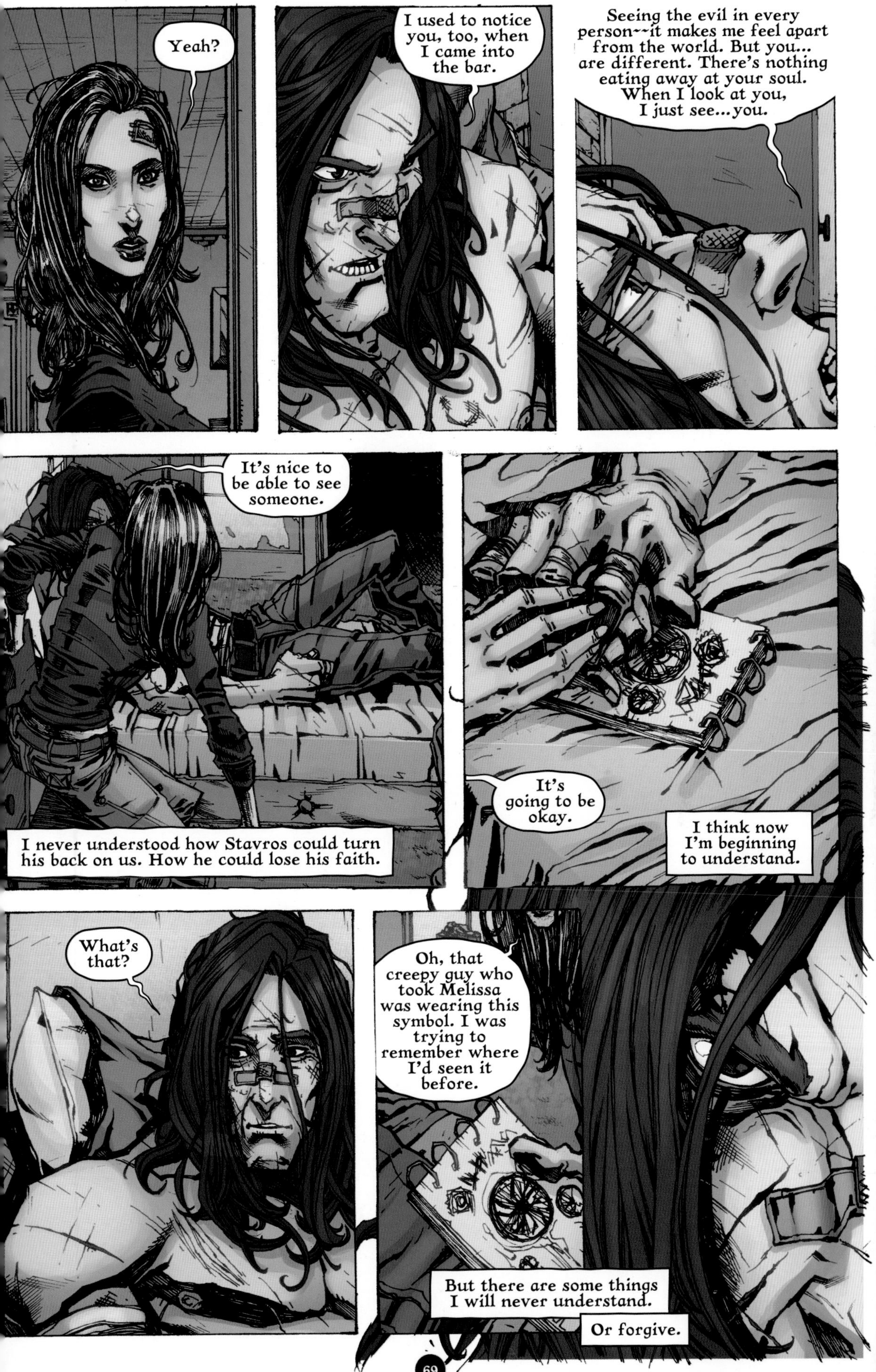
Yeah?
I used to notice you, too, when I came into the bar.
Seeing the evil in every person--it makes me feel apart from the world. But you... are different. There's nothing eating away at your soul. When I look at you, I just see...you.
It's nice to be able to see someone.
I never understood how Stavros could turn his back on us. How he could lose his faith.
It's going to be okay.
I think now I'm beginning to understand.
What's that?
Oh, that creepy guy who took Melissa was wearing this symbol. I was trying to remember where I'd seen it before.
But there are some things I will never understand.
Or forgive.

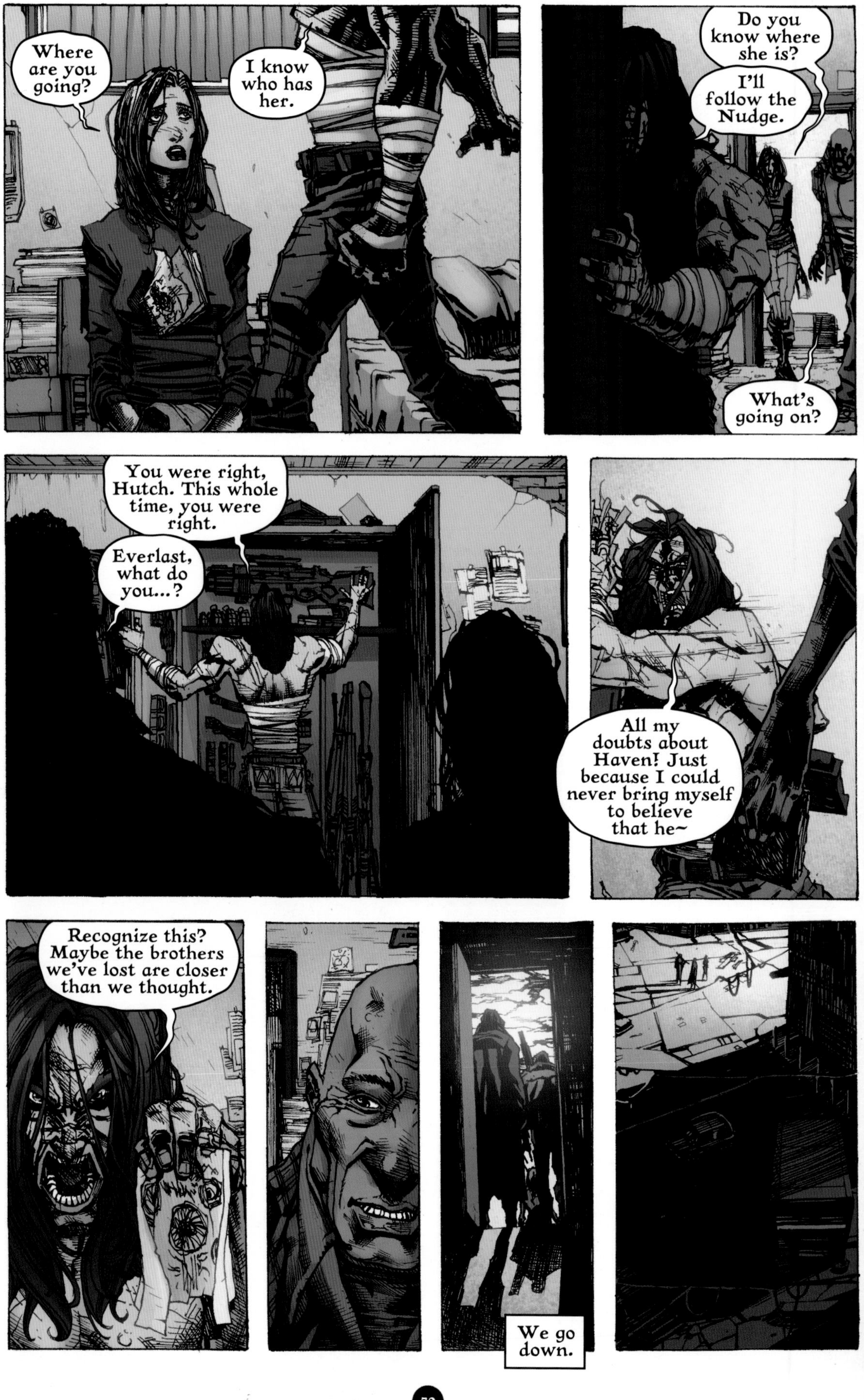

Where are you going?
I know who has her.
Do you know where she is?
I'll follow the Nudge.
What's going on?
You were right, Hutch. This whole time, you were right.
Everlast, what do you...?
All my doubts about Haven! Just because I could never bring myself to believe that he~
Recognize this? Maybe the brothers we've lost are closer than we thought.
We go down.

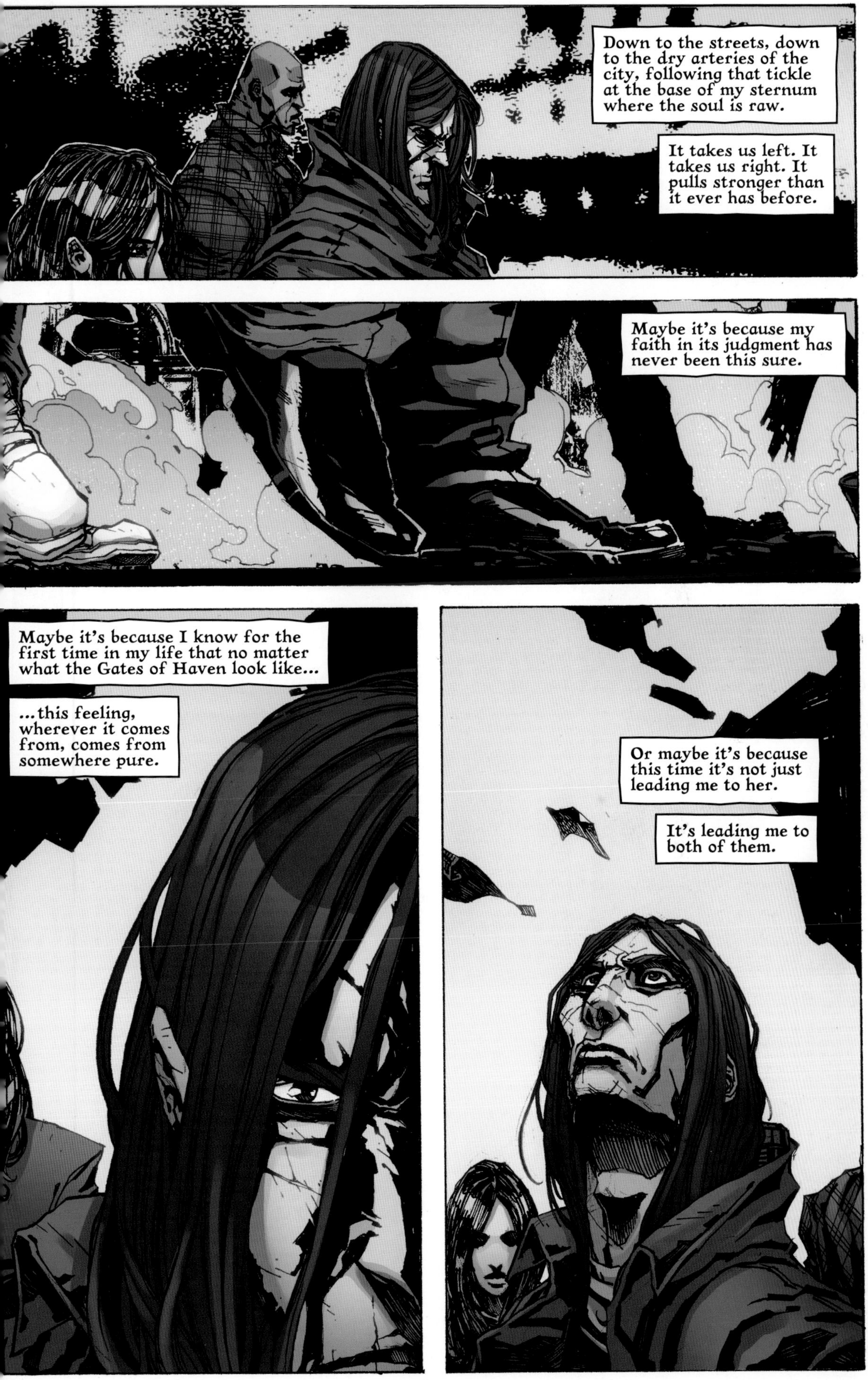
Down to the streets, down to the dry arteries of the city, following that tickle at the base of my sternum where the soul is raw.
It takes us left. It takes us right. It pulls stronger than it ever has before.
Maybe it's because my faith in its judgment has never been this sure.
Maybe it's because I know for the first time in my life that no matter what the Gates of Haven look like...
...this feeling, wherever it comes from, comes from somewhere pure.
Or maybe it's because this time it's not just leading me to her.
It's leading me to both of them.

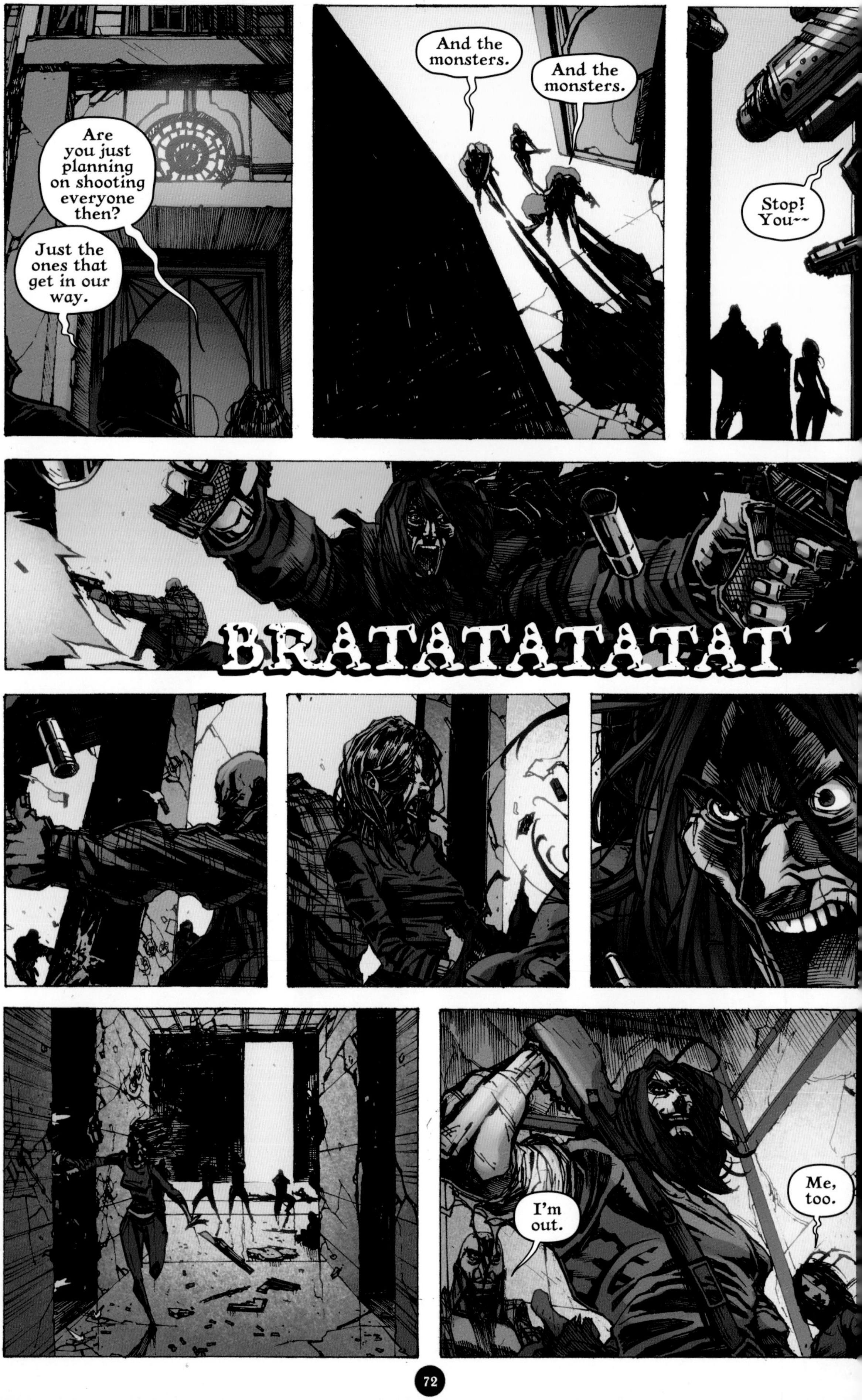
Are you just planning on shooting everyone then?
Just the ones that get in our way.
And the monsters.
And the monsters.
Stop! You--
BRATATATATAT
I'm out.
Me, too.

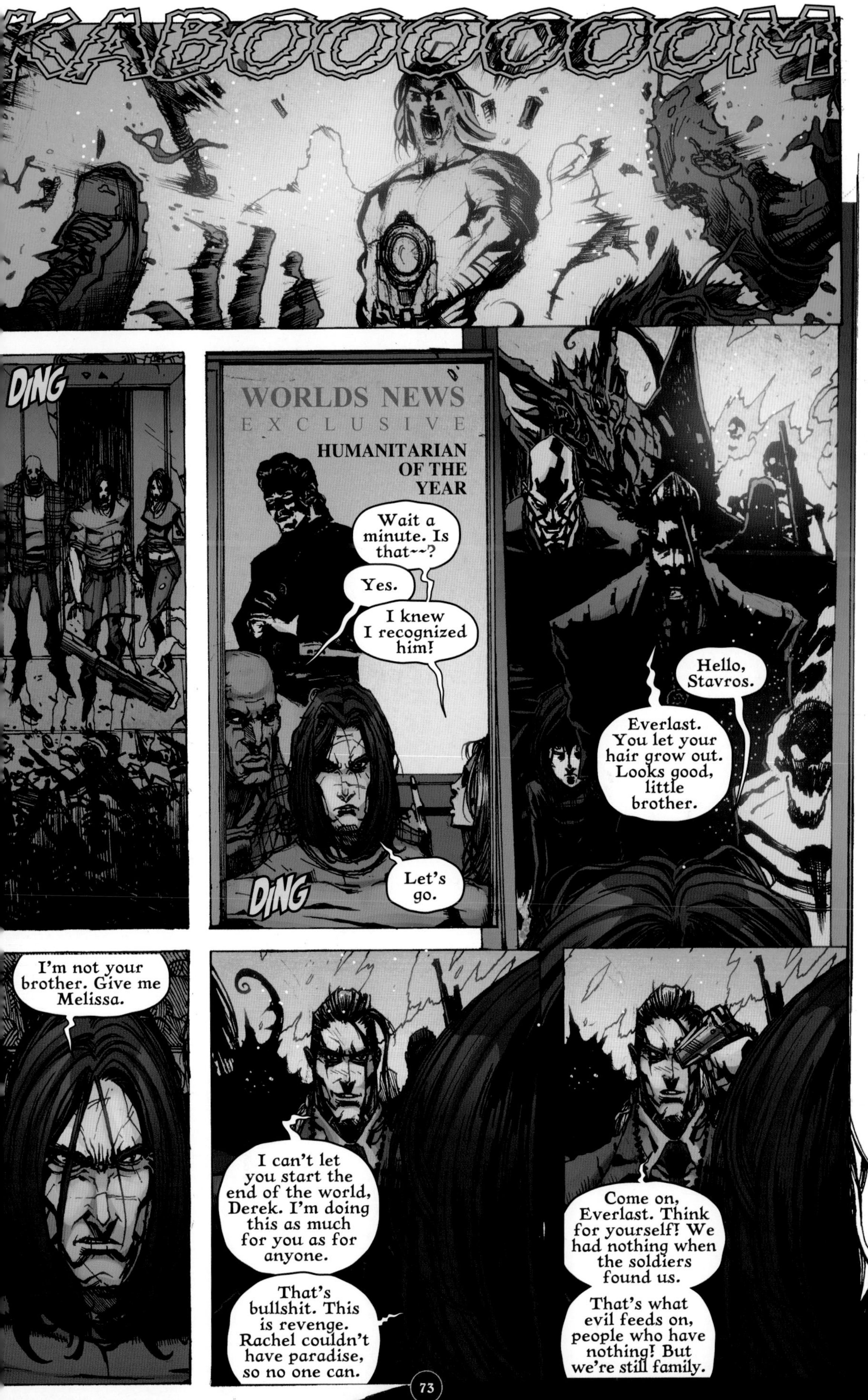
KABOOOOOOOM!
DING
WORLDS NEWS
EXCLUSIVE
HUMANITARIAN OF THE YEAR
Wait a minute. Is that--?
Yes.
I knew I recognized him!
DING
Let's go.
Hello, Stavros.
Everlast. You let your hair grow out. Looks good, little brother.
I'm not your brother. Give me Melissa.
I can't let you start the end of the world, Derek. I'm doing this as much for you as for anyone.
That's bullshit. This is revenge. Rachel couldn't have paradise, so no one can.
Come on, Everlast. Think for yourself! We had nothing when the soldiers found us.
That's what evil feeds on, people who have nothing! But we're still family.

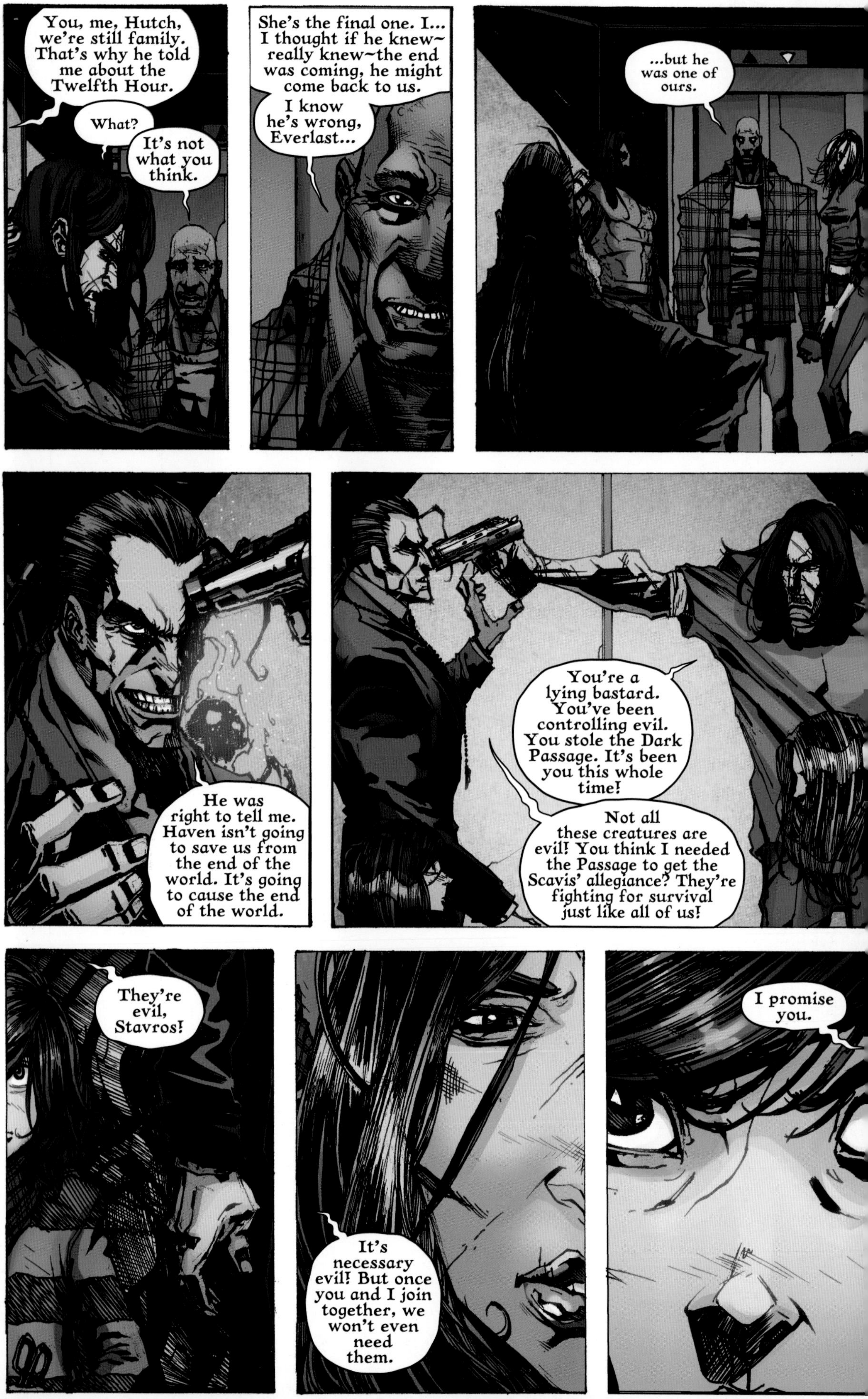
You, me, Hutch, we're still family. That's why he told me about the Twelfth Hour.
What?
It's not what you think.
She's the final one. I... I thought if he knew~ really knew~the end was coming, he might come back to us.
I know he's wrong, Everlast...
...but he was one of ours.
He was right to tell me. Haven isn't going to save us from the end of the world. It's going to cause the end of the world.
You're a lying bastard. You've been controlling evil. You stole the Dark Passage. It's been you this whole time!
Not all these creatures are evil! You think I needed the Passage to get the Scavis' allegiance? They're fighting for survival just like all of us!
They're evil, Stavros!
It's necessary evil! But once you and I join together, we won't even need them.
I promise you.

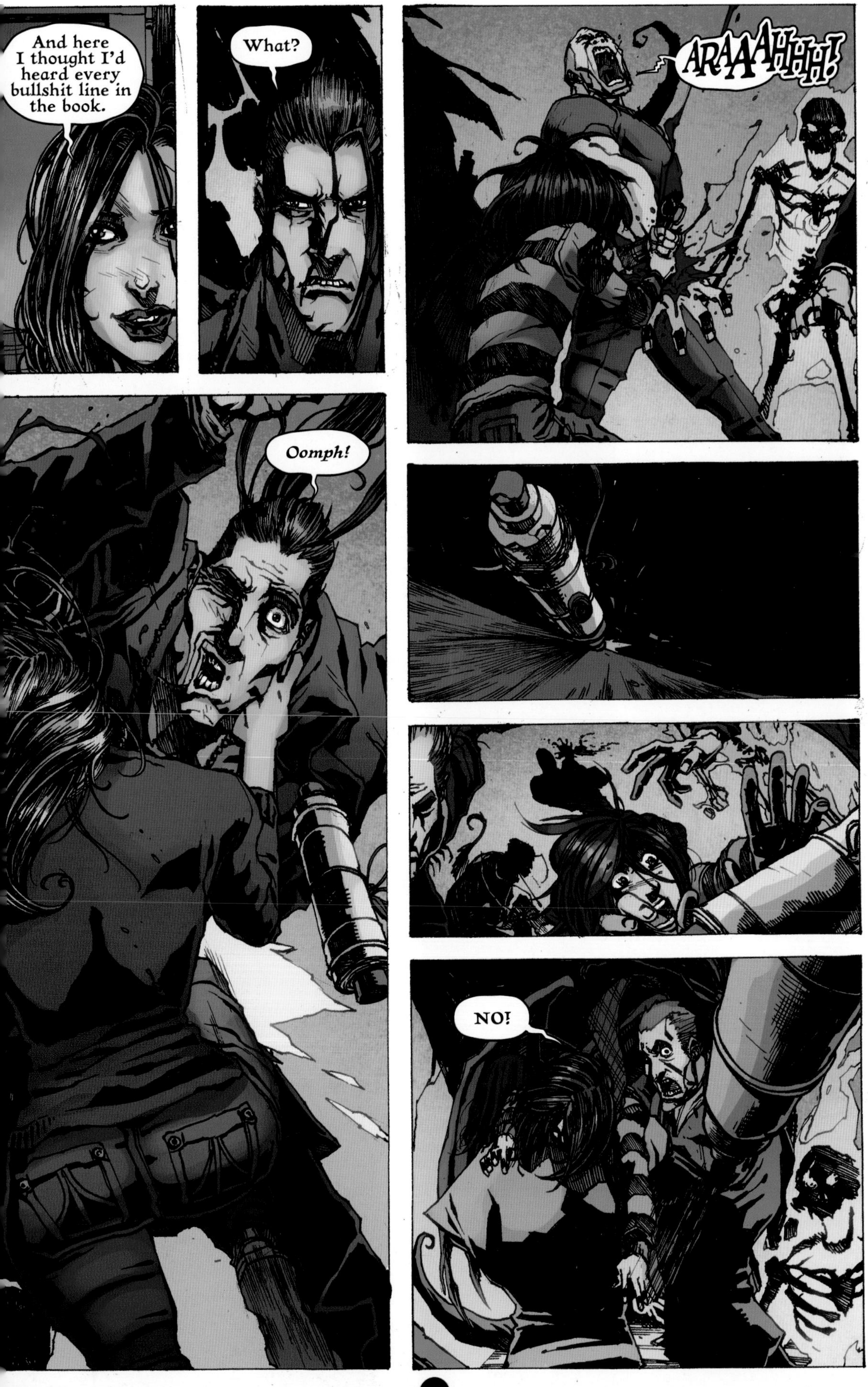
And here I thought I'd heard every bullshit line in the book.
What?
ARAAAHHH!
Oomph!
NO!

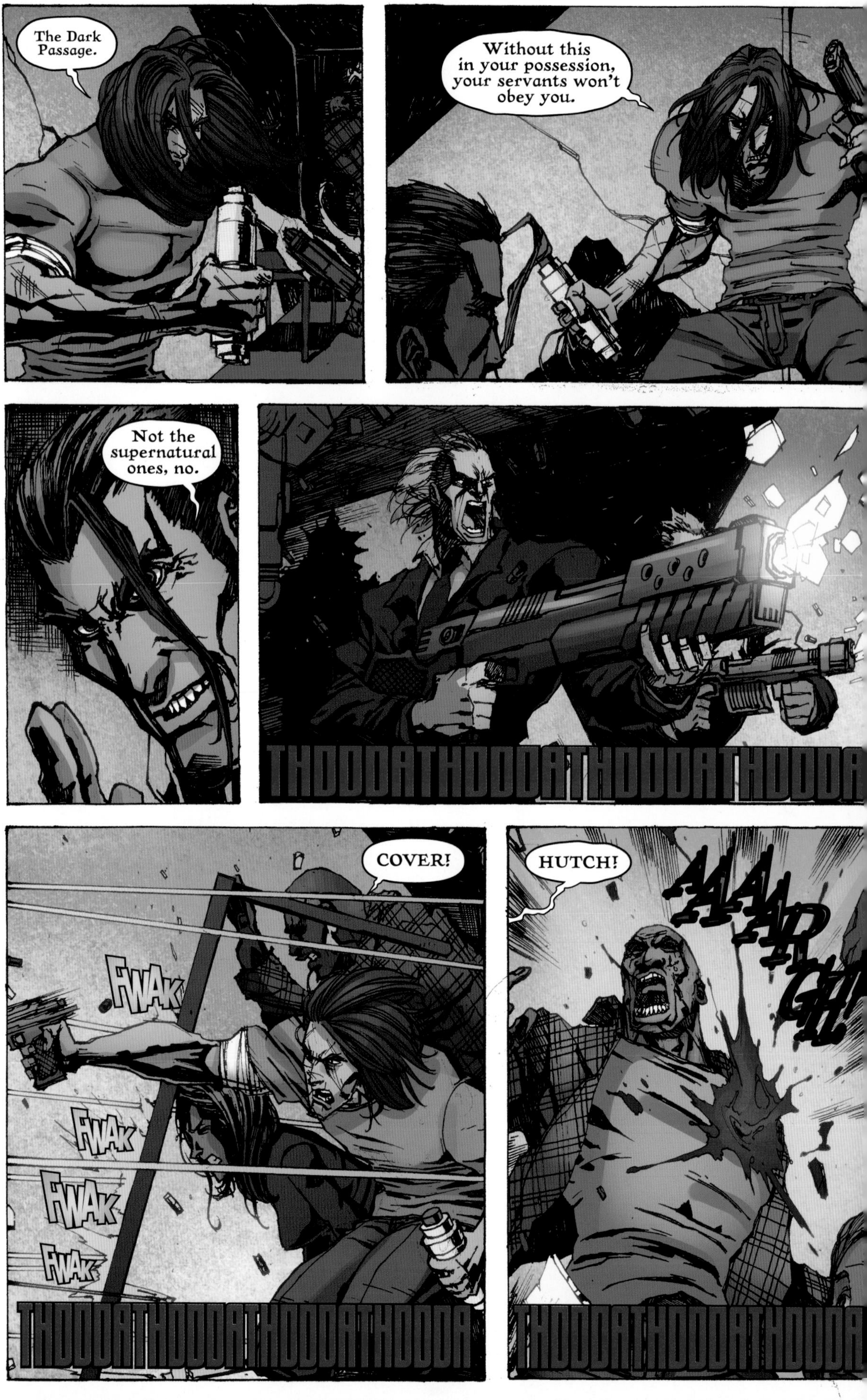

The Dark Passage.
Without this in your possession, your servants won't obey you.
Not the supernatural ones, no.
THDDDATHDDDATHDDDATHDDDA
COVER!
FWAK
FWAK
FWAK
FWAK
THDDDATHDDDATHDDDATHDDDA
HUTCH!
AAAARGH!
THDDDATHDDDATHDDDA

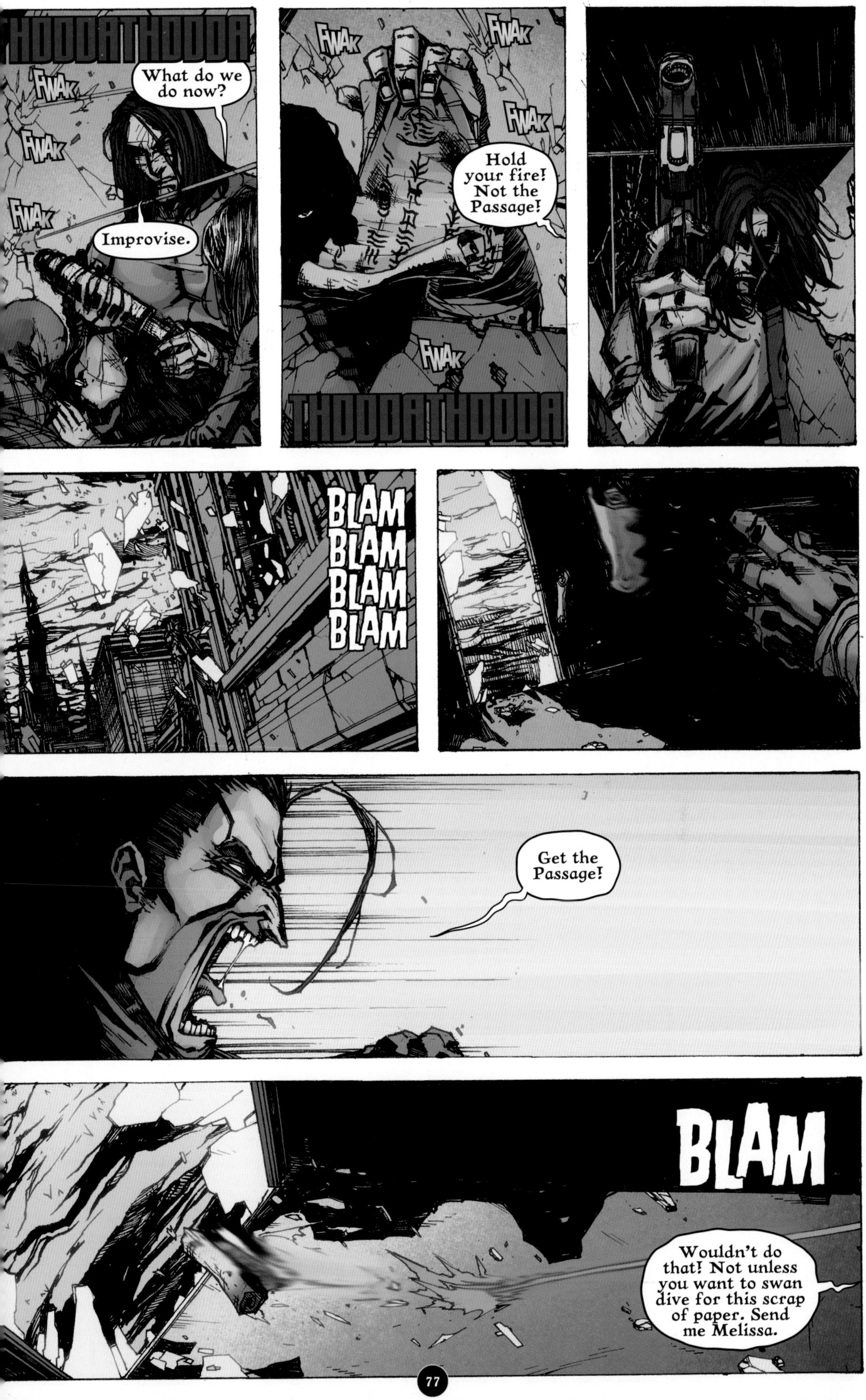
THODDATHODDA
What do we do now?
FWAK
FWAK
FWAK
Improvise.
FWAK
FWAK
FWAK
Hold your fire! Not the Passage!
FWAK
THODDATHODDA
BLAM BLAM BLAM BLAM
Get the Passage!
BLAM
Wouldn't do that! Not unless you want to swan dive for this scrap of paper. Send me Melissa.

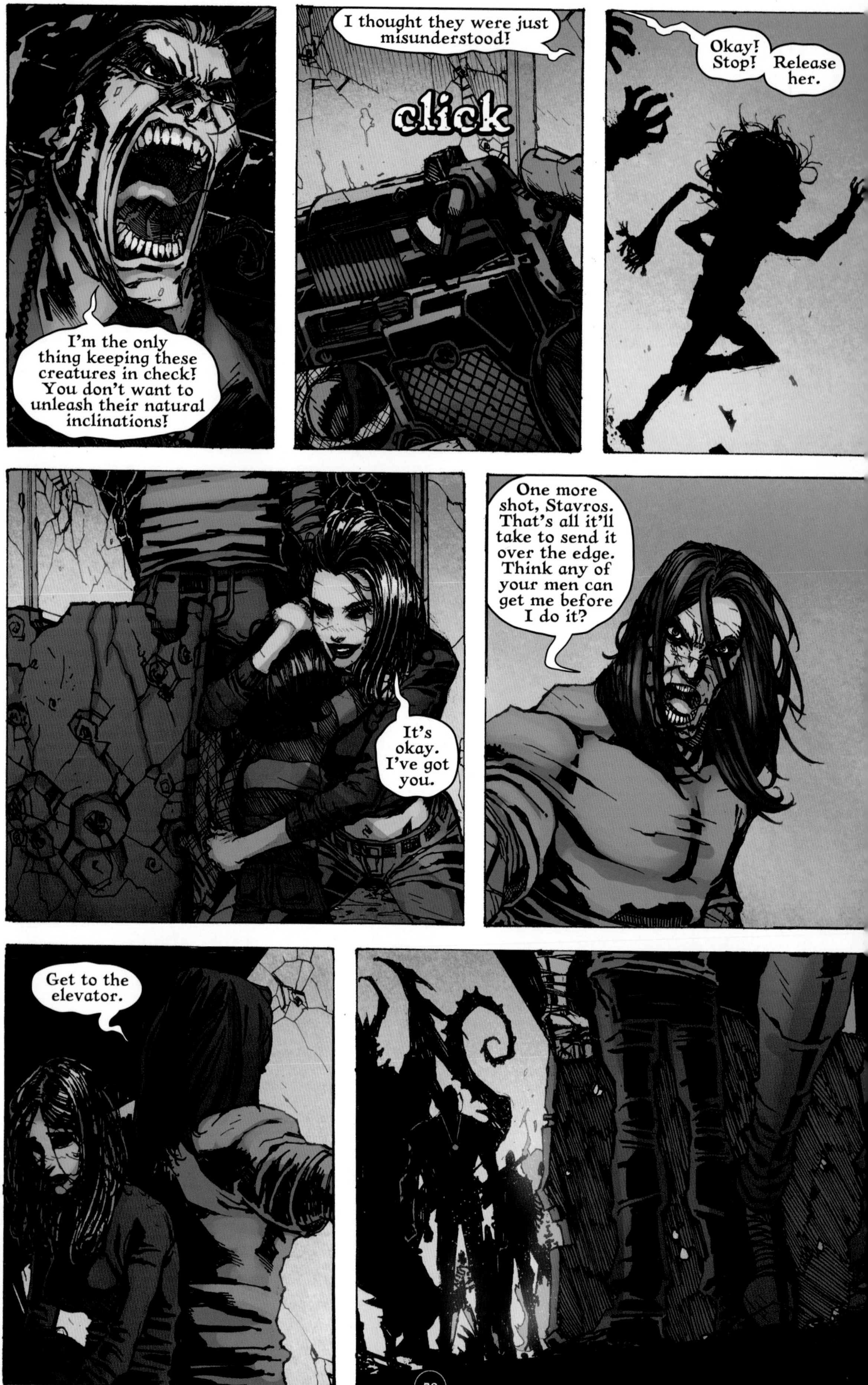
I'm the only thing keeping these creatures in check! You don't want to unleash their natural inclinations!
I thought they were just misunderstood!
click
Okay! Stop!
Release her.
It's okay. I've got you.
One more shot, Stavros. That's all it'll take to send it over the edge. Think any of your men can get me before I do it?
Get to the elevator.

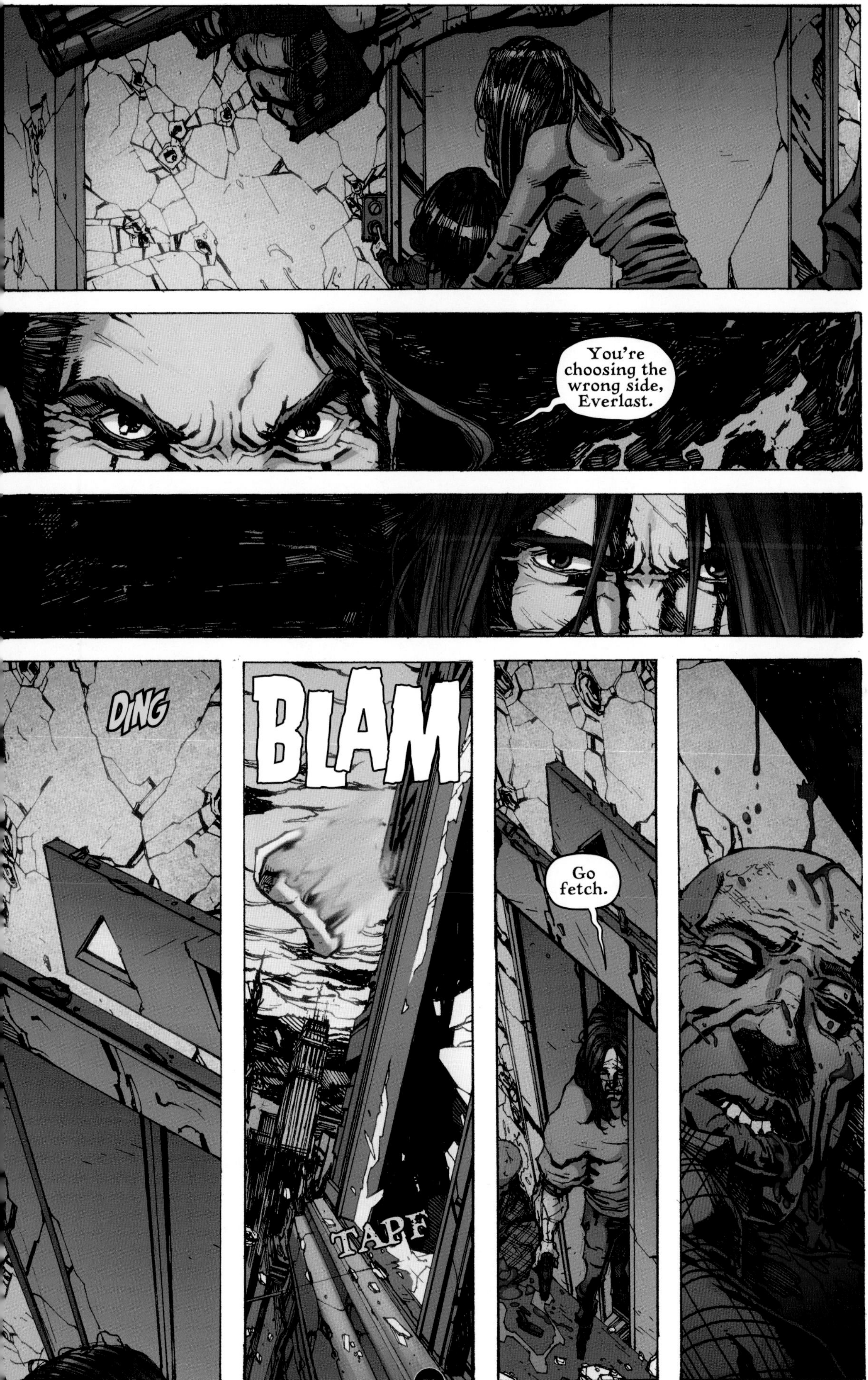
You're choosing the wrong side, Everlast.
DING
BLAM
TAPF
Go fetch.

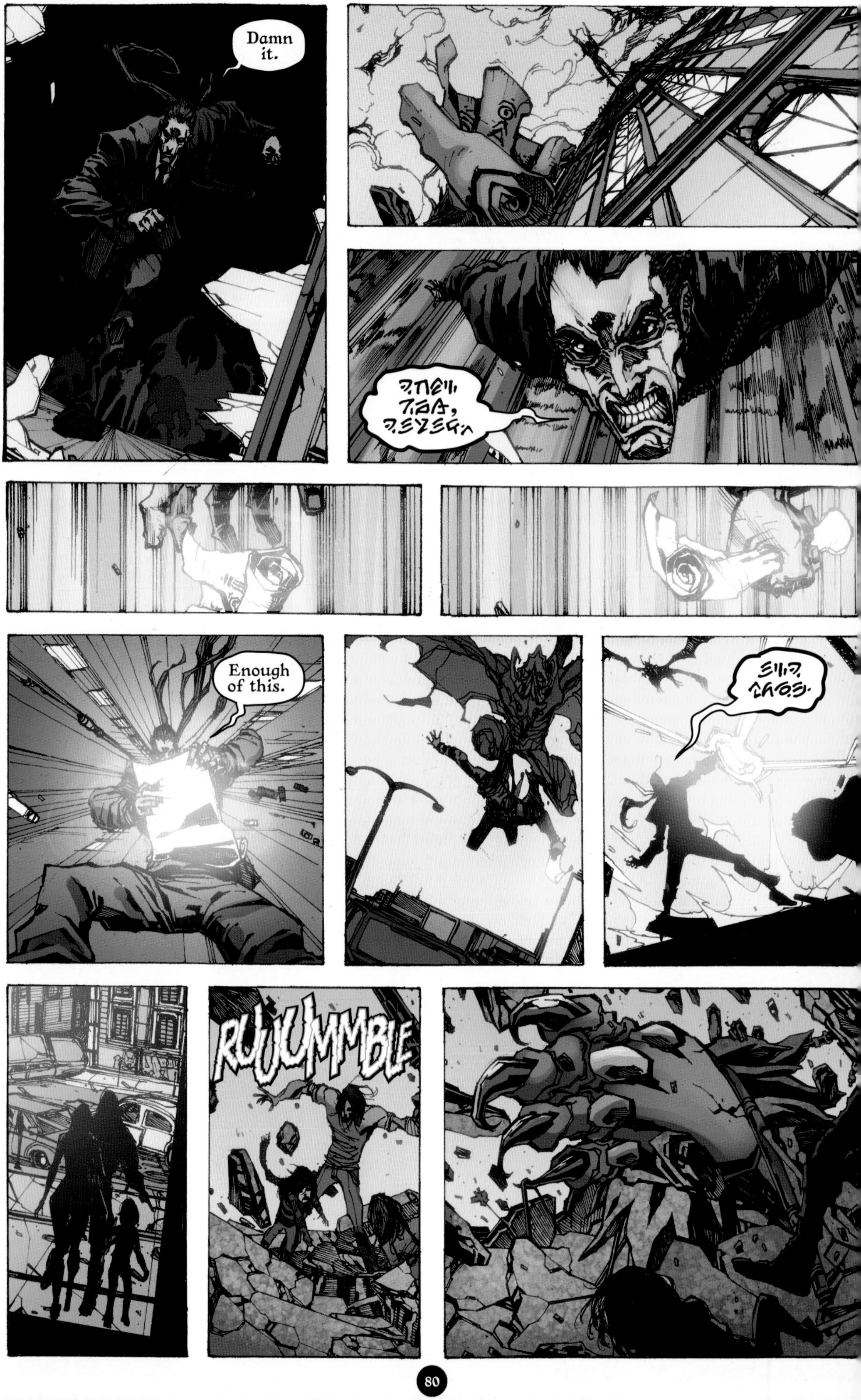
Damn it.
Enough of this.
RUUUMMBLE

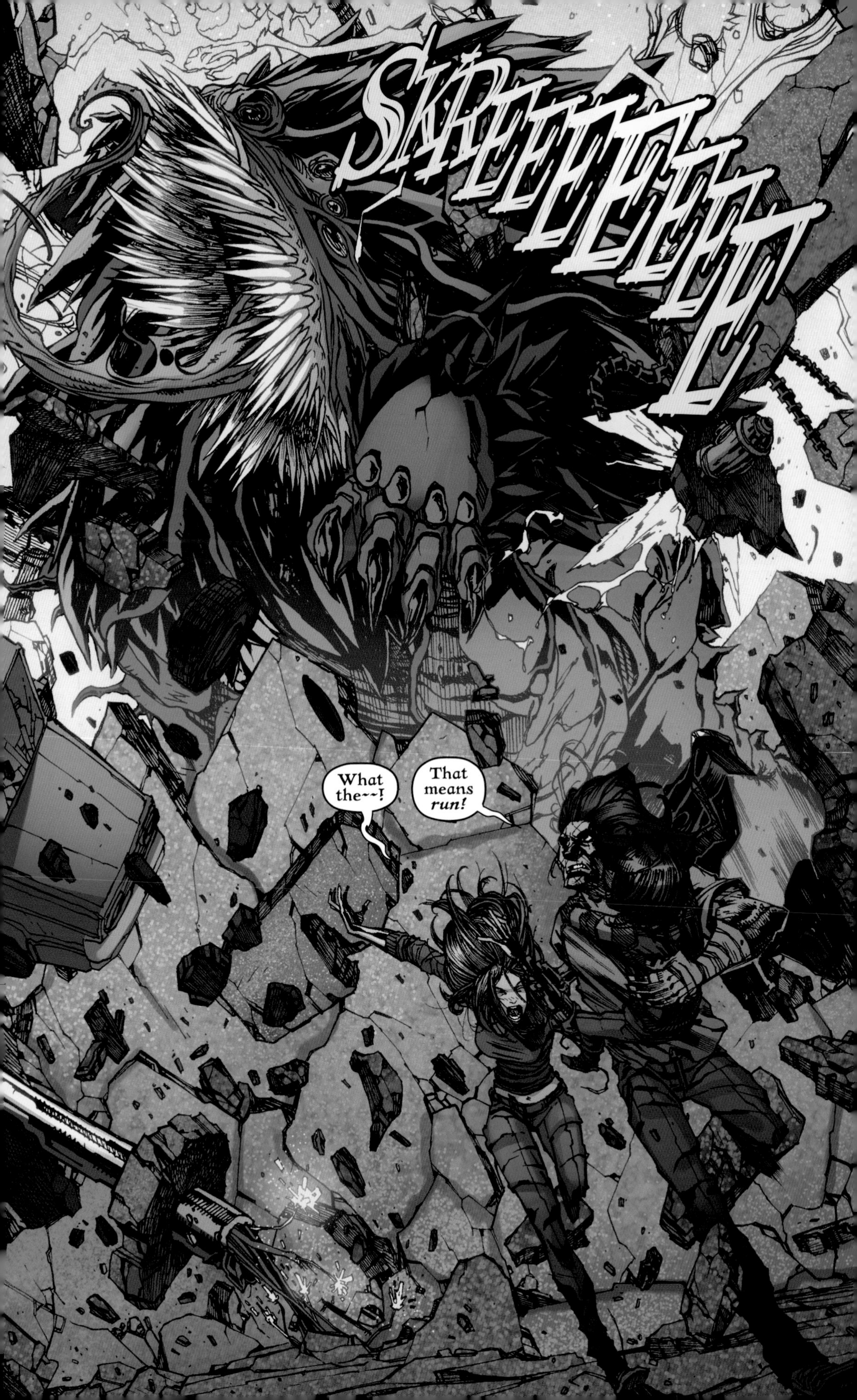
SKREEEEEEEE
What the--!
That means *run!*

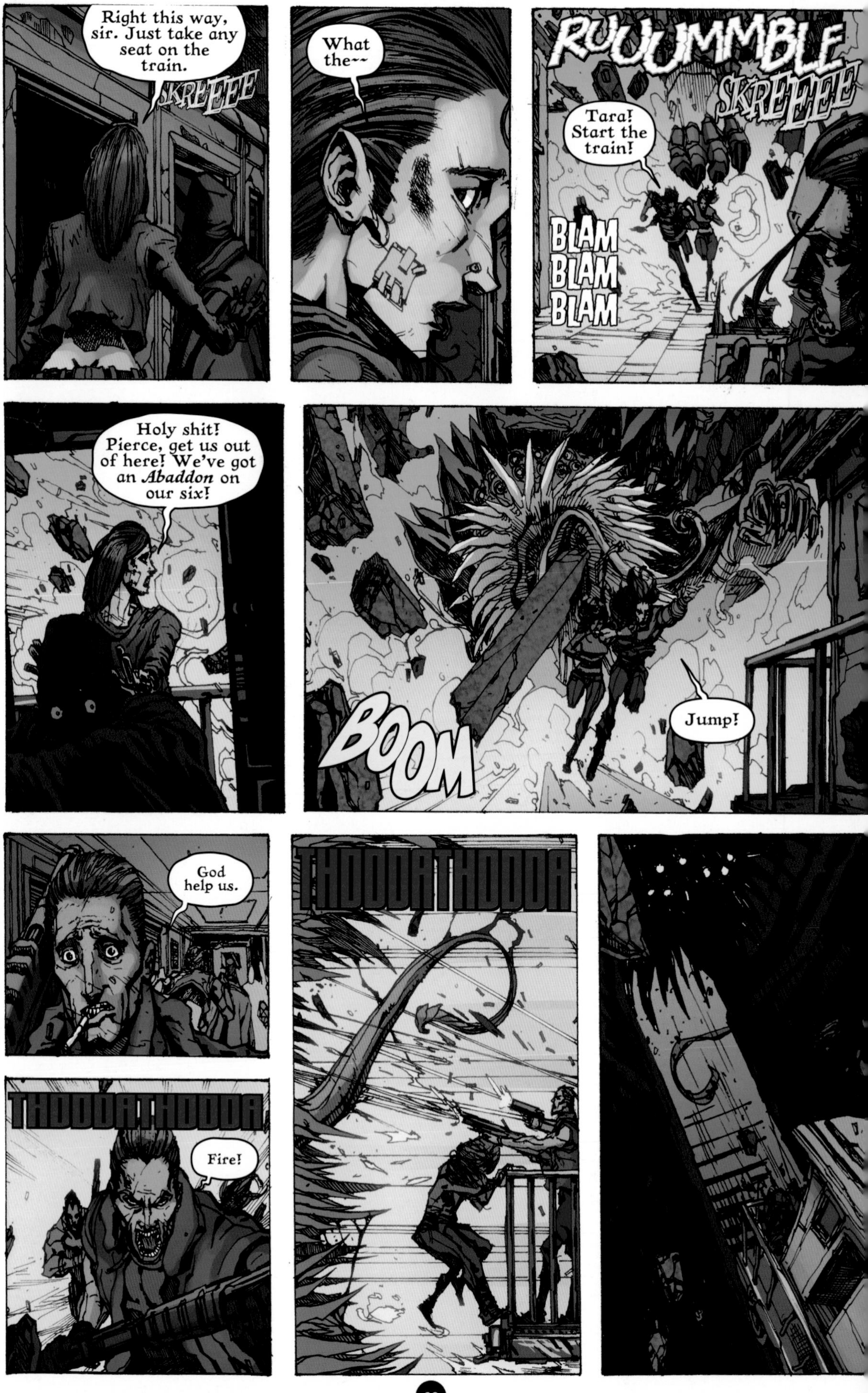
Right this way, sir. Just take any seat on the train.
SKREEEE
What the--
RUUUMMBLE
SKREEEE
Tara! Start the train!
BLAM
BLAM
BLAM
Holy shit! Pierce, get us out of here! We've got an *Abaddon* on our six!
BOOM
Jump!
God help us.
THDDDATHDDDA
Fire!
THDDDATHDDDA

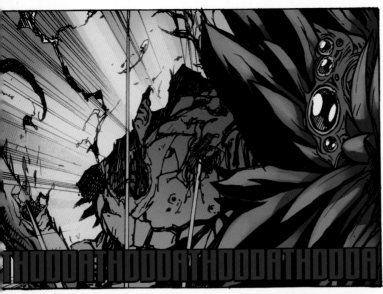

It's breaking apart!

THDDDATHDDDATHDDDATHDDDATHDDDA THDDDATHDDDA

THUMMMMMMMMMMMMM

THUMMM

AAAIIEEEE!

Almost there!

Quickly! Get to the water!

Jump!

THUMMM

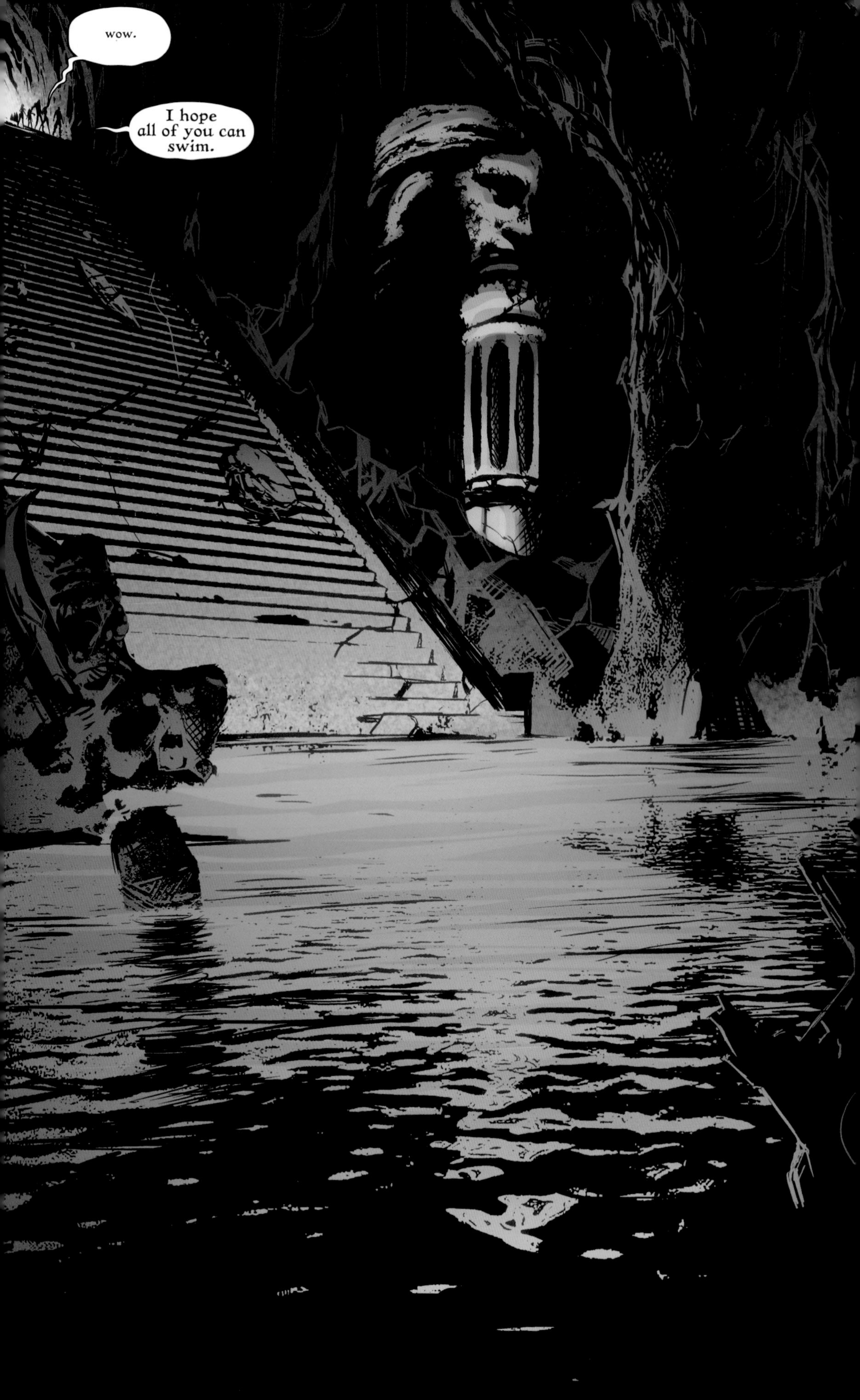
wow.
I hope all of you can swim.

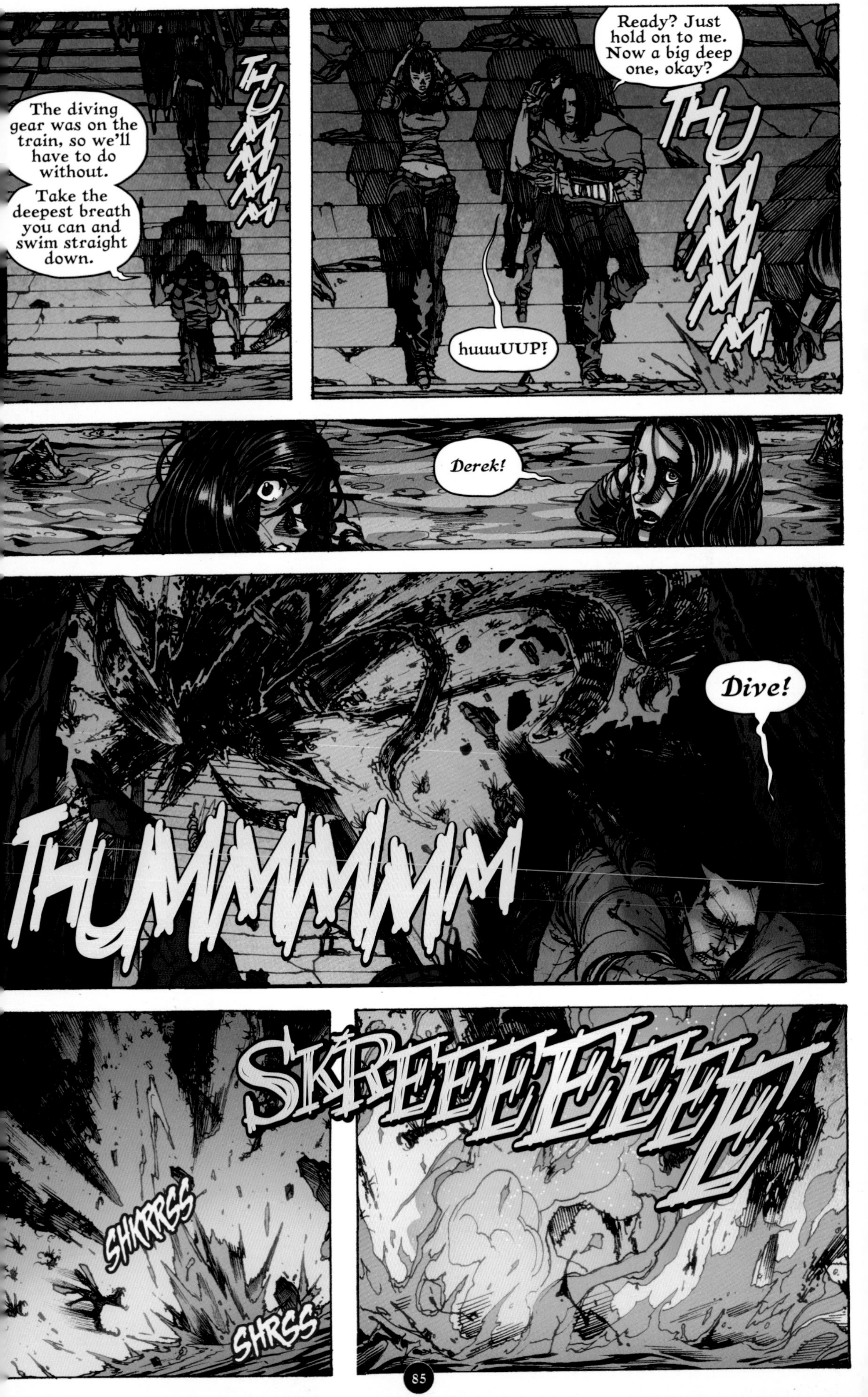

THUMMMM
The diving gear was on the train, so we'll have to do without.
Take the deepest breath you can and swim straight down.
Ready? Just hold on to me. Now a big deep one, okay?
THUMMMM
huuuUUP!
Derek!
Dive!
THUMMMMMM
SKREEEEEEEL
SHKRRSS
SHRSS

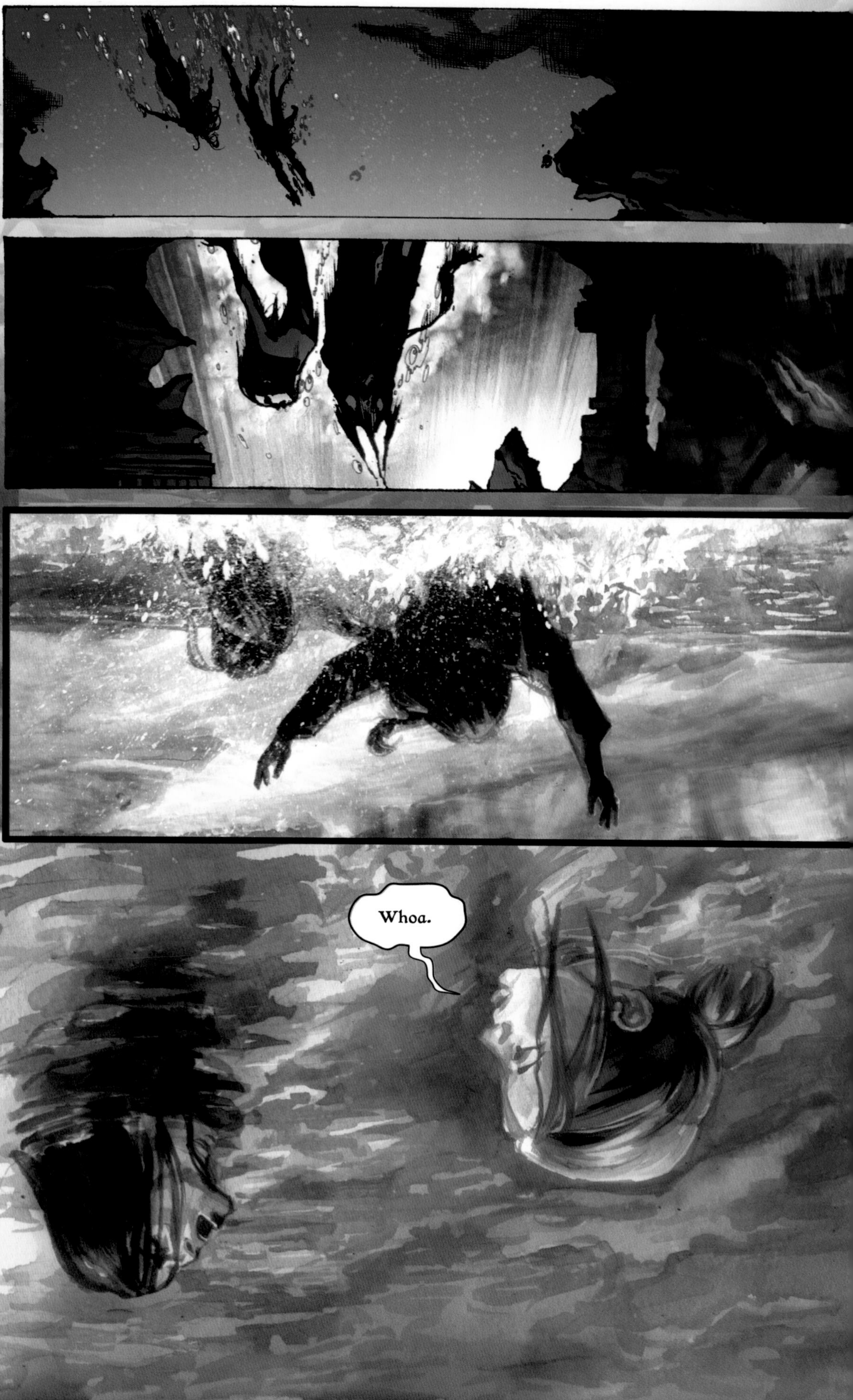
Whoa.

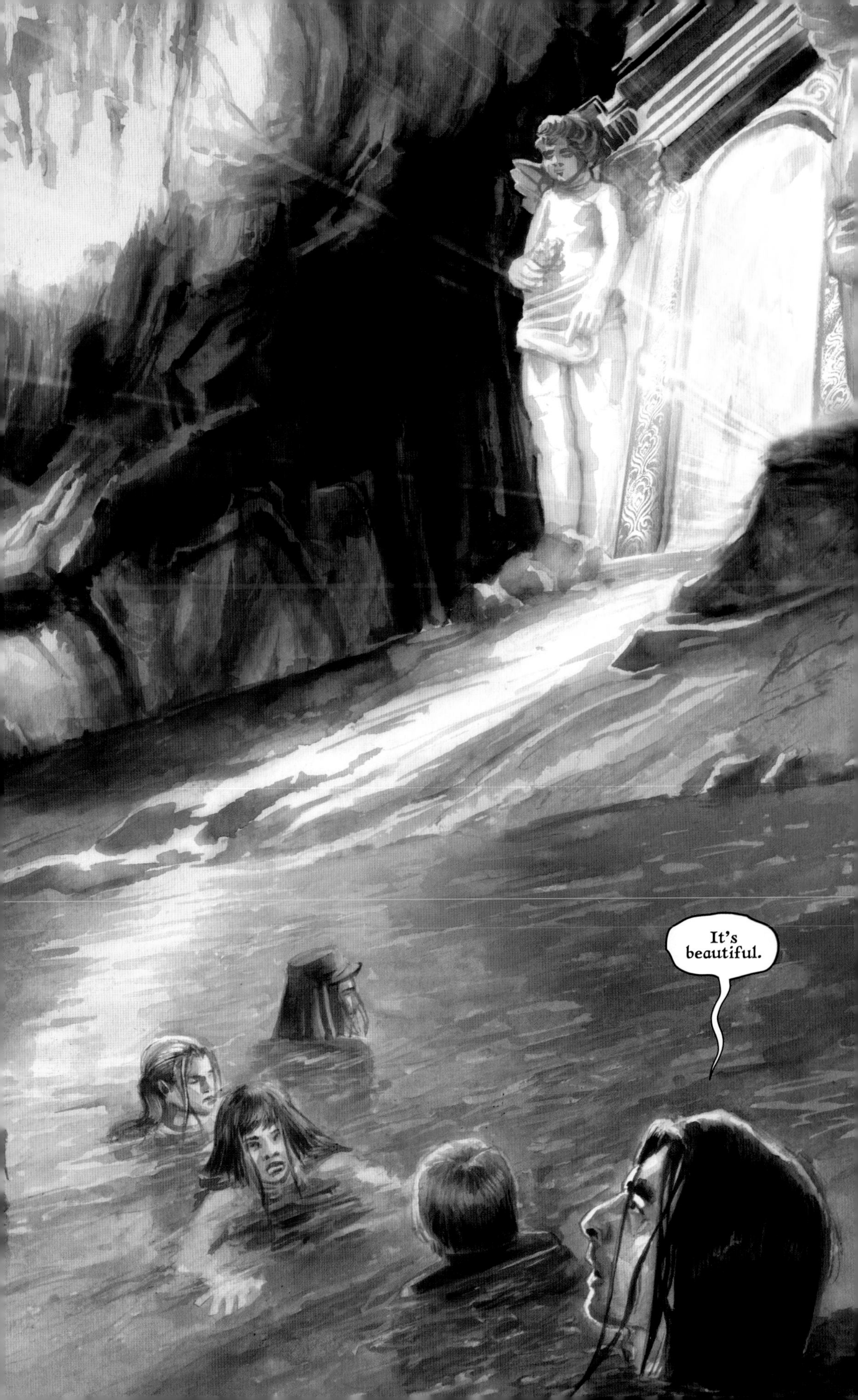
It's beautiful.

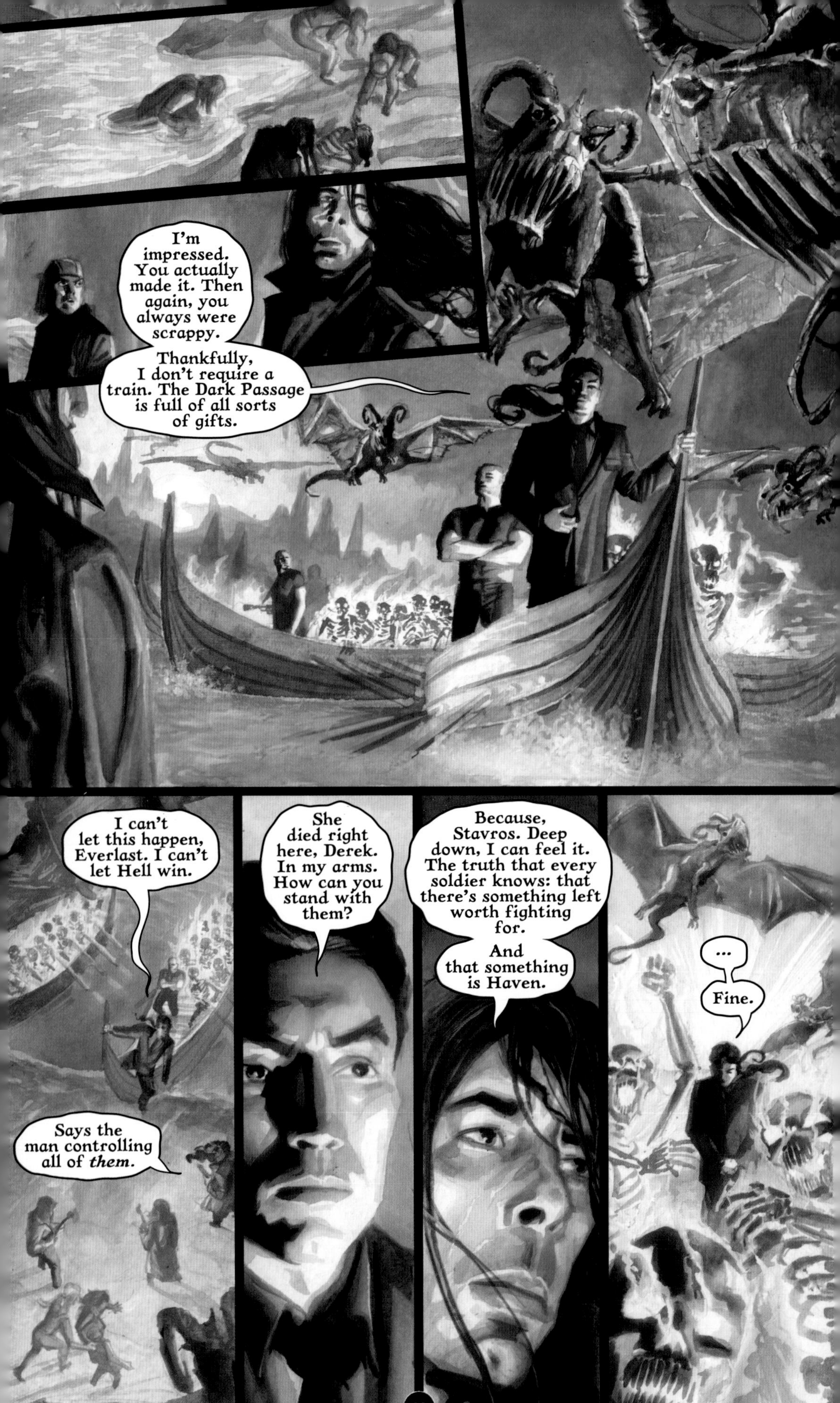
I'm impressed. You actually made it. Then again, you always were scrappy.
Thankfully, I don't require a train. The Dark Passage is full of all sorts of gifts.
I can't let this happen, Everlast. I can't let Hell win.
Says the man controlling all of *them*.
She died right here, Derek. In my arms. How can you stand with them?
Because, Stavros. Deep down, I can feel it. The truth that every soldier knows: that there's something left worth fighting for.
And that something is Haven.
...
Fine.

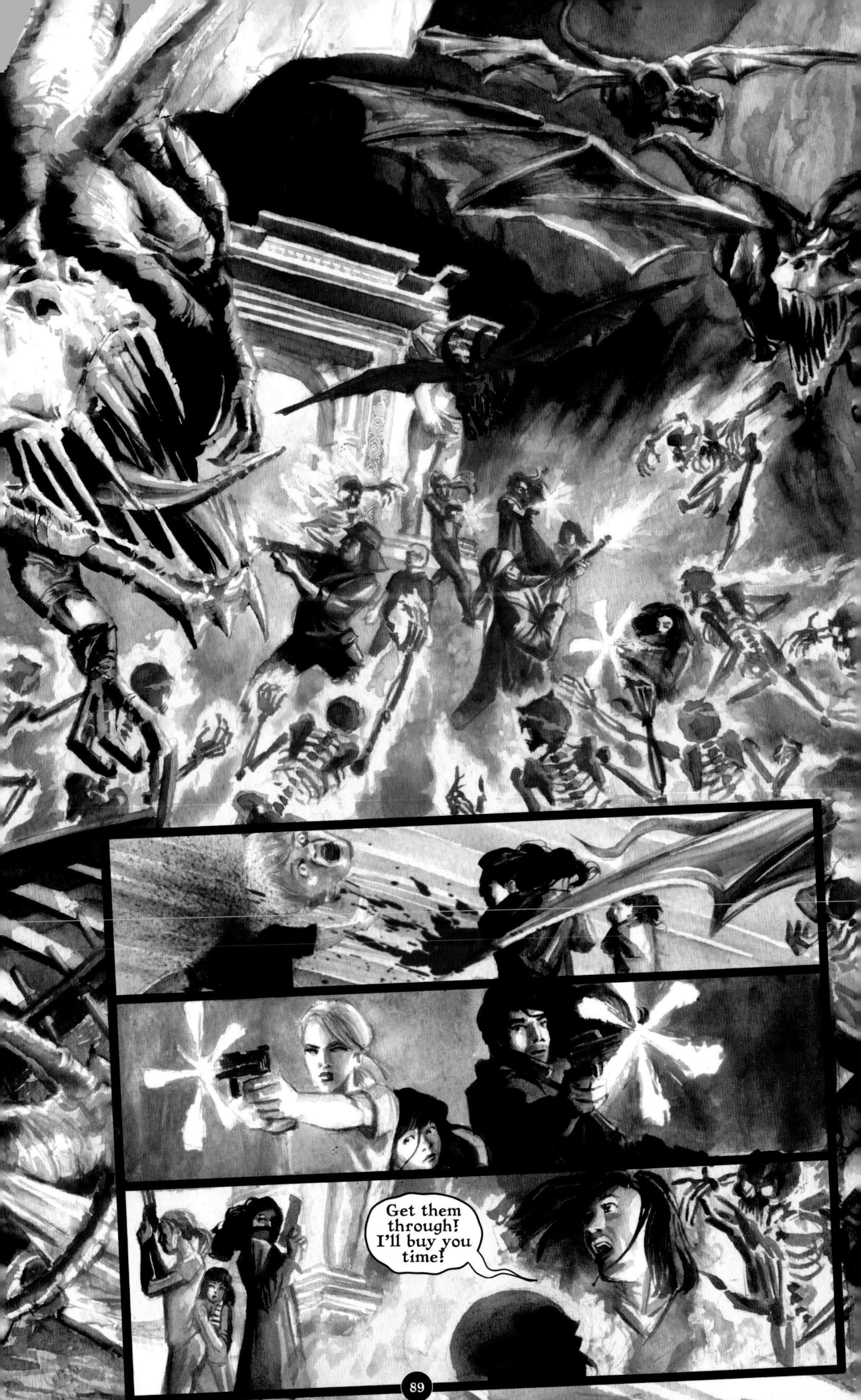
Get them through! I'll buy you time!

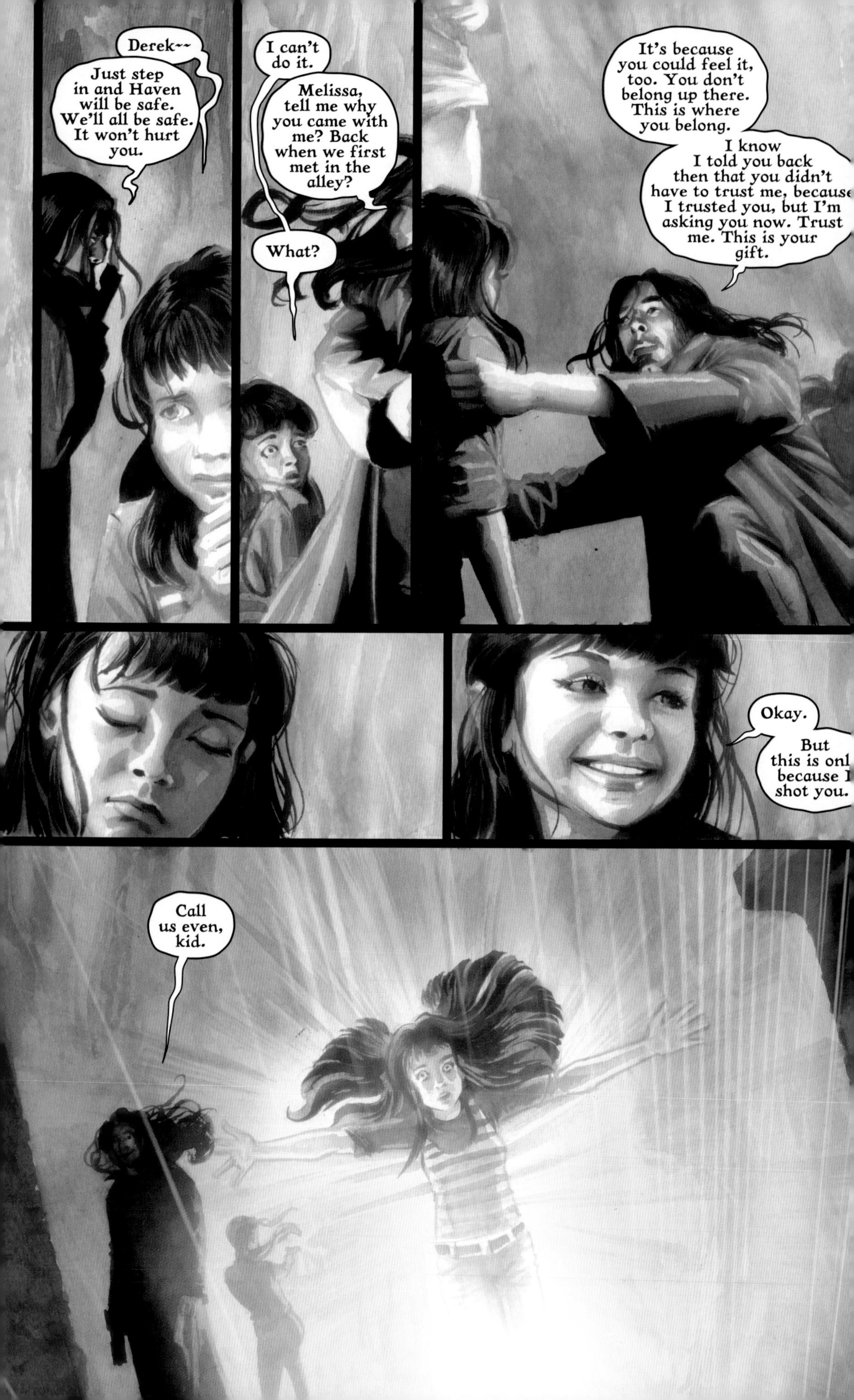
Derek--
Just step in and Haven will be safe. We'll all be safe. It won't hurt you.
I can't do it.
Melissa, tell me why you came with me? Back when we first met in the alley?
What?
It's because you could feel it, too. You don't belong up there. This is where you belong.
I know I told you back then that you didn't have to trust me, because I trusted you, but I'm asking you now. Trust me. This is your gift.
Okay.
But this is onl because I shot you.
Call us even, kid.

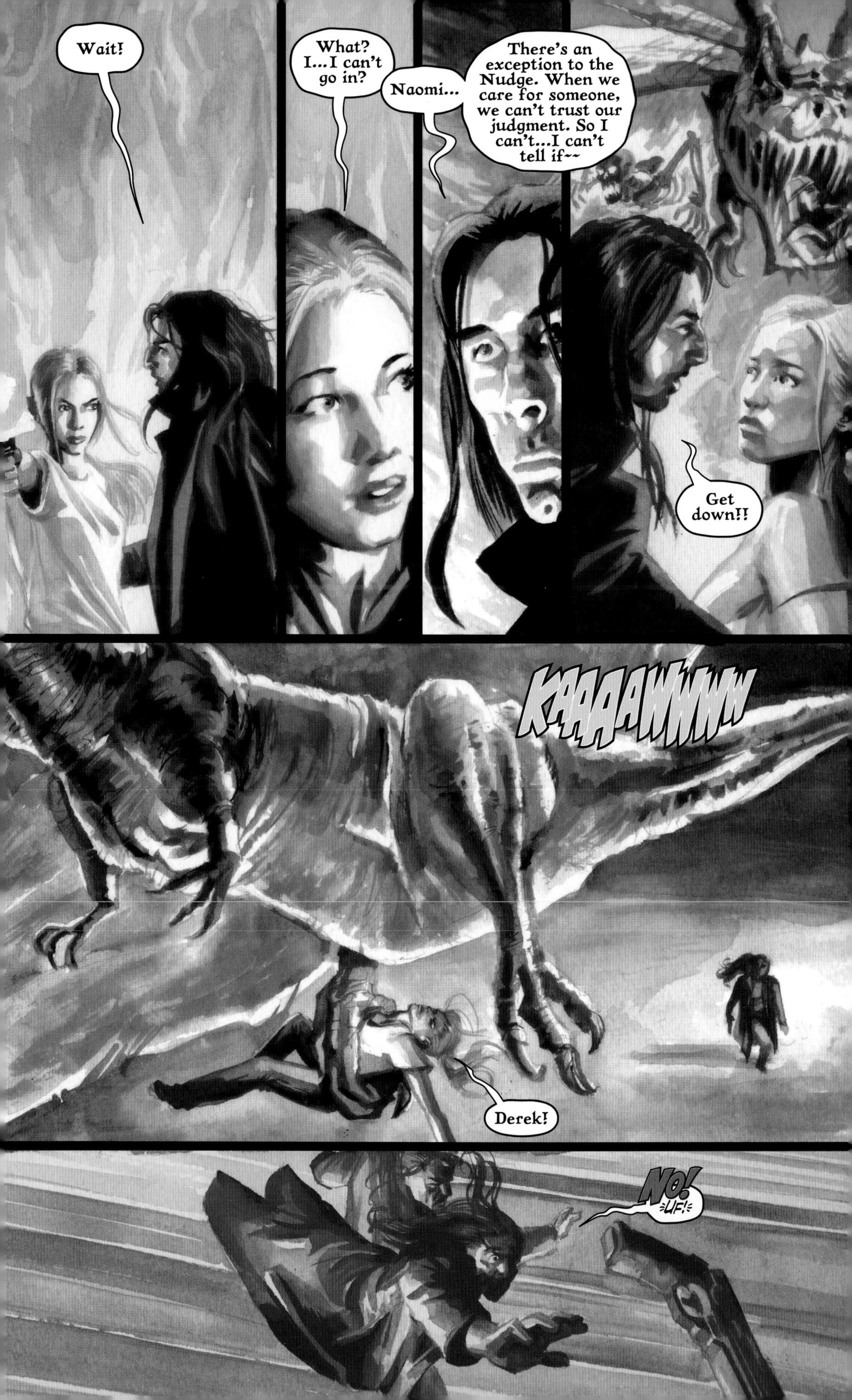
Wait!
What? I...I can't go in?
Naomi...
There's an exception to the Nudge. When we care for someone, we can't trust our judgment. So I can't...I can't tell if--
Get down!!
KAAAAWWWW
Derek!
NO!
UF!

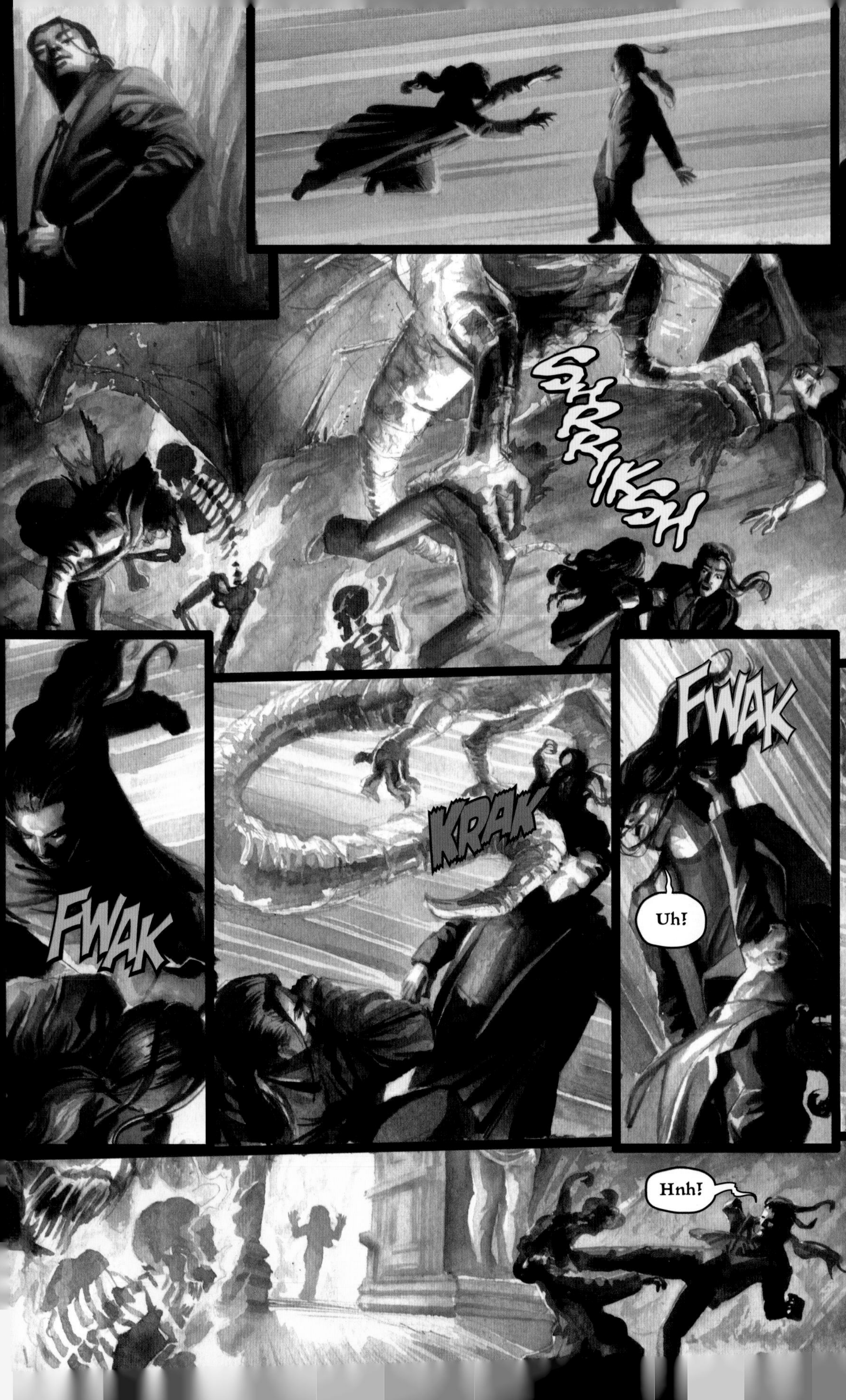
SHRIKSH
FWAK
KRAK
FWAK
Uh!
Hnh!

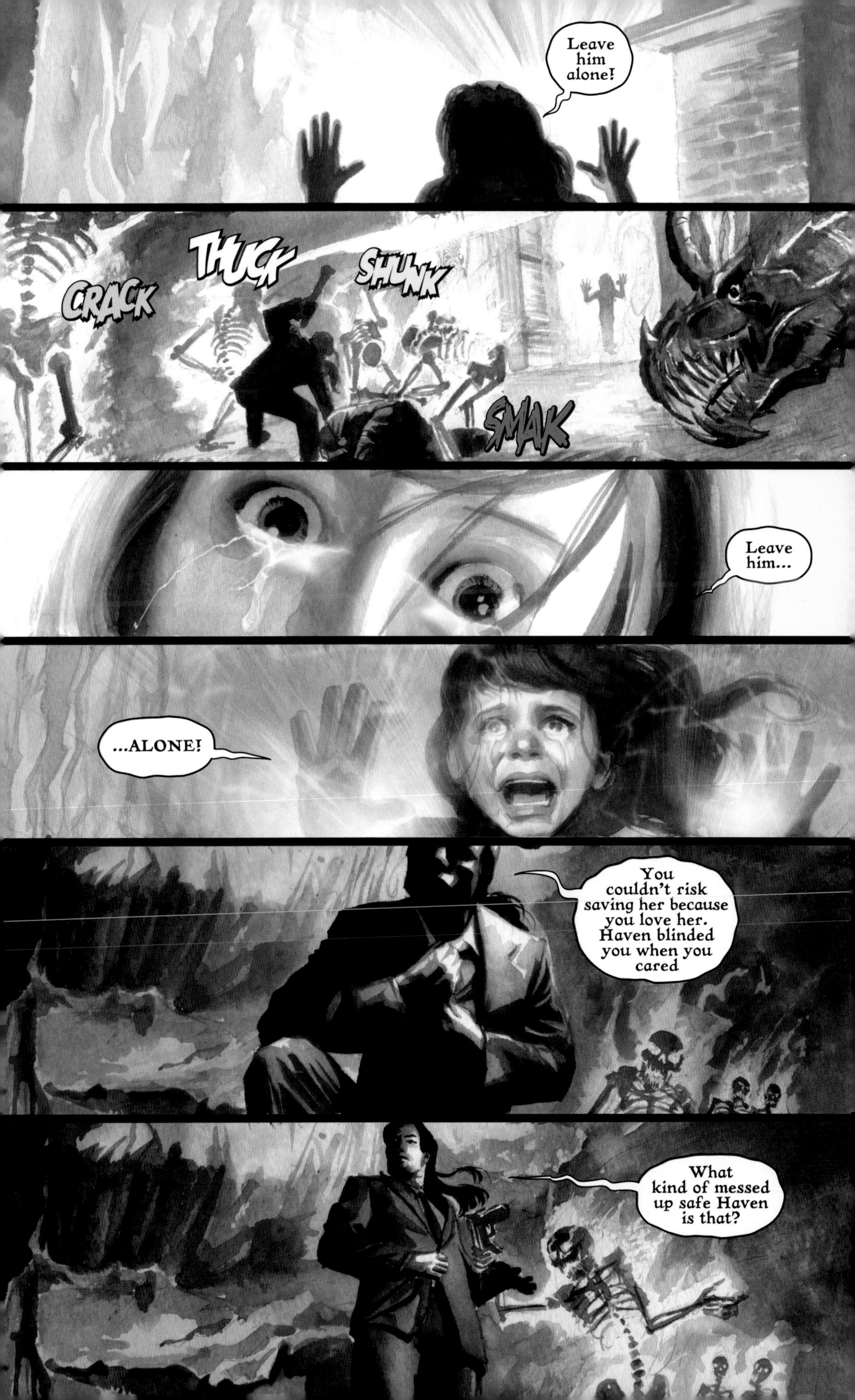
Leave him alone!
CRACK
THUCK
SHUNK
SMAK
Leave him...
...ALONE!
You couldn't risk saving her because you love her. Haven blinded you when you cared
What kind of messed up safe Haven is that?

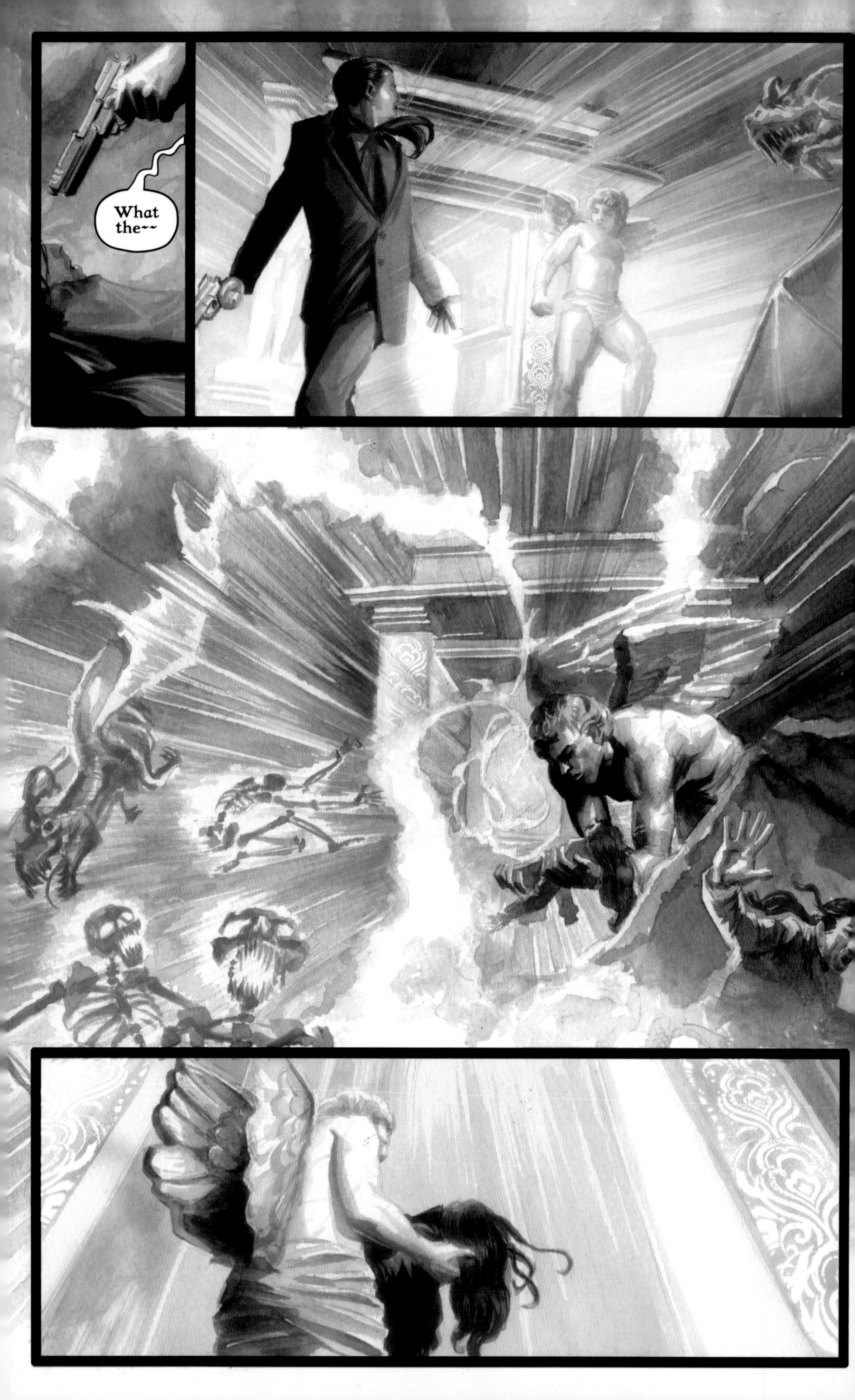
What the~~

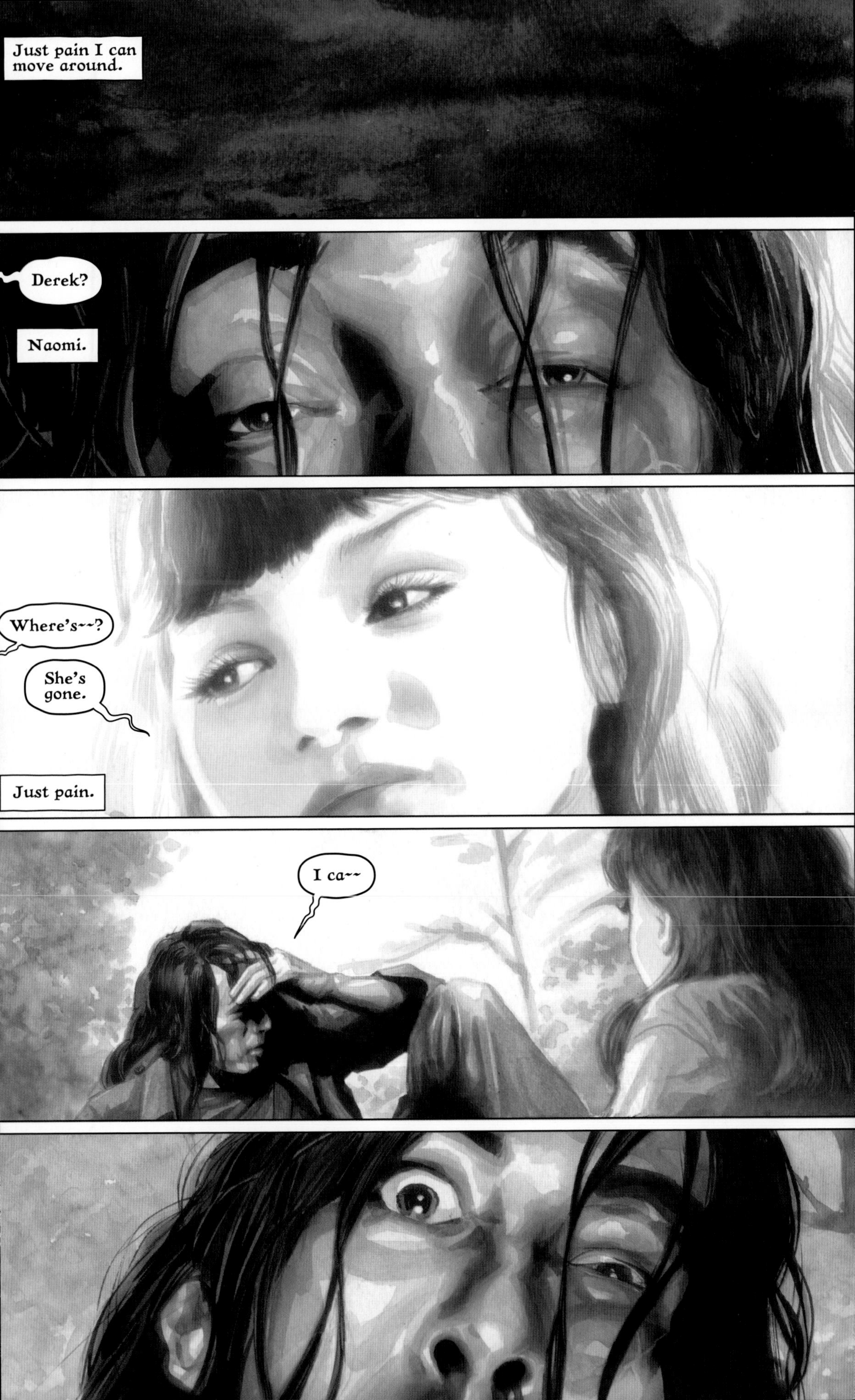
Just pain I can move around.
Derek?
Naomi.
Where's--?
She's gone.
Just pain.
I ca--

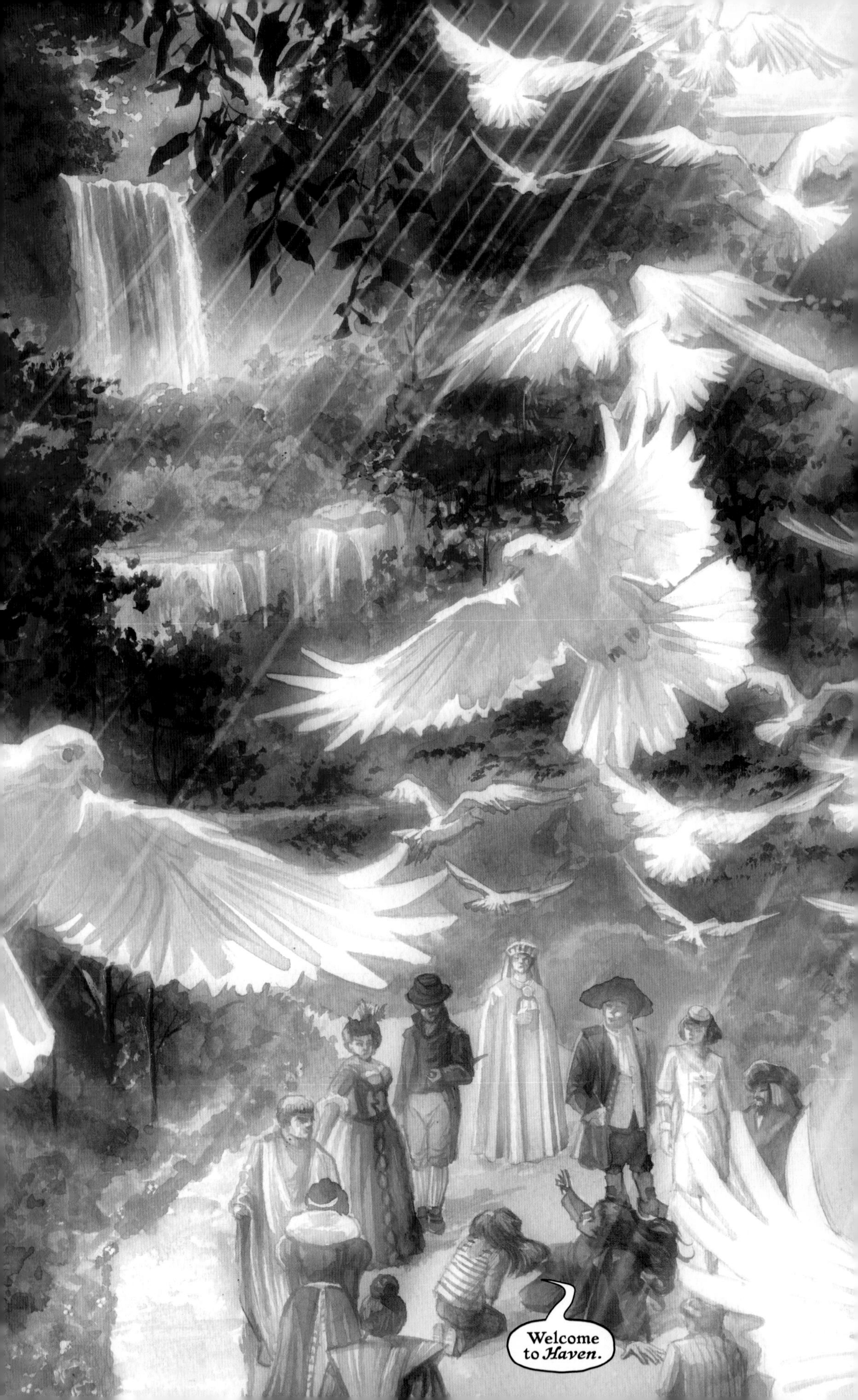
Welcome to *Haven*.

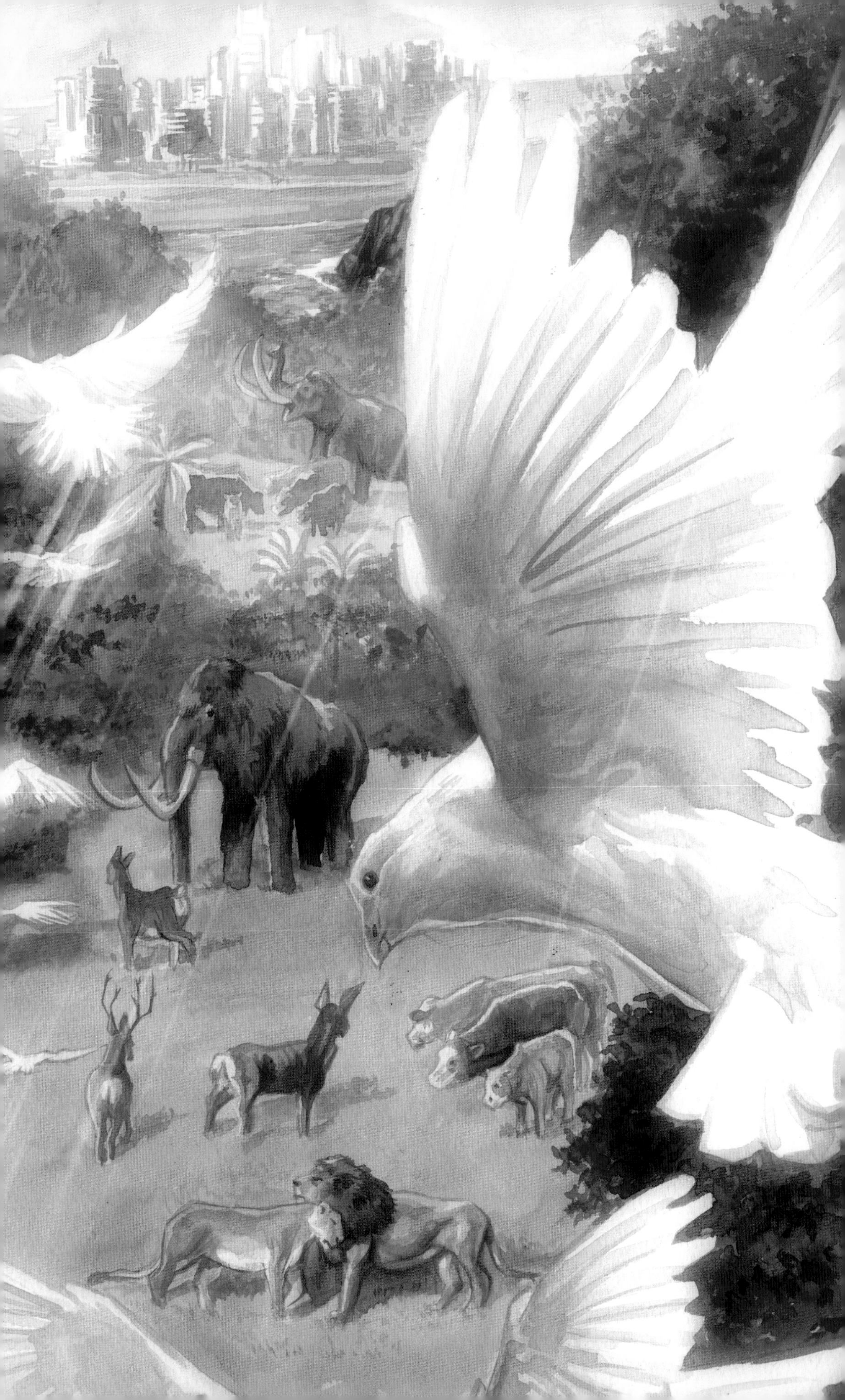

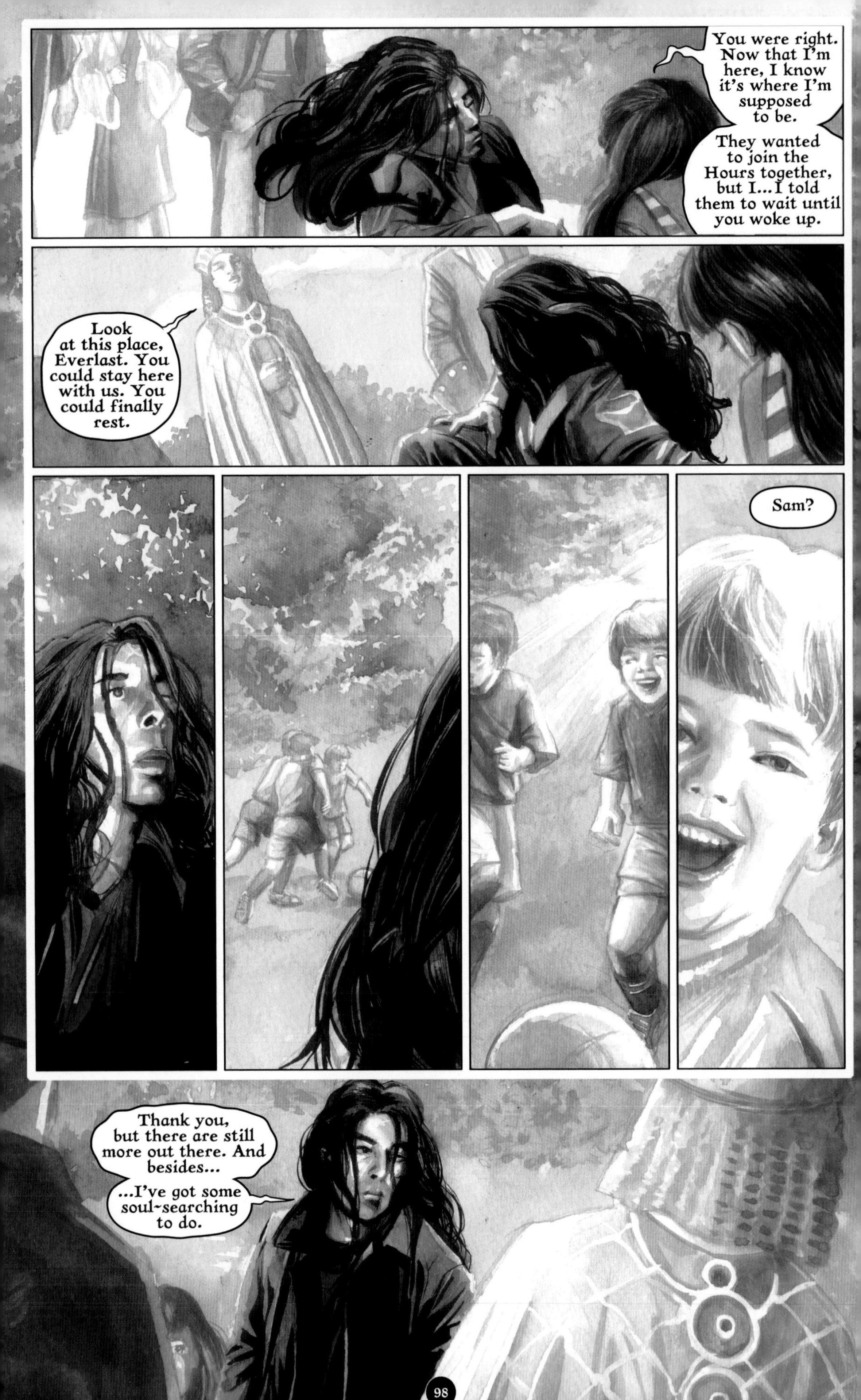
You were right. Now that I'm here, I know it's where I'm supposed to be.
They wanted to join the Hours together, but I...I told them to wait until you woke up.
Look at this place, Everlast. You could stay here with us. You could finally rest.
Sam?
Thank you, but there are still more out there. And besides...
...I've got some soul-searching to do.

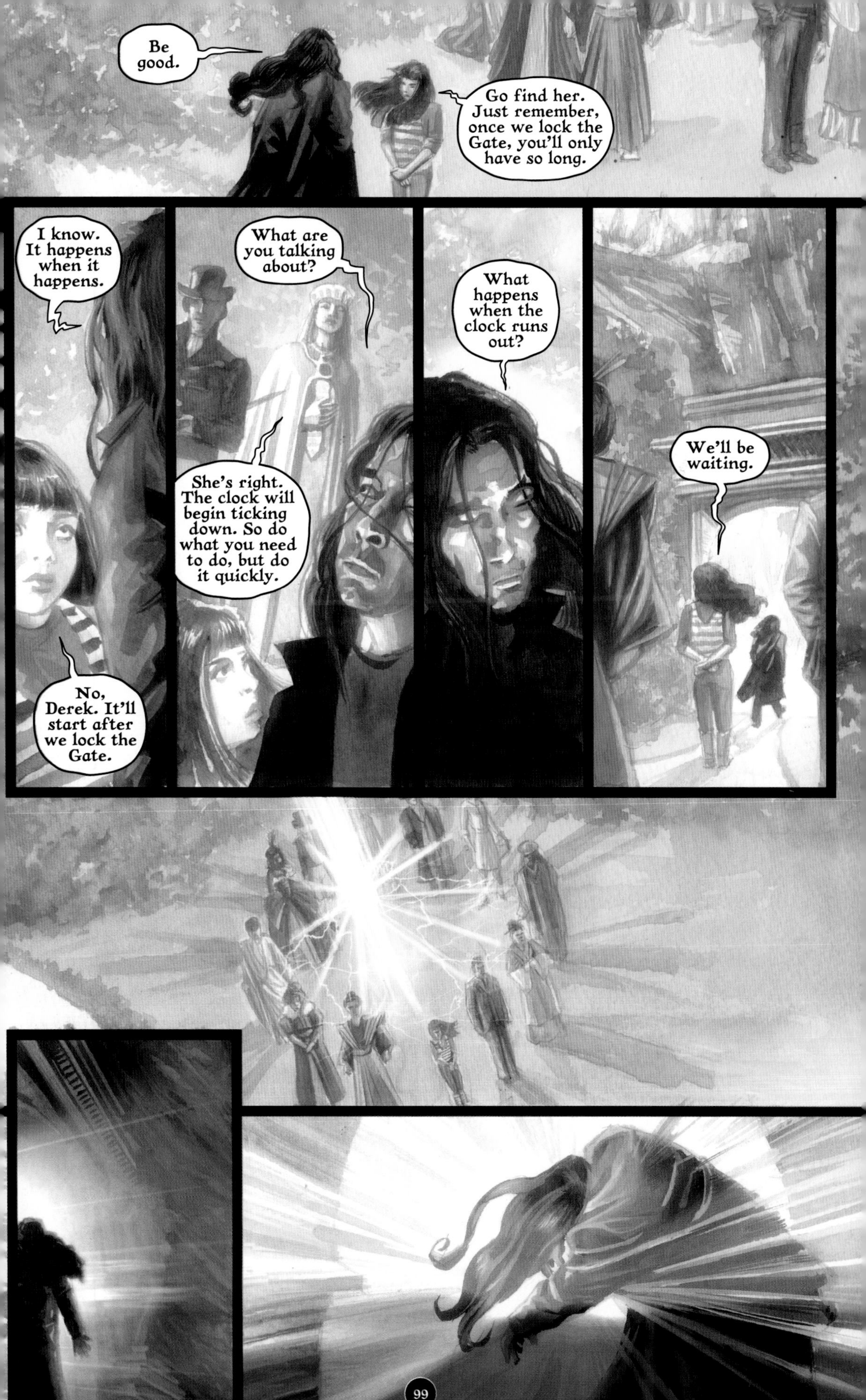
Be good.
Go find her. Just remember, once we lock the Gate, you'll only have so long.
I know. It happens when it happens.
No, Derek. It'll start after we lock the Gate.
What are you talking about?
She's right. The clock will begin ticking down. So do what you need to do, but do it quickly.
What happens when the clock runs out?
We'll be waiting.

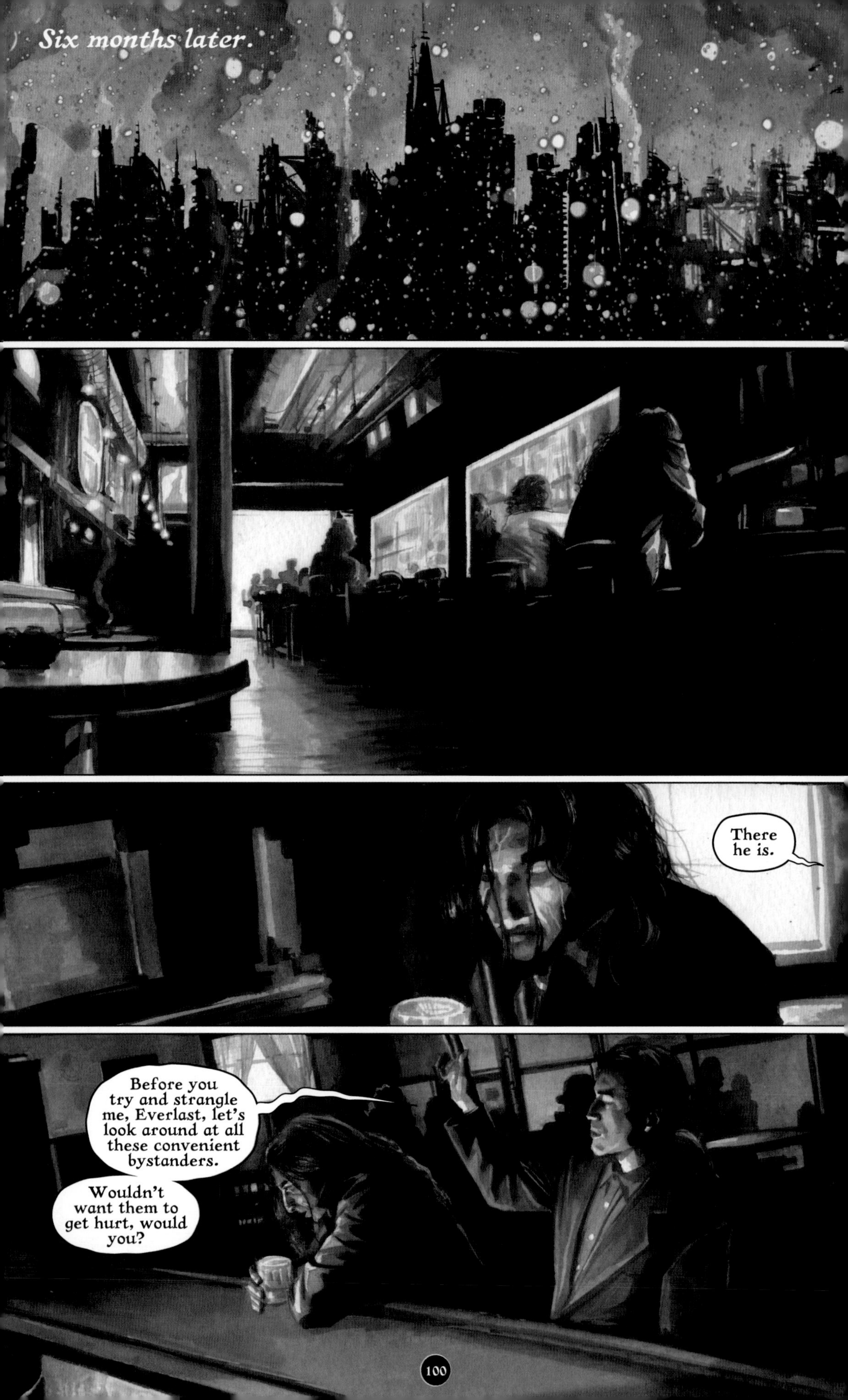
Six months later.
There he is.
Before you try and strangle me, Everlast, let's look around at all these convenient bystanders.
Wouldn't want them to get hurt, would you?

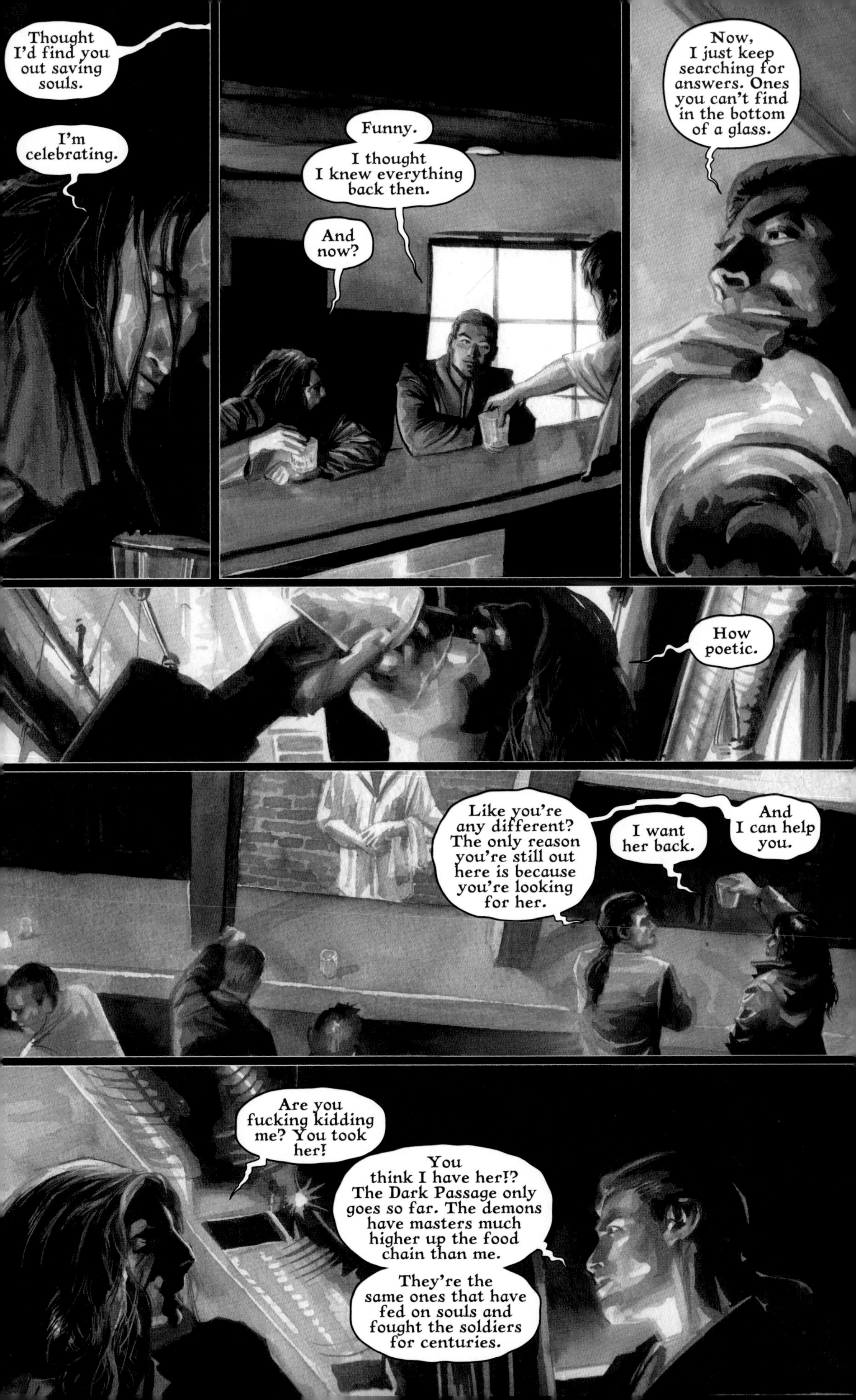
Thought I'd find you out saving souls.
I'm celebrating.
Funny.
I thought I knew everything back then.
And now?
Now, I just keep searching for answers. Ones you can't find in the bottom of a glass.
How poetic.
Like you're any different? The only reason you're still out here is because you're looking for her.
I want her back.
And I can help you.
Are you fucking kidding me? You took her!
You think I have her!? The Dark Passage only goes so far. The demons have masters much higher up the food chain than me.
They're the same ones that have fed on souls and fought the soldiers for centuries.

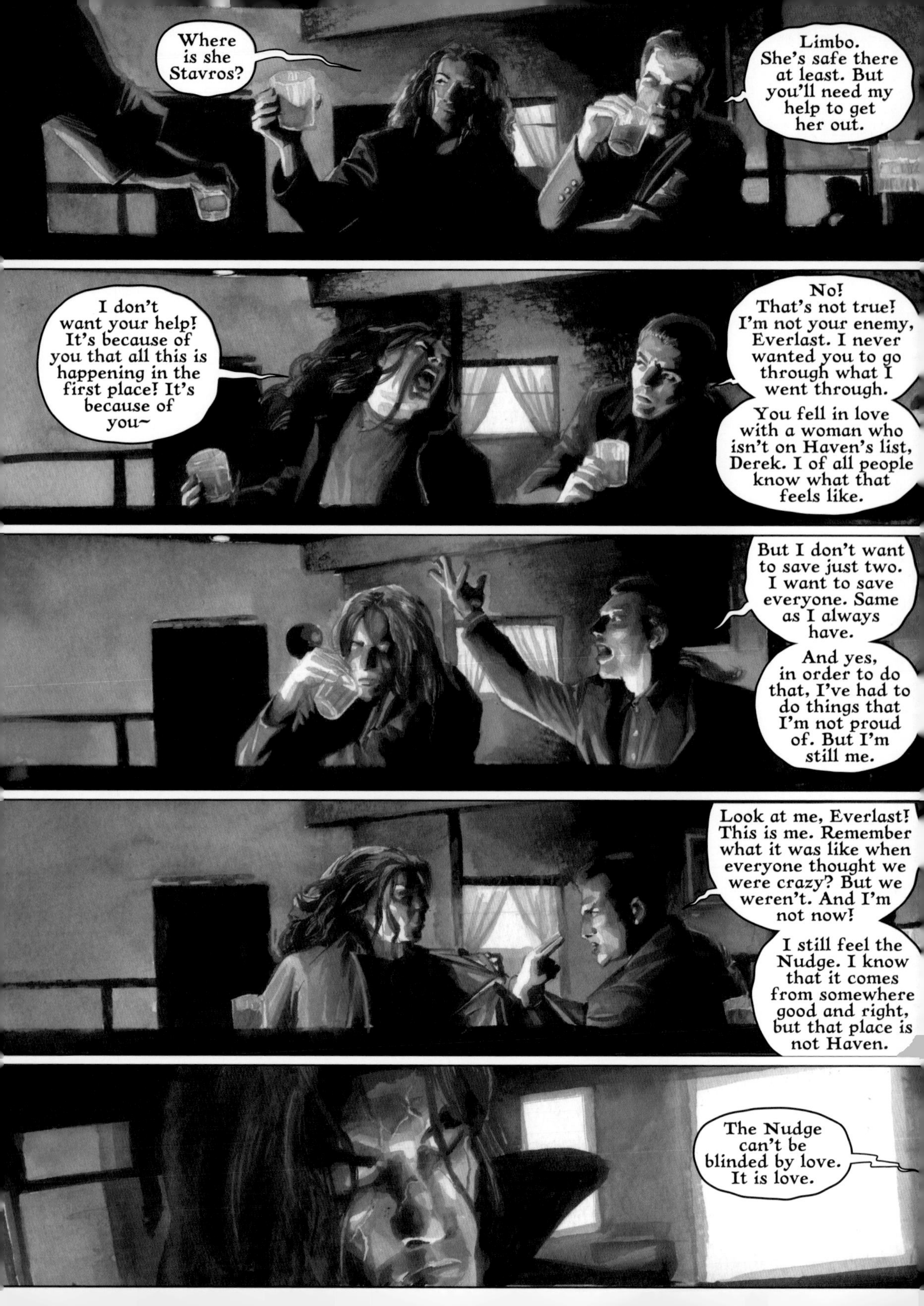
Where is she Stavros?
Limbo. She's safe there at least. But you'll need my help to get her out.
I don't want your help! It's because of you that all this is happening in the first place! It's because of you~
No! That's not true! I'm not your enemy, Everlast. I never wanted you to go through what I went through.
You fell in love with a woman who isn't on Haven's list, Derek. I of all people know what that feels like.
But I don't want to save just two. I want to save everyone. Same as I always have.
And yes, in order to do that, I've had to do things that I'm not proud of. But I'm still me.
Look at me, Everlast! This is me. Remember what it was like when everyone thought we were crazy? But we weren't. And I'm not now!
I still feel the Nudge. I know that it comes from somewhere good and right, but that place is not Haven.
The Nudge can't be blinded by love. It is love.

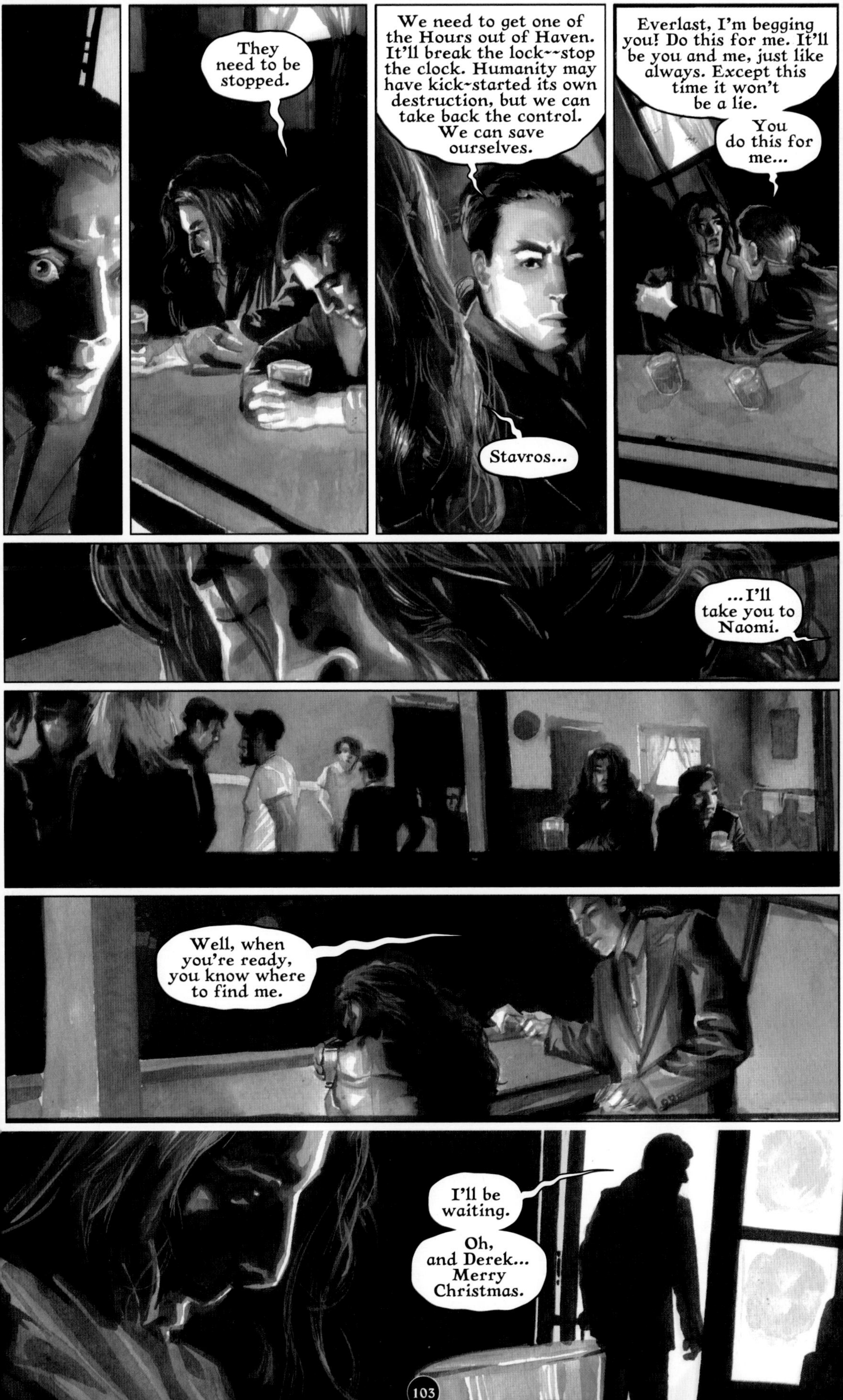
They need to be stopped.
We need to get one of the Hours out of Haven. It'll break the lock--stop the clock. Humanity may have kick-started its own destruction, but we can take back the control. We can save ourselves.
Stavros...
Everlast, I'm begging you! Do this for me. It'll be you and me, just like always. Except this time it won't be a lie.
You do this for me...
...I'll take you to Naomi.
Well, when you're ready, you know where to find me.
I'll be waiting.
Oh, and Derek... Merry Christmas.

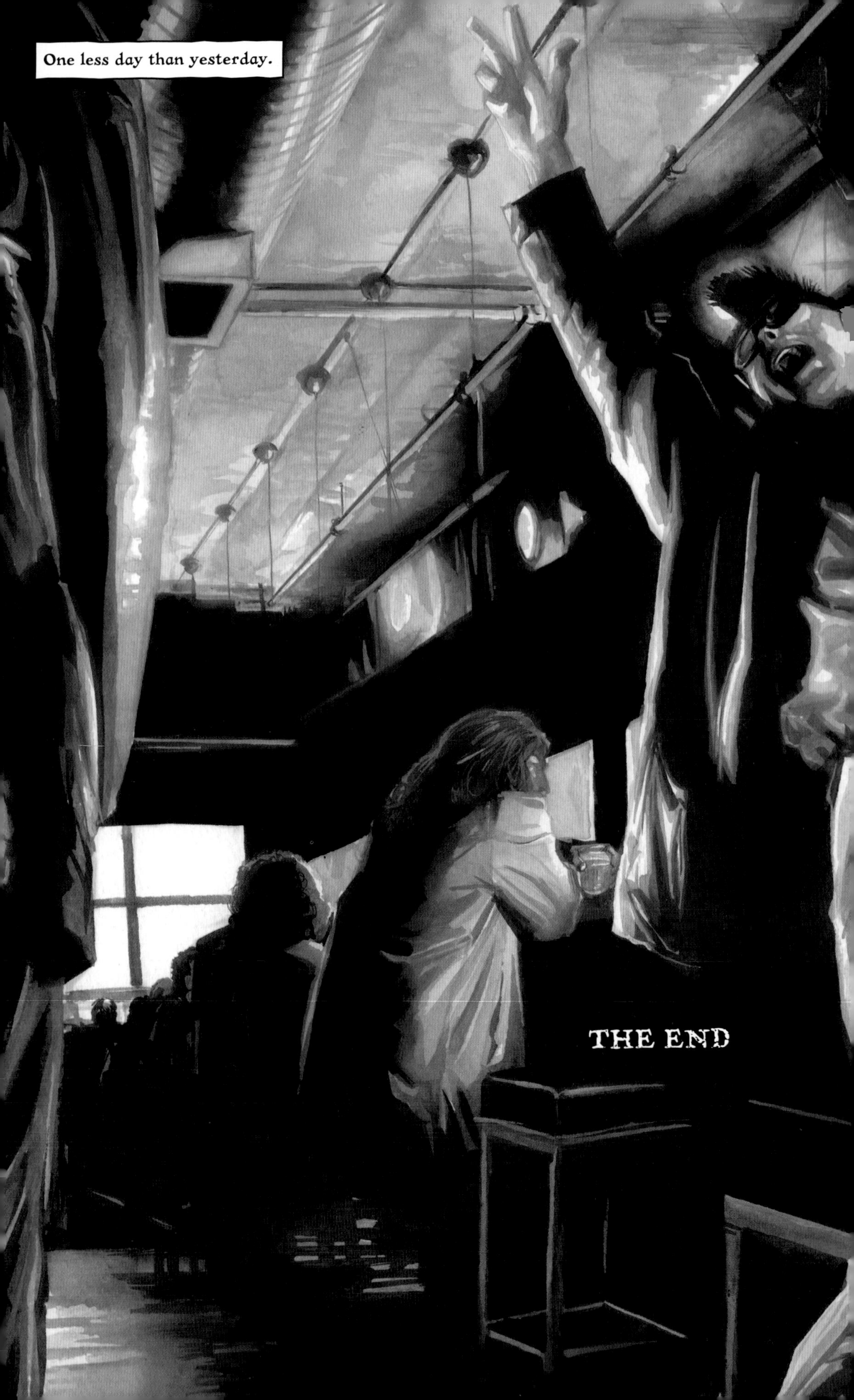
One less day than yesterday.
THE END

PHOENIX
AN EVERLAST SHORT

WRITTEN BY
CHAD MICHAEL MURRAY

ILLUSTRATIONS BY
JK WOODWARD

The city hung quietly in the blue light of early morning. This was Derek Everlast's favorite time of day. This was the time when the world was at its cleanest, its most pure. Walking the streets in the hush of dawn was like catching the world before it was properly dressed, when it was all natural and sleepy and full of hope.

With a spark of orange, the sun pierced the horizon, reflecting harshly off the glass high-rises. As the humid city air began to heat up, steam billowing out of sewer grates and the masses of morning commuters poured out onto the streets, Everlast put his head down and continued to wander through the maze of avenues and alleyways, like a cold grey ember floating on a heat wave.

All these people, Everlast thought. All of them so caught up in their own routines, their own endless cycles of vanity and survival tactics. It was like watching eight million people greedily climb eight million stepladders straight up into the sky and knowing that they'd find only dark clouds and a sharp drop. What most people never slowed down to realize was that all the fresh, early morning promises of hope and choice and chances to rebuild were right in their grasp, if only they would hold on tightly enough.

There were only a few people left who held on that tightly, and it was Everlast's job to find them. He'd been following the Nudge since around midnight, turning this way and that. It'd started soft, a gentle brush against his consciousness, but now it was stronger, its mysterious energy tingling down to every nerve ending. Turning onto a new street, Everlast finally felt the Nudge pointing him to his new save.

He regarded the man the Nudge had led him to. He appeared to be homeless, passing out slips of paper to passers by from his spot on the sidewalk. Disheveled, but not intimidating, he wore forest green corduroys and a brown rumpled jacket. His dark, weathered face carried a silver scruff, and there were flecks of grey in his close-cropped hair. A cardboard sign next to him read, "Poems in exchange for kindness," in a steady, almost elegant penmanship. Slightly hunched over, he gently called out, "Today be the day. Today be your day for a gift. All you need is a smile."

One pedestrian accepted a poem and promptly crumpled it, letting it drop to the ground. The homeless man hobbled over to it painfully, showing years of harsh reality, and bent down to retrieve it. Everlast watched as a passing woman, dressed primly in a blue sundress, leaned down and picked up the poem, handing it back to the man. Their eyes met for a moment—a small smile on her face, a look of surprise on his. He extended his hand slowly, not for the poem, but to shake.

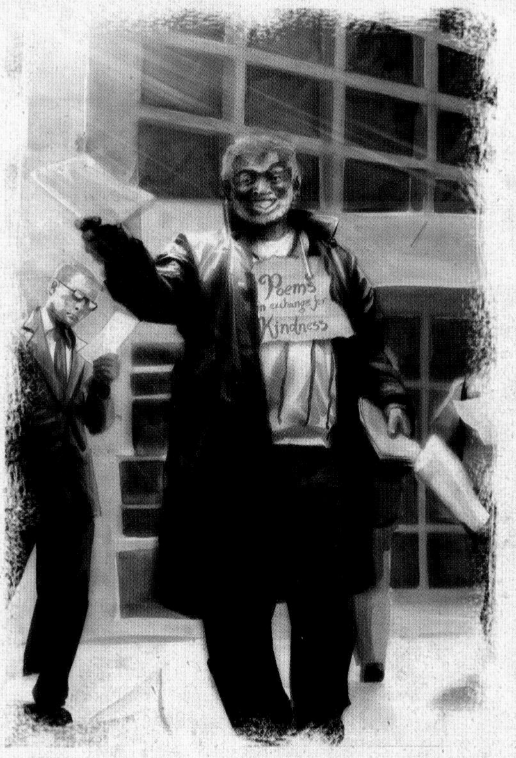
Poems
n exchange for
Kindness

"Thank you much, m'am. I wrote that one for you. You go on and keep it. My name's Henry. Henry Wolf," he said. His accent was Southern, with a surprising lightness to it. For a flash of a second, Everlast saw a much younger man behind his brown eyes.

The woman's smile disappeared suddenly as she looked at the hand, regarding it like a masticated animal. Awkwardly, she started to shuffle through her purse. Henry slowly pulled his hand back, wiping it against his jacket. He shook his head at her emphatically.

"No money needed, m'am. Just the warmth of your smile this morning." The woman managed another small smile and headed off down the sidewalk, removing hand sanitizer from her purse as she went. As Henry sat back down at his little street shop, a man in a grey business suit kicked the cardboard sign aside. Henry's head dropped in disappointment. He returned it to its place carefully, as if it were a fragile flower arrangement.

Everlast shook his head, took a deep breath and walked purposefully across the street. He smiled at Henry, who smiled back. He offered a poem, which Everlast took.

"Thank you."

"To send you on your way—a poem and a smile for the rest of your day!"

Everlast rarely smiled, but innocents like Henry made it easier. He smiled down at Henry as warmly as he knew how and said, "Henry, it's time to go."

Henry froze. "You death?" The fear quickly softened across his face, and he pointed up to Everlast. "You've got more skin than I figured you'd have."

Everlast laughed. "I'm not death, sir."

"You sure?" he questioned with one eyebrow raised. "I hear you knowing my name and saying 'It's time.' Those're the kind of things a man figures for death to say."

"I'm a soldier," replied Everlast. "I fight for a place created long, long ago for people like you."

"People like me, you say? What's that mean, 'people like me?'"

"Good people." Everlast looked at Henry's skeptical eyes and smirked. "I've done this enough times to know that I sound crazy. I also know that you've probably heard a lot of crazy in your life and maybe this time there's a part of you that's saying I'm not crazy. That you've been waiting for me."

Henry started to scoot backwards quietly. "I'm not going back to one of those homes. You can't make me. I haven't hurt nobody!"

Everlast took a step forward, but stopped as a shriek ripped across the sky. He turned quickly and scanned the skyline, Henry still cowering behind him. Everlast turned back. "Look, I believe you, and in about five seconds you're going to believe me, but right now I need you to just stay calm."

Everlast turned and readied himself for action as another shriek echoed off the towering buildings. Henry's eyes went wide as the sound got closer, looking back and forth at the other pedestrians, none of whom seemed to notice

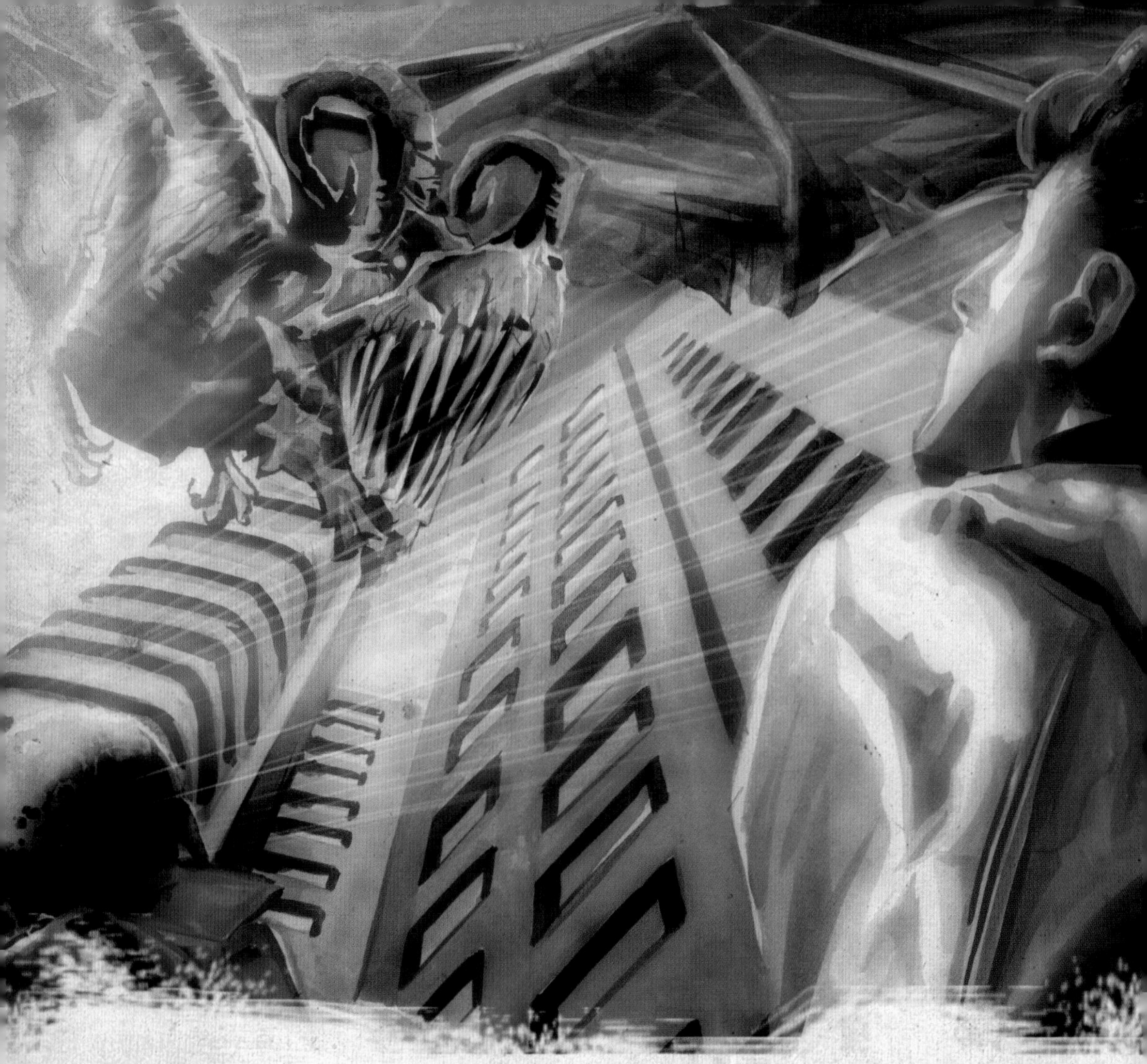

anything unusual. Everlast slowly bent down and grabbed a fist full of dirt from the base of the young honeylocust tree planted along the sidewalk.

Suddenly, the approaching creature broke around a skyscraper—a massive gargoyle bird with razor sharp, stone talons and a scythe-like beak full of polished, black teeth. "Scavi," growled Everlast.

Seeing them, the scavi, a vicious scavenger of souls, dove, shrieking its battle cry. Its stone wings cut through the humid morning air, hurtling it over the heads of oblivious pedestrians. Everlast shifted his feet as it dove closer, closer. Henry threw out his arms, but couldn't look away. At the last moment, when the monster was so close they could see the sharp orange sunlight glinting off its cold, stone eyes, it shrieked, and Everlast threw his handful of soil into its open mouth.

The scavi's scream was cut short and in a flash its stone body crumbled into soil. Everlast threw his trenchcoat over himself and Henry as the creature exploded into a burst of gravel and dust all around them.

As the dust settled, Henry coughed and looked up at Everlast with awe and fear. Everlast casually dusted himself off and looked back at him. "Believe me now?"

Henry looked with wide eyes back and forth at the passers by. Everlast shook the last of the dust out of his collar. "All they saw was a quick dust storm. Still, we should go. Or do you still need convincing?"

Henry stared at him for a moment before shaking his head and letting out a low whistle. "No, sir," he said finally, reaching out for a hand up. "If you have something more convincing than that, I for certain do not want to see it."

Everlast led Henry down to the sewers, through the subterranean catacombs of the city. Henry, for one, felt respected as an equal for the first time in a long time. After a while of walking in silence, he began to talk.

"I wasn't always like this, you know."

"Nothing wrong with it, even if you were," said Everlast.

"I was a soldier, too. Yes, sir. That's where I got this shuffle-step of mine. I used to make up them poems for the other soldiers in the hospital. They'd look to me and say, 'Hey Henry, you got one of them poems I could hear?'"

Everlast just listened, continuing on down the tunnels. Lots of innocents tried to explain themselves, as if they thought he'd take them back if he knew their life's story.

"The hospital, that's where I met my Beatrice. She was our nurse. You never saw a lovelier woman than her, inside and out. No, sir. I saw her, and the poetry, well, it just started pouring out of me, you know? Like it'd already been written somewhere and I was just the hand putting it to the paper."

Everlast nodded. "I know the feeling."

"Well," said Henry. "She was my muse, for sure. I wrote all my best ones for her."

They walked quietly for a while. The rest of the story was coming. Everlast waited.

"She was working late one night, and I wanted to surprise her. I lit candles and wrote her a new poem. She used to keep them all in a shoebox." Henry looked up, wistfully. "But I'd forgotten to get her flowers, and she loved daisies, so I rushed out. I figured I could get back before she came home. When I came back, though…"

He went quiet and Everlast turned them down an old subway tunnel. Henry kept his head down, watching his steps, caught in memory.

"They say the fire was started by a candle catching on a piece of paper on the table. My poem…can you believe that?"

"I'm sorry," replied Everlast.

Henry sighed. "I checked out after that, just went on and waited for death to bring me back to her. Then one night she came to visit me—saw her clear as day. And right then she told me to get up, to stop feeling sorry for myself, and to use what God gave me to help make this crazy world a little bit better. So that's why I pass out my poems, you see? Even if I make one person smile, well, that's when I see my Beatrice again."

Everlast took the story in as they continued down the tunnels. After a while, they came upon the old abandoned subway train with tracks leading straight to the center of the Earth. A man with a backwards hat and holding a large gun stepped off the train. The scars on his face were weathered and purple, but his smile was warm and friendly. He yelled out to them in a gravely voice, "Everlast! 'Bout time. You got a good one for me?"

"One of the best," Everlast called back. He looked at Henry. "Pierce here is going to take you the rest of the way. That train runs straight to the gates."

"What about you?"

Everlast smiled wearily. "Too much work still left to do up here."

Henry's forehead furrowed, and he suddenly looked very pensive. Everlast clapped a hand on his shoulder. "Don't worry. It's nothing but peace from here on out. I promise. Now, come on. Don't want the train to leave without you."

Henry nodded and extended a hand. Everlast glanced at it and then back at Henry. Shyly, Henry started to pull it back when he found himself pulled into an embrace.

"Good luck, Henry," Everlast said quietly, releasing the old man to Pierce, who took Henry by the elbow and led him gently to the train platform. Staring at the last few steps onto the train, Henry stopped and took a deep breath. Then, suddenly, he smiled, and instead of continuing forward, he turned back to Everlast.

Everlast frowned. "What's wrong? I swear to you, I'm not crazy."

Henry laughed softly. "Oh, it's not that. You were right, I can feel it; I know there's something out there calling me somewhere, but…well, it's like you said: there's still more for me to do upstairs. I know it's not as almighty as what you folks do, but I still think it's important. With all the filth in the world, some of us good ones have to stick around if we're going to have a fighting chance, don't you think?"

He smiled again. "Besides, up there, in those smiles, that's the only place I get to see my Beatrice. I'm sure your place down there is beautiful, but she's not there. And that thing that's calling to me, it's calling me from wherever she is. If I know one thing, I know that."

Everlast and Pierce exchanged glances. Henry stood upright, preparing himself for a fight. Finally, Pierce broke the silence. "You know, Everlast, I think you're right about this one. He is special. I ain't ever seen anybody say no to Haven."

Henry's face relaxed. Pierce stepped forward

and removed a rustic, silver chain from around his neck. From it hung a stone pendant that seemed to glow softly from within. He carefully placed it in Henry's weathered palm and gripped his shoulder warmly.

"That there's a ward stone. No scavi's gonna find you with that around your neck. You'll get more use of it up there than me down here. Besides, those suckers know not to mess with me if they know what's good for them!"

Henry grinned and put the stone around his neck. Slowly, he turned to Everlast, his posture hesitant, but the look in his eyes showing no regret. "I'm truly sorry to make you walk all the way down here for nothing. I hope you know I don't mean to be difficult."

Everlast smiled at him and gestured back towards the sewers. "Truth be told, it'll be nice to have some company for the walk up."

A few weeks later, Everlast found himself once again wandering the streets of the decayed city. Most times when he found his feet carrying him somewhere without knowing why, it was from the Nudge. This time, though, he didn't know what it was until, upon turning down one familiar street, he heard a light Southern accent over the noise of the crowd.

"Lemme give you a pleasant way to start your day! Pay with a smile that'll carry you that extra mile! Poetry from the heart and for the soul!"

Everlast watched as Henry, smiling with greater brightness and purpose than ever before, tried to spread that smile of his to each person passing by his little sidewalk shop. It was food for thought, the case of Henry, thought Everlast. Haven had always taught him that the world was getting worse despite the innocents like Henry. Was it possible that it was getting worse because he and the soldiers were helping the few good people that were left jump ship? Was it possible that maybe there was something left worth saving up here?

As the day wore on, Everlast left the smiling Henry to his poems in search of more souls like him, winding himself like a cat through the back alleys of the city. Finally, just as the sun tucked itself below the horizon and left the world to the lavender light of dusk, a strong gust of wind blew across the street towards him. Leaves shivered on the trees, and Everlast looked up curiously, feeling the energy of the moment. It was a melancholy energy; his nerves tingled, every pinprick of his skin on edge.

The wind continued on down the street,

leaving behind a stale vibration in the air. Everlast started to walk faster, trying to catch up with the gust. The walk turned to a jog, then to a sprint. The same way he could feel the Nudge telling him which way to turn, he felt as if the wind was leading him to something he had to see, something he was missing.

He slowed his pace as he came upon a bridge. The gust had turned now to a gentle breeze, blowing back against his face, brushing his long hair over his shoulder. Everlast looked around and suddenly froze. Under the bridge, covered by a pile of moth-eaten blankets, lay a man. Everlast approached slowly, almost reverently. Reaching the figure, he bent down and pulled the blankets back.

Henry's weathered face looked peaceful, a content smile on his lips. Everlast checked his pulse. Nothing.

The gust of wind suddenly returned, sweeping under the bridge and rattling the dry leaves of the honeylocust tree growing near the underpass. Everlast looked up as the leaves scattered. The energy that had scared him before was there, filling him up all the way from his fingertips where they wrapped around Henry's cold wrist to the back of his spine. Only this time, he wasn't afraid. Instead, it filled him with a calm he had not felt in a very long time. It was a feeling of certainty even stronger than the Nudge—a certainty that everything was going to be all right.

Everlast looked down at Henry's peaceful face in awe. "Whoever out there wanted you must have big plans for you," he said quietly. "I hope you're with her now."

Everlast pulled the tattered blankets up, tucking Henry in to his final resting place. Someway, somehow, Everlast felt as if a small part of him long forgotten had mended. If there was a power out there—a power that guided him, that had picked him—that wanted people like Henry, then that power must be good.

Everlast removed Pierce's stone pendant from around Henry's neck, and with one last whispered prayer, stood and walked off into the night.

"Sleep well, Henry."

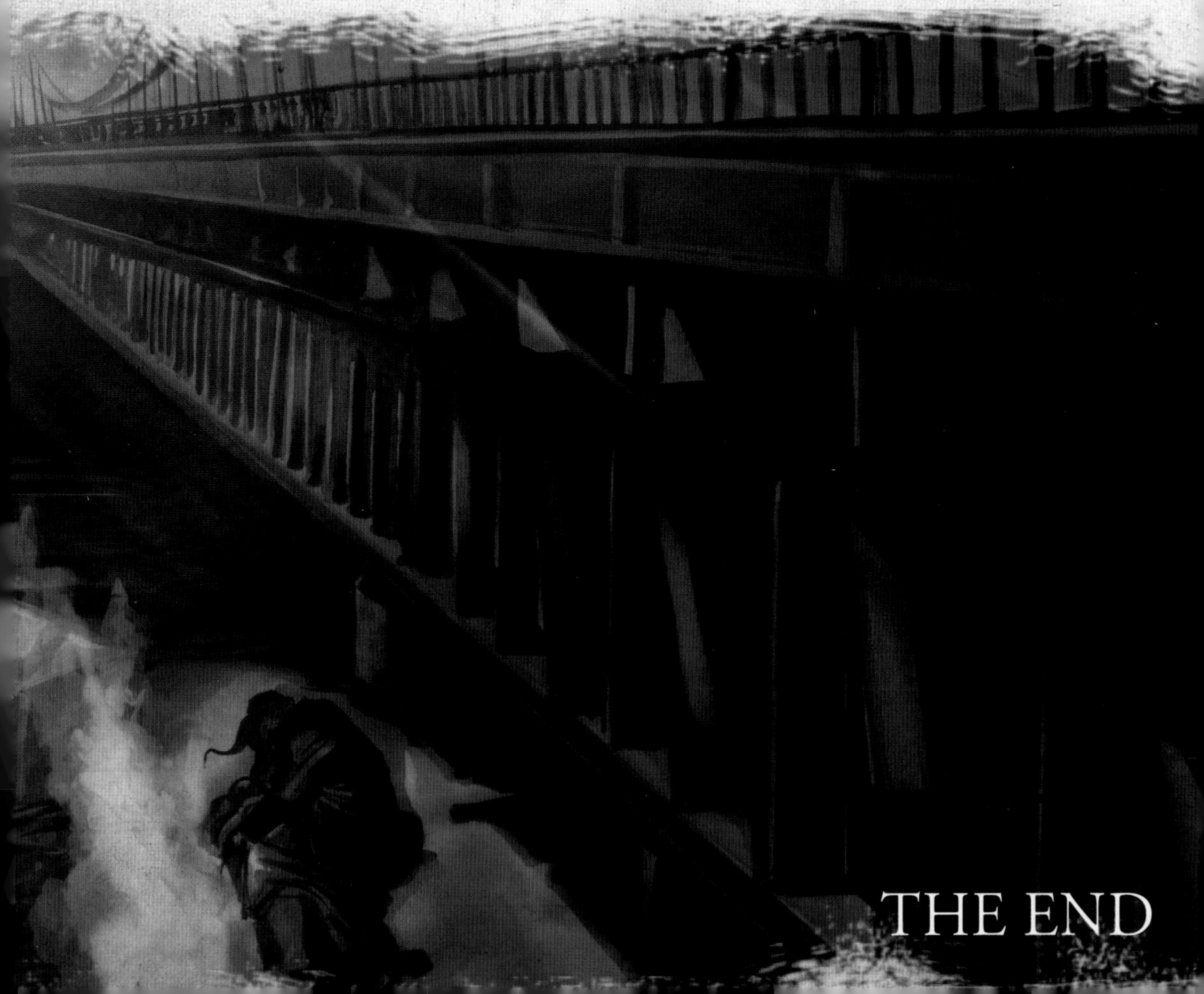
THE END

ABOUT THE AUTHORS

CHAD MICHAEL MURRAY was born in Buffalo, New York, in 1981. He began his acting career in Hollywood at the age of 18, going on to star in both film and television. He is best known for his role as Lucas Scott on the CW's *One Tree Hill*. Among his box office hits are *A Cinderella Story, Freaky Friday,* and *House of Wax*. He currently lives in Los Angeles, California. This is his first graphic novel.

DANIJEL ZEZELJ is a graphic artist, painter, illustrator and author of more than twenty graphic novels. He studied at the Academy of Fine Arts in Zagreb, Croatia, and his comics and illustrations have been published in magazines and anthologies all over the world. He was nominated for the Eisner Award in 2010, for his work on the graphic novel *Luna Park* (DC Vertigo). He lives and works in Brooklyn.

ROBBI RODRIGUEZ was born in Waco, Texas, and has been a cartoonist since 2004. You can find him at www.robbirodriguez.com or at the Chick-fil-A in the Del Amo Mall, where he will be putting together a plan to escape Los Angeles, CA.

Born and raised in California, **ANDREW HUERTA** is a Hip-Hop head, visual artist and a student at the Academy of Art University in San Francisco. He has worked for IDW Publishing, BOOM! Studios, Archaia Entertainment, Los Angeles Times, and NYU Press. Currently he is working on a new comic book series. www.andrewhuerta.com

J.K. (James Kenneth) WOODWARD has been illustrating comics since 2003. He's best known for his continuing work on Peter David's *Fallen Angel*, *Star Trek* and *X-men Origins: Beast*. He resides in NYC with his fiancé and fat, lazy cat who really likes cheese.

TREVOR HAIRSINE works in a very nice shed at the bottom of his garden in Sheffield in the UK. Over the last 18 years, he's drawn everything from *Judge Dredd* to *X-men* and very much enjoyed himself doing so.

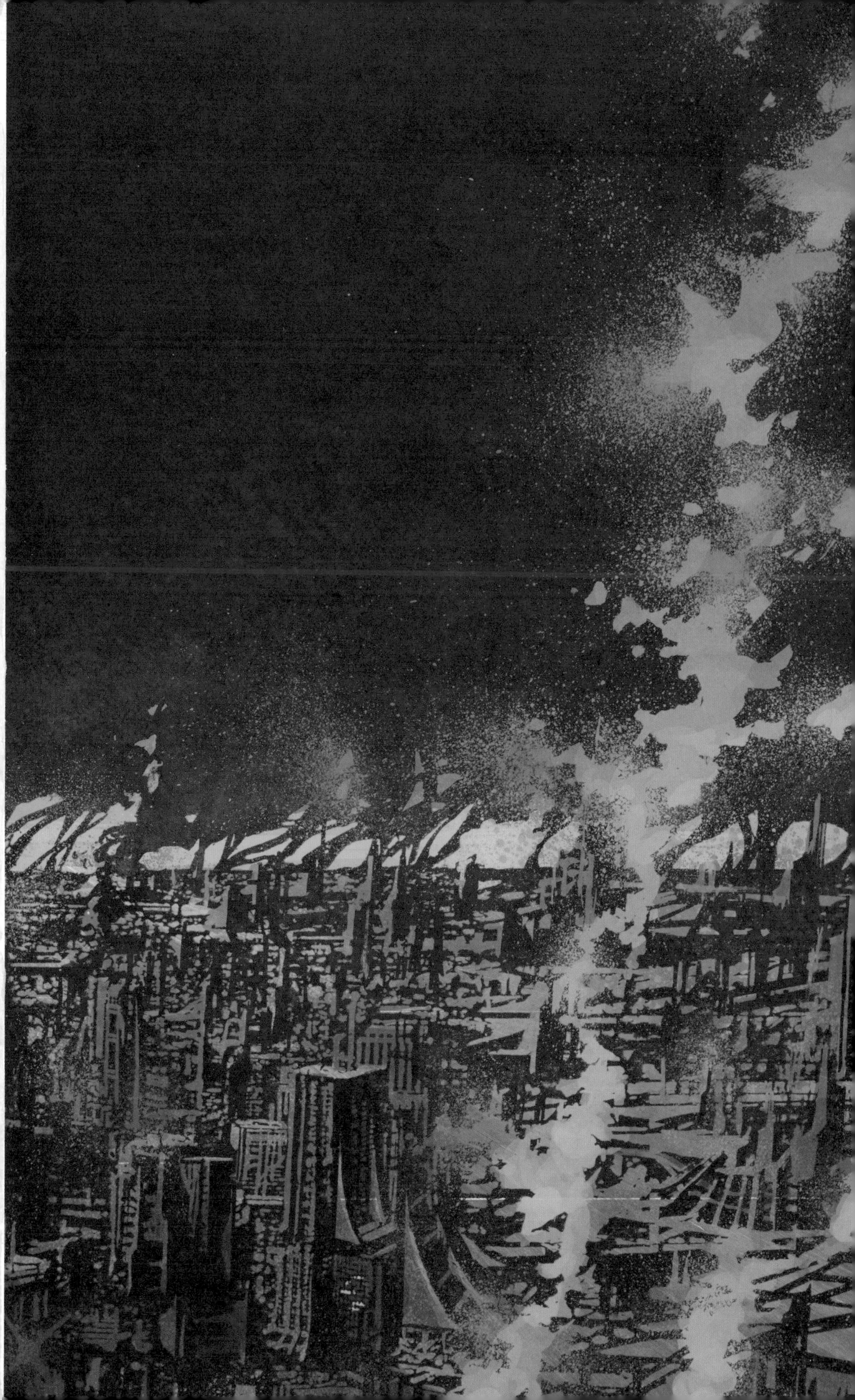

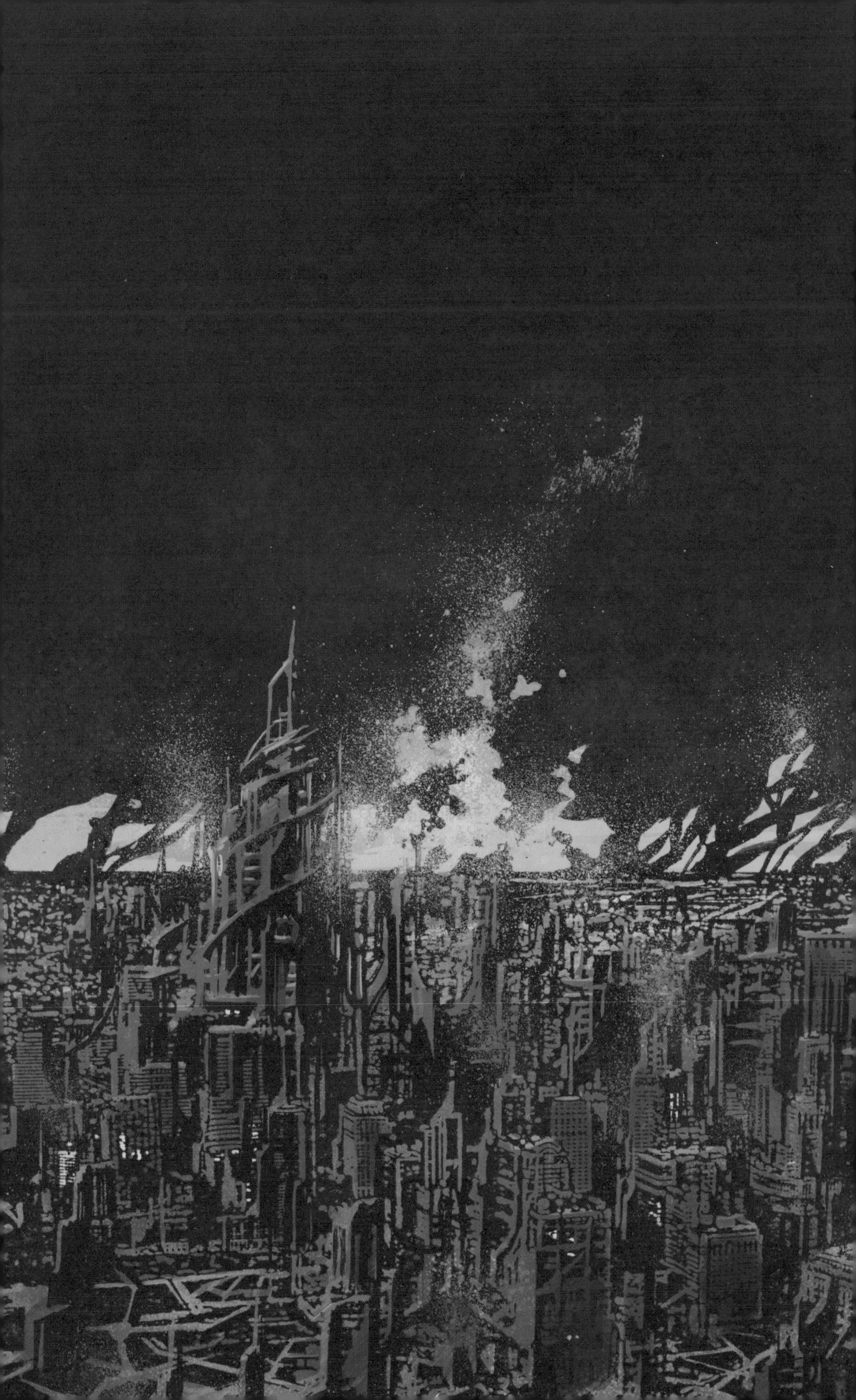